1986

Natural
Emphasis

Natural Emphasis
ENGLISH VERSIFICATION FROM
CHAUCER TO DRYDEN

by Susanne Woods

THE HUNTINGTON LIBRARY · SAN MARINO

1984

Copyright 1985 by the Huntington Library
Designed by Ward Ritchie
ISBN 0-87328-085-7
Printed in the United States of America

Library of Congress Cataloging in Publication Data

Woods, Susanne, 1943-
  Natural emphasis.

  Includes bibliographies and index.
  1. English language—Versification. 2. English
poetry—Early modern, 1500-1700—History and
criticism. 3. English poetry—Middle English, 1100-1500
—History and criticism. I. Title.
PE1505.W66 1985   821'.009   84-28854
ISBN 0-87328-085-7

To the memory of my Mother,
Gertrude Cullom Woods
1912-1977

LIST OF ILLUSTRATIONS

*All illustrations are from the collections of the Henry E. Huntington
Library and are reproduced with permission.*

Contents

Whan that Aprill with his shoures soote
The droghte of March hath perced to the roote,
And bathed every veyne in swich licour
Of which vertu engendred is the flour;
Whan Zephirus eek with his sweete breeth
Inspired hath in every holt and heeth

The tendre croppes, and the yonge sonne
Hath in the Ram his halve cours yronne,
And smale foweles maken melodye,
That slepen al the nyght with open ye
So priketh hem nature in hir corages;
Thanne longen folk to goon on pilgrimages,
And palmeres for to seken straunge strondes,
To ferne halwes, kowthe in sondry londes;
And specially from every shires ende
Of Engelond to Caunterbury they wende,
The hooly blisful martir for to seke,
That hem hath holpen whan that they were seeke.

Bifil that in that seson on a day,
In Southwerk at the Tabard as I lay
Redy to wenden on my pilgrymage
To Caunterbury with ful devout corage,
At nyght was come into that hostelrye
Wel nyne and twenty in a compaignye,
Of sondry folk, by aventure yfalle
In felaweshipe, and pilgrimes were they alle,
That toward Caunterbury wolden ryde.
The chambres and the stables weren wyde,
And wel we weren esed atte beste.
And shortly, whan the sonne was to reste,
So hadde I spoken with hem everichon
That I was of hir felaweshipe anon,
And made forward erly for to ryse,
To take oure wey ther as I yow devyse.
But nathelees, whil I have tyme and space,
Er that I ferther in this tale pace,
Me thynketh it acordaunt to resoun
To telle yow al the condicioun
Of ech of hem, so as it semed me,
And whiche they weren, and of what degree,
And eek in what array that they were inne;
And at a knyght than wol I first bigynne.

A knyght ther was, and that a worthy man,
That fro the tyme that he first bigan
To riden out, he loved chivalrie,
Trouthe and honour, fredom and curteisie.
Ful worthy was he in his lordes werre,
And therto hadde he riden, no man ferre,

Preface

*And in your verses remembre to
place everie worde in his
natural* Emphasis *or sound.*

Gascoigne, "Certayne Notes of Instruction," 1575

This book is intended for readers interested in Renaissance poetry as well as those interested in versification and poetic form. Its approach is to trace the development of English versification as practiced by the important and influential poets of the English Renaissance. Its primary purpose is to serve as a historical guide to the interaction of theory and practice in English verse from Chaucer, who is for many reasons the father of verse in Modern English, through Dryden. A second purpose is to identify and describe the characteristic, innovative, or influential verse techniques of major poets of the period. Chaucer and Wyatt, as the most problematic of the poets who affect the development of iambic pentameter, are discussed in somewhat greater detail than the rest, but I have tried to define at least the principal contributions of Surrey, Gascoigne, Sidney, Spenser, Shakespeare, Donne, and Jonson, among others. I have not sought to attempt an exhaustive treatment of their poetry or even of the full range of their versification, but rather to provide a context for seeing these poets in relation to the history of verse making in English, and, within the limits of that focus, in relation to each other.

No extensive study of the history of English versification has been undertaken since George Saintsbury's monumental three-volume *History of English Prosody* (1906-10), although John Thompson provided a useful but limited survey of the central part of this period in 1961 *(The Founding of English Metre)*, Catherine Ing reviewed some of the prosodic issues relevant to the lyric *(Elizabethan Lyrics*, 1951), and there have been a number of summaries of the history of English verse in the context of both traditional and structural linguistic approaches to English versification. Paul Fussell's outline of English verse history appears in the *Encyclopedia of Poetry and Poetics* (ed. Alex Preminger, 1965), in *Versification: Major Language Types* (ed. W. K. Wimsatt, 1972), and in his introduction to the analysis of meter and form, *Poetic Meter and Poetic Form* (revised edition, 1979, 62-75). It may fairly be taken as the current standard approach to English meters, but it is avowedly condensed. John Hollander offers enlightening and more detailed discussion of certain limited aspects of Renaissance English meter in several of the essays in *Vision and Resonance* (1975). From the perspective of structural linguistics, Morris Halle and S. Jay Keyser have done extensive work on both the Anglo-Saxon alliterative line and iambic pentameter (as in *English Stress: Its Form, Its Growth, and Its Role in Verse*, 1971, 147-80) but have not attempted a coherent history. Marlina Tarlinskaya, in *English Verse: Theory and History* (1976), does offer a historical sketch of English verse with an emphasis on phonology. None of these focuses specifically on the development of English versification in the Renaissance, however, though Thompson's book documents some of the facts of change. The linguistic studies, for all their value in specifying and defining relevant phonological phenomena, provide at best only a very basic approach to the aesthetics of versification.

In addition to these works, many recent studies of individual authors or of poetic genres in the late Middle Ages and Renaissance have enriched the resources for a survey of the development of verse in this crucial formative period. My debt to them and to both linguists and literary critics will be clear in the following pages. I have sometimes found myself in disagreement, however, with either the literary critics or the linguists, and occasionally with both. While I agree with the traditional view that the history of the iambic pentameter line is of central and dominating importance in this period, for example, my conclusions about its origin and development differ from those of Halle and Keyser, Tarlinskaya, and other linguists, who tend to see it as continuing from the time of Chaucer. I also disagree with traditional theorists like Saintsbury and Fussell, who see iambic pentameter as disappearing between Chaucer and Surrey. I find it appearing for the first time in Surrey, although elements that contributed to it (experimentation with French and Italian decasyllabic verse and English accent-meters) were handled with great skill by Chaucer. This view demands an important modification in the usual perspective. For the most part both critics and linguists have sought to read Chaucer and the fifteenth-century poets in terms of Elizabethan iambic pentameter.

Since the study of versification is complex, subtleties often matter. Throughout I have tried to balance theory and practice, as the Renaissance poets themselves often did. Above all I have tried to keep a clear focus on the development of English versification, which has meant sometimes emphasizing theory, and sometimes practice, as those two contributed sometimes together, and sometimes separately, to the evolution of English poetic form.

A premise of this study is that ideas affect experience and theory affects practice, although not always in precisely the ways the theoreticians originally envisioned.

Acknowledgments

The conventional statement that a book owes far more debts than can possibly be acknowledged is in this instance profoundly true. A great many friends, colleagues, teachers, and students have enriched this book. It is not possible to list them all. Those named contributed perhaps most directly, but this project would nonetheless have been impossible without years of stimulating interaction with the rest. You know who you are.

Among those whom it would be a rudeness bordering on barbarism not to thank by name is my sister, Virginia Woods, who tolerated years of my absorption in arcane subjects and contributed her own extensive learning and enthusiasm for knowledge; she is also to be blamed for introducing me to (metrical) poetry. Sister Ellen Stephen of the Episcopal Order of Saint Helena (then Ellen de Young Kay) and Charles B. Gullans of UCLA introduced me to the study of versification. Without their clear and challenging presentation of a topic they persuaded me was central to the study of poetry, this project would never have been conceived. The late William Nelson of Columbia University taught me respect for the Renaissance context and the late John Crow of the University of London introduced me to Renaissance bibliography and textual criticism. Many friends and colleagues have made suggestions or offered various kinds of pertinent assistance over the years, among them G. B. Harrison, John Hollander, Marjorie Perloff, John T. Shawcross, Paul Sheats, Hallett Smith, Stanley Stewart, and Edward Weismiller.

Several scholars have taken time away from their own work to read all or part of the manuscript. Of these, I am particularly grateful to my Brown University (or then Brown University) colleagues, Elizabeth D. Kirk and Barbara K. Lewalski, whose comments were especially helpful, and whose friendship I greatly value. Judith Anderson, Edward Doughtie, Roland Greene, William B. Hunter, James Riddell, William Ringler, Jr., and Edward W. Tayler also made many useful comments and suggestions. I owe a very great deal to all these conscientious readers; remaining errors or obstinancies are my own.

Portions of chapters 1 and 8 appeared in different form in *Studies in the Literary Imagination* and the *George Herbert Journal.* Much of the material on Jonson and Bacon in chapter 7 appeared as "Ben Jonson's Formalism," in *Classic and Cavalier: Jonson and the Sons of Ben,* ed. Ted-Larry Pebworth and Claude J. Summers (1982).

Research for this book was supported by grants from Brown University, the William Andrews Clark Memorial Library, and the Henry E. Huntington Library.

I am especially grateful to James Thorpe, Director of the Huntington Library during the years this book took shape, and to Martin Ridge, problem solver *par excellence.* Mary Isabel Fry and Virginia Renner, along with their incomparable Reader Services staffs, have been central to the amazing ease with which a scholar settles into the Huntington community. My many friends among the staff and readers, especially Janet Hawkins, Noelle Jackson, Debbie Smith, Mary Wright, and the splendid editor of Huntington Library Publications, Jane Evans, have made that community far more than an academic one. I also very much appreciate the editorial help of Susan Ringler. In Rhode Island, Elaine Brennan contributed invaluable help with editing and with the computer formatting that established the basis for typesetting this book.

I most especially want to thank Arlene Stiebel, whose ideas and judgment infuse all that is good in this work, and whose continuing friendship is most valuable of all.

Providence, Rhode Island, December 14, 1983

Chapter One

Terms and Approaches

'Tis with our judgments as our watches; none
Go just alike, yet each believes his own.

Alexander Pope, *Essay on Criticism*

Pope's observation about literary judgment is equally pertinent to that slippery branch of the study of poetry, versification. As with watches, so with the ears of most serious students of poetry: they differ from person to person and even the most courteous scholars can become heated over the particular justice of their own perceptions of verbal rhythms. Because individual perception is so basic to the study of verse rhythms, versification is a difficult art to objectify. The difficulty is compounded when the poetry is written in the deceptively familiar language of the late Middle Ages and Renaissance.

Yet what has conventionally distinguished poetry from prose is the greater objectivity of its form. Poetry, in contrast to prose, has traditionally been measured (as in the word *meter*) according to agreed-upon and recognizable linguistic units. The rhythmic and other phonological repetitions of poetry (such as rime and alliteration) have allowed for predictability on the part of the reader or listener, and control of language movement and rhythmic effect on the part of the author. Patterns of repetition allow anticipations fulfilled and surprised according to specific and accessible rules. Poetry has always been the most fully reg-

1

ulated of verbal arts, but versification has remained a controversial subject.

A simple explanation is that verse theory, like literary criticism generally, is subject to the fads and controversies that accompany a culture's more general intellectual activity. Although there has never been full agreement on the nature of English versification, dominant theories have tended to reflect their times. In the eighteenth century, for example, Edward Bysshe and others sought to codify English versification along the lines of French syllabic verse theories and the general Enlightenment insistence on logic.[1] English verse was to be measured by the number of syllables per line, and exceptions to established syllabic rules were limited, justified only when meaning was logically advanced by the exception. Pope's famous presentation of "Numbers" in his *Essay on Criticism* (1711) is a discussion, example, and criticism of eighteenth-century English syllabic verse.[2] The nineteenth century, characterized in art generally by the original asymmetries of individual passion, is represented in the history of English metrical theory by Edwin Guest, whose *History of English Rhythms* (1838) turned away from the precise syllabic counts of the French model and went back to the accentual verse of Anglo-Saxon.[3] For Guest, as for Coleridge writing *Christabel*, it was not the number of syllables per line that measured English verse, but the number of accented syllables per line.[4] Guest's work was based on a naive view of Anglo-Saxon verse and of its continuing influence on English, but it did emphasize the importance of accent for English meter and reaffirmed that merely counting syllables, even with sophisticated conventions of syllabification, was not sufficient to determine whether a line made good English verse.

The common nineteenth-century term for accentuation perceived as metrical (that is, as important to the measuring of the verse) was "ictus." The *OED* defines "ictus" as "stress on a particular syllable of a foot or verse; rhythmical or metrical stress." Other terms prominent in late nineteenth-century metrical theory include "arsis" and "thesis," although there was confusion over which of the two signified the relatively stressed syllable within a metrical foot. The *OED* cites varying usages, then concludes that "in modern acceptation" it is arsis that is "the strong syllable in English metre (or classical metre as read by Englishmen), the strong note in barred music; thus identical with the modern meaning of L.[atin] *ictus.*" This is not precisely true. "Arsis" and "thesis" are consistently associated with rising and falling pitch, while ictus comes from Latin "blow, strike, or thrust" and refers to beat or pulse. While the concepts of pitch and beat may be analogous, their equation illustrates a long-standing confusion about accent in English verse. In the Romance languages accent is traditionally associated with pitch (as in the rising and falling pitches of French accents *aigu* and *grave*), but English accent derives from the feature called stress, which has recently even replaced the word "accent" as the denoter of emphasis in English.[5]

In any case, the difference between accent and ictus allowed these nineteenth-century theorists to distinguish usefully between accent generally and accent as part of a system of versification, a distinction that continues in different terms today (see the definitions of stress and accent). But until very recently it was assumed that English, unlike Latin or German, did not have a predictable pattern of accentuation. Well before the turn of the century, however, J. B. Mayor and others recognized that patterns of relative accent among a few syllables could usually be agreed upon. Ictus could therefore be derived from the context of a specific line of verse, even when it was not possible to agree on which syllables were absolutely accented in the normal registers of language.[6] Relative accent is most readily apparent in polysyllabic words (most speakers would place the accent on the second syllable of "today," for example, and on the first syllable of "yesterday"), but it can also be determined in word groups. In "I want to go today" the even syllables (second, fourth, and sixth) are accented relative to the odd syllables (first, third, and fifth) in unemphatic speech. Given the general agreement over relative accentuation, Mayor was able to codify what had usually been assumed and occasionally made explicit from George Gascoigne's first description of English meter in 1575 forward: that the measurement of language appropriate to English verse depends both on the number of syllables in the line and on the position of relatively accented syllables.

Mayor, George Saintsbury, and most critics up to the present have combined eighteenth-century syllabification and nineteenth-century accentuation into a description of English verse as accentual-syllabic. W. K. Wimsatt and Monroe Beardsley reaffirmed the accentual-syllabic view of English versification in a 1959 article that has become the standard theoretical statement of the traditional approach to English meter.[7] That view has been generally supported by the work of linguists, most notably Morris Halle and S. Jay Keyser, who have done much to objectify the phonological bases for accentual-syllabic versification.[8] As a result of these and other recent studies, there is presently some agreement over the following features as most pertinent to the discussion of English versification:

Syllables: morphological units, hard to define but fairly easy to agree upon, which most languages have found useful for measuring lines of verse.[9] Syllables usually consist of a single vowel or dipthong often preceded, followed, or surrounded by consonants or consonant clusters. Conventions of elision (contracting two syllables into one) and synalepha (slurring two syllables together so that they may be perceived as one, although they remain phonetically distinct) occur commonly in poetics, and in some languages, such as French, are important features of rhythmic variety. Conventions of syllabic addition are more rare, though occasionally important. Syllabification of the final -e in Chaucer's poetry apparently continued after it was no longer heard in ordinary speech, and there is good evidence that Renaissance English poets through Milton felt free to count a final -ed as a syllable or not, depending on the needs of their meter. The spelling in Spenser's *Faerie Queene*, apparently supervised by the author, regularly distinguishes between the syllabic and non-syllabic -ed, as with "resolv'd" and "gushed" in I.i.23.

Stress: syllabic emphasis. Patterns of stress are a long-recognized feature of the English language. Nineteenth-century "accent" is synonymous with what we now refer to as stress.

4

According to Halle and Keyser, stress is objectively derivable from the relation of tense vowels to word and phrase patterns. Tense vowels are roughly analogous to what have usually been called "long" vowels in English.[10] Seymour Chatman has summarized studies of the phonological elements that contribute to what we perceive as stress, and has concluded that stress is primarily a confluence of change in pitch, loudness, and duration.[11] However it is defined, native English speakers usually know which syllables should be stressed in the normal, non-emphatic registers of language, and can recognize when stress is appropriate or inappropriate. Stress patterns are basic to clear communication in English, and are often difficult for the non-native speaker to master. They provide a logical and distinguishing feature for abstracting and formalizing poetic measure appropriate to English. Despite flirtations with purely syllabic meters from the thirteenth to the twentieth centuries, English poets have generally had what Sir Philip Sidney called "some regarde of the accent."

Accent: metrical stress, roughly equivalent to nineteenth-century ictus. This maintains the old distinction between a feature of language and that feature counted for purposes of meter, but with a confusing change in terminology. What was referred to in the nineteenth century as "accent" is called "stress," and what was referred to as "ictus" is what is usually meant by the term "accent." In other words, accent now means ictus, and stress now means accent. One needs to be alert to this switch in terminology as one moves from Mayor to Wimsatt and Beardsley. This book assumes the modern terminology, using "stress" to mean an objective feature of the language and "accent" to mean a syllable counted as emphasized for purposes of the meter.

If the distinction is not immediately clear, it emerges in traditional verse scansion. In a conventional binary scansion of the opening line of Shakespeare's Sonnet 30 (an example Wimsatt and Beardsley found useful), "sweet" is a stressed syllable but not an accented one, and "of" is not a stressed syllable but it is accented:

5

Natural Emphasis

```
  /  x  x  /   x  /   x  /  x   /
When to | the ses | sions of | sweet si | lent thought
```

Here "x" designates a syllable relatively unstressed within the conventional syllabic grouping or "foot," and is therefore unaccented (a designation sometimes made by the classical symbol for a short syllable, "‿"). "/" designates the syllable which is stressed relative to the other or others in the foot, and which is therefore considered accented even though it may be an unstressed or (in Halle and Keyser's term) "weak" syllable in ordinary conversation, or in relation to a stressed syllable in another foot.

Foot: an intralinear unit of two or three syllables with their syllabic relationships defined for metrical purposes. The concept of the foot is borrowed from classical meter, which defined syllables as long or short, and used their juxtapositions to allow for complex syllabification. In classical verse two short syllables are the equivalent of one long syllable, so that a spondee, or two long syllables, for example, may be replaced by a dactyl, or one long followed by two short syllables. The English analogue of allowing two unstressed syllables to be the equivalent of one stressed syllable did not become common practice until the Romantic poets, notably Coleridge and Shelley. Some modern theorists, including Otto Jesperson early in this century and Halle and Keyser more recently, reject the concept of the foot for English meter. For them the metrical unit is the line. I accept the concept of the foot, despite its non-English origins and its limited usefulness for describing the appearance of syllabic variety before the Romantics. The Renaissance poets themselves were well aware of classical foot meter, and from early on appeared to be working toward an English version of it (see the discussions of Gascoigne and Harvey in chapter 4).

In English, a foot may be considered a unit of stress relationships between two or among three syllables, not precisely tied to syntax or meaning but with some phonological independence. In other words, it is a unit that focuses on the rhythm of language apart from (though inevitably still somewhat dependent upon) meaning and syntax. Foot meter assumes that language

6

has rhythmic components more abstract or artificial than the phrase, but smaller than the line. The number and patterns of feet determine the kind of line, or kinds of lines, the poem is written in (English iambic pentameter describes five stress-iambic feet, trochaic tetrameter describes four stress-trochaic feet, and so forth), and provide a conceptual framework that allows for what John Hollander and others have referred to as the metrical contract between poet and reader.

Meter: the measure of a line of verse. In English accentual-syllabic poetry the meter is a function of the number of syllables in the line and the pattern of relatively stressed and unstressed syllables within individual feet. Shakespeare's line has ten syllables, which may most easily be described as iambically patterned. Meter describes the metrical pattern derivable from a given line of verse, and recognizes only two levels of stress: accented or unaccented. It depends on the reader's recognition of pattern, and therefore posits a reader's experience with verse and ability to conceptualize form. Since meter is determined foot by foot, according to formal patterns of relatively stressed and relatively unstressed syllables, metrical accents may sometimes appear at odds with the normal patterns of prose or conversation. So it is in the Shakespeare line, where "of" is relatively stressed within its foot while the stronger syllable, "sweet," is relatively unstressed within its foot. The inherent artificiality of a metrical pattern is at once its strength and weakness: its strength, because meter is almost completely objectifiable when derived foot by foot, and can lead the reader to see a contrastive or emphatic stress that might be missed in prose; its weakness, because alone it cannot describe the effect of living language in a given line of verse. Sometimes, as in "When to the sessions of sweet silent thought," it is in discernible tension with the regular emphasis of the language in units larger than the single foot.

Rhythm: the movement of a line of verse. Rhythm refers to the actual, as opposed to the abstract, patterns of emphasis and repetition in a given line of verse. H. L. Trager and G. L. Smith posited four readily-discernible levels of English stress, providing a useful technique for observing the more complex

7

patterns of language movement in a poem.[12] If meter is determined foot by foot, rhythm is a function of the whole line and sometimes a pair or set of lines. Rhythm is the interaction between the prose and normal stress and sound patterns of the language on the one hand, as they might be analyzed according to Trager and Smith's four levels of stress, and the conceptual direction of the abstract pattern on the other hand. For example, a legitimate question about "When to the sessions of sweet silent thought" is whether "of" or "sweet" should receive emphasis. The metrical answer is "of," since it is accented and "sweet" is not. But in most ordinary circumstances the answer would have to be "sweet," since it is a more important word both semantically and phonologically. The rhythmic answer is that both words are emphasized, though in the context of the whole line "sweet" naturally receives greater emphasis. A reading of the line according to both the metrical scansion and Trager and Smith's four levels of stress would produce the following (where 1 = greatest stress and 4 = least stress):

```
    /   x   x   /   x   /   x   /  x       /
When to | the ses | sions of | sweet si | lent thought
    2   3   4   1   4   3   2   1   4       1
```

Two lines from one of Sidney's renunciation sonnets illustrate how the rhythmic resolution of meter and the ordinary stress patterns of prose discourse may affect tone and even meaning. In the poem's first line, a metrical derivation of iambic pentameter would seem to promote stress on "but," a word usually unemphatic:

```
    /    x x /     x   /   x  /  x  /
Leave me | o love, | which reach | est but | to dust
```

The rhythm of the line does encourage a fairly brisk progress from the heavily emphasized first four syllables, especially "love," to the "dust" into which "love" degenerates. Still, "but" must receive some emphasis; the meter demands it. As the poem proceeds, the reader recognizes that the speaker is pointing to two kinds of love, one that reaches "*but* to dust," and one "which never taketh rust" (l. 3). The former is associated with fire, the latter with an illuminating beacon to heaven. In line 9 the distinction between the two loves is affirmed by an apparent direct conflict between the established meter and normal speech patterns:

O take fast hold, let that light be thy guide

In modern terms, the line may seem unmetrical. It appears to consist of four rather than five feet, the last two anapestic:

```
x  /    x   /    x  x  /     x  x  /
O take | fast hold, | let that light | be thy guide
```

If we assume that the received meter will help the line resolve into its true rhythm, however, we discover a contrastive stress important to the meaning and tone of the poem:

```
x   /   x   /    x  /   x   /    x  /
O take | fast hold, | let that | light be | thy guide
        4      1        3        2
```

It continues to be common to confuse or try to conflate meter and rhythm, a practice given some legitimacy by Jesperson who in 1901 sought to correct the admittedly stultifying tendency of Bernhard ten Brink (and others) to wrench language rhythm into preconceived foot meters. Some modern readers do not hear the influence of meter on a line of verse. Others more deliberately collapse the distinction between meter and rhythm.

Natural Emphasis

Anthony Easthope, for example, insists that "it is not the case that the official pattern is a metrical 'abstraction' and its practice in counterpoint an 'actualization' of this abstraction; rather, the counterpoint *is* the meter." Easthope defines counterpoint as "the vector between the two axes" of abstract pattern and living language. I would say instead that what he calls "counterpoint" is the rhythm.[13] Rhythm is a function of both idea and verbal reality, a fusion of the abstract and concrete into living art. It carries the artist's control over the enactment, the individual performance, of the poem. The poem is a dead object until it is enacted in the mind's eye of the reader or the ear of the listener, and then it becomes more than Keats's cold pastoral although it remains something other than his living hand. Rhythm is the artist's control over the performance of the poem.[14]

Yet it is precisely on the level of performance that controversy has most raged. Line 9 of the Sidney poem could be scanned as four feet. So, perhaps, could the Shakespeare line, as it was by a colleague of mine:

/ x x / x x / xx /
When to | the ses | sions of sweet | silent thought

I reject this very lyrical reading because it denies the reasonable expectation of stress on the first syllable of "silent," it does not support the tone implied by the statement, and it tends to equate meter with rhythm, since it depends almost entirely on a reading of the whole line. In addition, it challenges the experienced reader's expectation of a metrical contract between poet and reader by first denying the expected sonnet meter (in itself not unheard of) and then returning to it in the next line. Most poets, especially Renaissance poets, simply do not work that way. My colleague nonetheless remains unpersuaded.

If two experienced scholars of versification who are more often in agreement than not can have such a thoroughgoing disagreement over so famous a line, then to what extent is a poet's intended performance decipherable, objectifiable, and repeatable?

10

The answer is: somewhat. There will always be differences among individual performances, a fact more to be lauded than damned. I once saw two great performances of *King Lear* within a couple of years of each other, one with Morris Carnovsky and the other with Eric Porter. I preferred Porter, but both actors showed me things I had not seen before, or had not considered in quite the way they presented them. Although I thought Porter's interpretation more "right" than Carnovsky's, neither was "wrong." Nor were the productions distorted, as for example in the eighteenth century when Nahum Tate rewrote the play to allow Lear to live and Cordelia to marry Edgar. This changes the material altogether, but to allow for individual performance of the same material is not to deny objective standards of performance nor the goal of serving the art.

Whatever strictly individualized pleasures may come from idiosyncratic or socially popular performances of plays or poems, it remains a fundamental duty of scholars and critics to serve as faithfully as may be the author's text. The goal should not be the reconstruction and presentation of what is archaic and irrelevant, but rather the revivification of art in its own terms. With that in mind, there are some things about which we can be objective in the study of versification. One purpose of this book is to provide a context and a perspective for hearing, and for properly re-enacting, the art of Renaissance poetry. This is not to deny that there is some range for individual readings, but to help make all readings more alive to the text.

A thesis of this book is that the history of English verse since 1066 is the history of the tensions and accommodations between the Germanic and the Romance, mainly the French, verse traditions. When Mayor recognized that English verse could best be described as accentual-syllabic, he was tacitly recognizing the English fusion of the Germanic-accentual with the French-syllabic traditions. In addition to these tensions and accommodations, English verse has from time to time been subject to an overlay of quantitative or temporal verse theories and practices. The late sixteenth-century effort to discard rime and create an English verse based entirely on classical Greek and

11

Natural Emphasis

Latin models is an important example.[15] There have also been various attempts, notably in this century, to describe English verse by musical notation or extended analogues with music.[16] These efforts tend to be well away from the mainstream of English verse, however, and I will touch on them only when they have directly influenced central theory or practice.

Throughout I depend primarily on the standard accentual-syllabic scansion with which most students of poetry are familiar and which is readily accessible in the *Encyclopedia of Poetry and Poetics*, Paul Fussell's *Poetic Meter and Poetic Form*, Hollander's *Rhyme's Reason*, or any of a number of handbooks on poetry.[17] Explanations and notation may vary slightly among these, but anyone familiar with one of them should have no difficulty in following my scansions. Dependence on standard scansion is not only intended as a convenience for the non-specialist but also as an affirmation of the emergence of foot meter as central to the development of English verse in the Renaissance. Since that emergence is not immediate, I will also have occasion to use Halle and Keyser's system for English scansion and my own notation for the accentual aspect of late medieval verse, but these will be explained as appropriate and will require no special background.

In addition to these technical matters, I should also indicate some of the underlying assumptions of this book and anticipate broader concepts that will appear in the course of it. These begin with the philosophical assumption that poetry is, among other things, a universal response to the problem of time, and lines of verse are a direct reflection and conceptualization of that response. In particular, they respond to three ways in which human experience seeks to alter or overcome its subjection to the dynamic of time: by incantation, by making records, and by providing repeatable experiences.

Poetry has long been associated with religion and its verses with the rhythmic incantations of both literate and preliterate cultures.[18] In this context verse is a cousin of both prophecy and mysticism – prophecy through the oracular significance of figurative language and the predictability of rhythm that meter

12

allows, and mysticism through the hypnotic effects of repeated rhythmic phrasing and the mood of contemplative concentration and time-space transcendence that such formulas may sometimes invoke. This poetic response to the tyranny of time is a subject for metaphysicians and social scientists, and I will make very little reference to it in this book.

More to our purpose is the fact that poetry, like all art, makes records of experience, real or feigned. "This day is holy; doe ye write it downe," says Spenser in the *Epithalamion*, "That ye for ever it remember may." Record-making acknowledges that in a temporal universe permanence resides in memory, and recording has therefore been a simple but essential social function of art. It was so acknowledged by the fame ethic of classical Rome, and by the Renaissance reflection of that ethic.[19] Even more basic is the mnemonic aspect of verse, which allows for extended record-keeping, as in genealogies and cultural histories, among preliterate cultures.

The repeatability of the artistic experience is related to the making of records but the two are not precisely the same. It is true that something must in some way be recorded before it can be repeated, but art as replication provides more than evidence that something once happened or someone once thought or felt something. It provides for that "once" to happen again, for experience to be relived.[20] A poem by Ben Jonson is not only a record of the virtues of the Countess of Bedford or Sir Henry Morison; it is also a repeatable affirmation of those virtues, and repeatable not only as a speech act Jonson once feigned to utter but also, through Jonson's artistic voice, as an experience of the subject of the poem. Poetry as repeatable experience is even more clear in drama or dramatic lyrics, as in the works of Shakespeare or Donne, where the performer and the reader are invited to enact experience.

Rhythmic elements are crucial not only for the incantatory aspect of verse but also for this enactment. When meter is sufficiently objective it allows for a base structure which the poet can use to control emphasis and phrasing even more precisely than in carefully constructed prose. In addition, by affecting

13

tone and conveying a complex of attitudes and feelings, the poet directs not only the speech patterns of the poem but also the experience it enacts, so that a fictive or long-gone reality may be felt along the pulse. Rhythm creates an experience from what would otherwise be simply a record.

Insofar as a poem is a record it serves the classical function of providing permanence through time by enduring in the memory of succeeding generations. Insofar as a poem provides a repeatable experience, experience which can in some sense be lived *now*, it approaches the eternal, which theologians have defined as infinite present. The former is basic to Humanist classicism; the latter is a feature of Christian Humanism. Renaissance poets such as Spenser and Jonson were aware that poetry brought fame and that it had a transcendent dimension. It both extended through time and imitated the eternal now. However much they and their colleagues emphasized the more pragmatic function of teaching by delighting, poetry was understood to be an eternizing force.[21]

Verse is the emblem for poetry's complementary dual function of record and reenactment. The line of verse must be read through time to establish rhythm. In English, the stress feature on which rhythm is based is relative to the sequence of syllables uttered through time. Rhythmic positions therefore require serio-temporality. But rhythm is also repetition, which requires return as well as sequence. The pattern of repetition and change, of repetition through time and understood by means of time, is both characteristic and defining of the poetic line on the one hand and crucial to the theory behind the production of poetry on the other. From this vantage the poetic line is more than the formal technique by which a certain art is conveyed. Linear rhythm is itself a reflection of an idea of art that has dominated Western culture at least since Aristotle, who perceived art as emanating from two basic human impulses: to imitate and to create harmony. The former implies a drive toward reenactment, and both involve repetition: "Poetry in general seems to have sprung from two causes, each of them lying deep in our nature. First, the instinct of imitation is implanted in

14

man from childhood, one difference between him and other animals being that he is the most imitative of living creatures, and through imitation learns his earliest lessons. And no less universal is the pleasure felt in things imitated. Next, there is the instinct for harmony and rhythm, – meters being manifestly sections of rhythm."[22]

To a certain extent the style of a poet or a period in the history of English verse may be described in terms of convenient dichotomies. Poetry as record and poetry as reenactment may be loosely associated with what are usually called public and private poetry, for example.[23] A distinction useful for this book is between what I call aesthetic and mimetic verse forms and rhythms.[24] These terms will appear throughout, and are meant to indicate tendencies rather than absolute categories or antagonisms.

By mimetic I mean forms and rhythms that directly imitate, represent, or promote the speaking voice the poem seeks to present or the statement the poem is making. By aesthetic I mean those forms and rhythms which are themselves somehow pleasurable and add to the total power of the poem, but which do not directly imitate, represent, or promote either the effect of the speaking voice or the lexical meaning of the poem's statement. Aesthetic rhythms are perceived as beautiful or as appropriate and just, without themselves signifying (in the usual sense of pointing to something other than themselves); as the philosophical meaning of "aesthetic" implies, aesthetic rhythms are pleasing for their design and proportion and for the interaction of sameness and variety. Program music and representational art are analogous to mimetic forms and rhythms in poetry; fugal music and abstract art are analogous to aesthetic forms and rhythms. Campion and Herrick are masters of the aesthetic, while Sidney is a master of mimetic rhythms and Herbert of mimetic forms, both of voice and of subject matter in each case.

The development of English versification in this crucial period of what John Thompson has quite properly called "the founding of English metre" may be roughly described as the interplay between the English language and its continental poetic

15

Natural Emphasis

models, especially the French and Italian, as explored by the variously aesthetic and mimetic talents of an impressive number of fine poets. The result of that development is an English versification appropriate to the newly established phonologies of Modern English and remarkable for its combination of objectivity and flexibility. The ultimate purpose of this study is to provide a basis for understanding both the objectivity and the flexibility of what we have come to call traditional English meters, and to diminish or at least clarify the areas of disagreement that have plagued the study of English versification.

We begin with Chaucer, whose English language had long been the companion of Anglo-Norman French and Medieval Latin.

NOTES

1. Edward Bysshe's *The Art of English Poetry* (1702), went through several editions. For its influence and a more extensive consideration of eighteenth-century prosodic theory, see Paul Fussell, Jr., *Theory of Prosody in Eighteenth-Century England* (New London: Connecticut College Monographs, 1954).

2. Pope also makes it clear that "equal syllables alone" and "the same unvaried chimes" are insufficient criteria for effective verse. See Jacob H. Adler, *The Reach of Art: A Study in the Prosody of Pope* (Gainesville, Fla.: Univ. of Florida Monographs, 1964).

3. Edwin Guest, *History of English Rhythms*, 2 vols. (London: William Pickering, 1838). His focus on accent affected his reading of eighteenth-century as well as of earlier poets. In a reference to Pope's description of swift Camilla (in the "Numbers" section of the *Essay on Criticism*), who "Flies o'er th'unbending corn: and skims along the main," Guest entirely misses the sophistication of Pope's carefully elided alexandrine. He says that Pope "seems to have thought, that, to represent rapid motion, it was sufficient to crowd his verse with syllables; and for this purpose he even added to the number of accents! Who can wonder at his failure?" (1:168).

4. Coleridge was a master of traditional versification who experimented with complex analogues of classical feet as well as hearkening back to an early English accentual tradition. The result is a loose iambic movement in the "mystery" poems – *Rime of the Ancient Mariner*, "Kubla Khan," and *Christabel* – with the last (1816) an explicit experiment in accentual verse.

16

5. The confusion of English accent with pitch goes back at least as far as the first treatise on English metrics (George Gascoigne's "Certayne Notes of Instruction Concerning the Making of Verse or Ryme in English," *Posies of George Gascoigne*, 1575), and has tended to blur the distinction between English and continental or classical versification.

6. J. B. Mayor, *Chapters on English Metre* (Cambridge: Cambridge Univ. Press, 1901). See also George Saintsbury, *A History of English Prosody*, 3 vols. (London: Macmillan, 1906-10). Saintsbury's theoretical basis is a muddier version of Mayor's work, which Saintsbury admired.

7. W. K. Wimsatt and Monroe Beardsley, "The Concept of Meter: An Exercise in Abstraction," *Publications of the Modern Language Association of America*, 74(1959):585-98; rpt. *Essays on the Language of Literature*, ed. Seymour Chatman and Samuel R. Levin (Boston: Houghton Mifflin, 1967), 91-114.

8. See especially Moris Halle and S. Jay Keyser's *English Stress: Its Form, Its Growth, and Its Role in Verse* (New York: Harper and Row, 1971). This work is based on Noam Chomsky and Morris Halle, *The Sound Pattern of English* (Cambridge, Mass.: MIT Press, 1968). Among other recent work, Paul Kiparsky's is an extension and revision of the Halle-Keyser theory in an effort to account for more complex aspects of verse rhythm. See "Stress, Syntax, and Meter," *Language*, 51(1975):576-616 and "The Rhythmic Structure of English Verse," *Linguistic Inquiry*, 8(1977):189-247. David Chisholm provides a thorough critique of Halle and Keyser and of Kiparsky in "Generative Prosody and English Verse," *Poetics*, n.s. 6(1977):111-53. Chisholm is a proponent of Karl Magnuson and Frank G. Ryder's generative theory, summarized by Magnuson in "Rules and Observations in Prosody: Positional Level and Base," *Poetics*, 12(1974):143-54. Largely for its accessibility to the majority of readers of Renaissance poetry, but also for its sufficiency in describing the development of English verse in the Renaissance, I am relying on what is usually called the traditional approach to English versification. Its relation to some aspects of generative linguistic metrics is well expressed by W. K. Wimsatt in "The Rule and the Norm: Halle and Keyser on Chaucer's Meter," *College English*, 31(1970):774-88, rpt. *Literary Style*, ed. Seymour Chatman (New York: Oxford Univ. Press, 1971), 197-215. See T. V. F. Brogan, *English Versification, 1570-1980: A Reference Guide with a Global Appendix* (Baltimore: Johns Hopkins Univ. Press, 1981), 233-318, for the bibliography relevant to further exploration of traditional and linguistic stress meters.

9. Cf. Sanford Schane, *Generative Phonology* (Englewood Cliffs, N.J.: Prentice-Hall, 1973), 9: "Ironically, the syllable as a unit has not been

satisfactorily defined, but that it plays a role in many kinds of phonological processes is undeniable."

10. Halle and Keyser, 3 ff. Tense vowels are those in "beat," "bait," and "boot," for example, as opposed to "bit," "bat," and "but."

11. Seymour Chatman, *A Theory of Meter* (The Hague: Mouton, 1965).

12. H. L. Trager and G. L. Smith, *An Outline of English Structure* (Norman, Okla.: Univ. of Oklahoma Press, 1951).

13. See Otto Jesperson's "Notes on Metre," rpt. *Essays on the Language of Literature*, 71-90; and Anthony Easthope, "Problematizing the Pentameter," *New Literary History*, 12(1981):475-92. Some of the confusion between meter and rhythm may also account for the apparent alienation from the mainstream that David Crystal's interesting work on prosodic intonation has suffered. He raises important questions in *Prosodic Systems and Intonation in English* (Cambridge: Cambridge Univ. Press, 1969) and "Intonation and Metrical Theory," *Transactions of the Philological Society*, 1971, 1-33. Although I disagree with his metrical claims, he offers substantial insights into the rhythms of phrasing and lineation in poetry, and suggests why some of these questions about the nature of meter and rhythm in English refuse to go away.

14. Derek Attridge's excellent *Rhythms of English Poetry* (London: Longman, 1982) arrived too late to consider its arguments in detail, but it also supports the recent trend toward rejecting foot meter for English, largely on the basis that foot meter is contrived and artificial. Attridge sees "meter" and "rhythm" as different in degree rather than kind (153-55). I would argue that what he calls "underlying rhythm" directs the codification of an abstraction which in turn acts as a conceptual direction for the realized rhythms of the line. That is, "underlying rhythm" directs us to the meter, which in turn helps to direct what I call the rhythm of the line. Attridge does not distinguish between metrical substitutions and rhythmic tensions (15), and in this and in the general confusion between meter (idea) and rhythm (realized language) he misses some of poetry's potential subtlety and ignores what are often explicit efforts by the poets who wrote in what we have come to think of as "traditional" verse. But the relation between foot and line is complex and problematic. It should be clear from this book that English foot meters did not arrive full grown out of the head of Chaucer, or anyone else, and an English meter based on accentual-syllabic (as opposed to quantitative) feet was a happy and perhaps coincidental derivation from a variety of influences. See chapter 3.

15. See Derek Attridge, *Well-Weighed Syllables: Elizabethan Verse in Classical Metres* (Cambridge: Cambridge Univ. Press, 1974).

16. Such analogues are probably as old as the two arts. In the Renaissance they were common, and best represented in English by Thomas Campion's *Observations in the Art of English Poesie* (London, 1602), a useful and interesting document despite its support of the losing side in the controversy over rime (see chapter 4). In this century some writers have used musical and poetic notation almost interchangeably, resulting in a distorted view of English verse. See, for example, M. A. Bayfield, *The Measures of the Poets* (Cambridge: Cambridge Univ. Press, 1919); Katherine M. Wilson, *Sound and Meaning in English Poetry* (New York: Jonathan Cape, 1930); and even Geoffrey N. Leech's generally excellent *Linguistic Guide to English Poetry* (London: Longman, 1969), 106-14. That there is some usefulness to analogies between these two serio-temporal arts is undeniable. The problem lies in the tendency to equate what is merely analogous, and to confuse terminologies and notations. For a listing of temporalist and musical theories and their responses, see Brogan, 193-225.

17. *Encyclopedia of Poetry and Poetics*, ed. Alex Preminger (Princeton: Princeton Univ. Press, 1965); Paul Fussell, Jr., *Poetic Meter and Poetic Form*, rev. ed. (New York: Random House, 1979); John Hollander, *Rhyme's Reason* (New Haven: Yale Univ. Press, 1981). Handbooks include those by Joseph Malof and George Woods. Most introductions to poetry include summaries of scansion techniques, and although they are not nearly as consistent or reliable as one would like, they are frequently useful at a basic level.

18. John M. Foley, in "The Ritual Nature of Traditional Oral Poetry," (Ph.D. diss., Univ. of Mass., 1974), observes metrical formulae associated with religious and social ritual.

19. The fame ethic may be an important feature of a legitimate separation between the Renaissance and the Middle Ages. Georges Poulet, in *Studies in Human Time*, tr. Elliott Coleman (Baltimore: Johns Hopkins Univ. Press, 1956), 3-38, sees the Renaissance and Reformation combining to eradicate theological concepts of time.

20. Cf. Hans Meyerhoff, *Time in Literature* (Berkeley and Los Angeles: Univ. of Calif. Press, 1960), 48: "Creative imagination is creative recall. Recollection is an activity. . . . To construct a work of art is to re-construct the world of experience and the self." See also 89-106 for his summary of the increasing importance of time in literature since Descartes.

21. For a summary of Renaissance attitudes toward time, see Ricardo Quinones, *The Renaissance Discovery of Time* (Cambridge, Mass.: Harvard Univ. Press, 1972), 3-27. "In his attempts to manage time, Renaissance

man strives to achieve by means of process what eternity possesses in stasis" (26).

22. Aristotle, *Poetics*, II, 4 (1448b), tr. S. H. Butcher, ed. with an introduction by Francis Fergusson (New York: Hill and Wang, 1961). For the attitudes of some twentieth-century symbolic and phenomenological aestheticians toward temporalism, see the several essays on time and art in *Reflections on Art*, ed. Susanne K. Langer (New York: Oxford Univ. Press, 1961), esp. Raymond Bayer, "The Essence of Rhythm," 186-201. Bayer states: *"Phenomena of the aesthetic order are all characterized, on every level, by a certain constancy: and this constancy is revealed to us by the study of rhythms"* (190). Italics are Bayer's.

23. It remains, of course, quite possible to create a public record of a private experience (as in the *Epithalamion)* or to emphasize private experience on a public occassion (as in Donne's "Good Friday, Riding Westward").

24. Susanne Woods, "Aesthetic and Mimetic Rhythms in the Verse of Gascoigne, Sidney, and Spenser," *Studies in the Literary Imagination*, 11(1978):31-44.

Chapter Two

Chaucer and the Fifteenth Century

Some vers faile in a sillable

Chaucer, *Hous of Fame*

During the latter half of the fourteenth century, when Geoffrey Chaucer (1343-1400) was pursuing his various public responsibilities and also writing poetry, there were no treatises on English verse. Chaucer was profoundly original. He took French and Italian models, his own familiarity with what had by then become an English poetic tradition, and the rising prestige of the London language, to establish virtually by himself an English poetry that would dominate subsequent generations despite the rapid change in the language.[1] The development of English versification through the Renaissance, therefore, begins with Chaucer, specifically with his theoretical and practical heritage, his transformation of it, and its transmission (not entirely intact) to the sixteenth century.

Although there were no treatises on English verse, there were by Chaucer's time many works on Latin and French verse, some written by Englishmen. As early as the scholar and poet Aldhelm (c. 639-705) medieval England produced treatises on Latin versification, the most important of which was *De Metrica Arte*, a textbook by the Venerable Bede (673-735).[2] The section "De Rithmo" is of particular relevance to the development of Romance versification, describing in new and appreciative detail

21

the essentially syllabic "rhythmic" verse of medieval Latin song. Unlike classical Latin quantitative verse, which allowed two short syllables to equal one long (according to conventional formulae), in rhythmic verse "every syllable is strictly counted and even elision is looked upon with doubtful eye."[3]

Bede's discussion "De Accentibus" begins its analysis of eight different kinds of accent with three that anticipate Romance pitch-accent and may also include elements of stress-accent:[4] acute, circumflex, and grave. He then goes on to discuss accent as quantity, starting with "long" and "short." His focus on the first three accents, which do not allow the interchange of two syllables for one as classical quantitative verse does, suggests the dominance of medieval rhythmic verse for Bede. In the "De Rithmo" section of his treatise, Bede goes on to observe how patterns of rhythmic accent often imitate patterns from quantitative verse. Syllables accented in rhythmic verse may also be conventionally "long," and unaccented syllables may be "short," but not necessarily. Thus, for example, Dag Norberg analyzes the following line taken from Bede:[5]

$$\backslash \quad x \; / \; x \quad \backslash \; x \; / \; x \quad /x \quad / \quad x \quad / \; x \; \backslash$$
Apparebit I repentina II dies magna Domini

Despite the analogue with classical meters, there is no room for variable syllabification, and the values accented/unaccented clearly dominate over rules for long and short. For example, the last syllable of "apparebit," combined with the first consonant of "repentina," would be considered long by convention (because its short vowel is followed by two consonants, even though across a word boundary). It is clearly to be treated as unaccented, however.

This early analogue to English accentual-syllabic meter does not appear to have made any immediate impact on English verse, which was at the time and remained for another three or

22

four hundred years the strong-stressed alliterative verse of Old English.[6] Rhythmic Latin verse, increasingly in rimed lyric forms, continued to be written and to gain acceptance, and had a major influence on the development of lyric forms and syllabic meters in the Romance languages.[7] After 1066 French forms especially were to have tremendous impact on English verse. By this circuitous route Bede's observations eventually returned to have an effect on the constantly changing language of his own country.

John of Garland's *Parisiana Poetria de Arte Prosaica, Metrica, et Rithmica* (c. 1235) illustrates the continuing importance of Latin rhythmic verse (the *Rithmica* as opposed to the *Metrica* of the title).[8] Garland was born in England, educated at Oxford, and taught at the University of Paris most of his life. An interesting exception is the three years he spent as Master of Grammar at the University of Toulouse during the full flourishing of Provençal vernacular lyrics (1229-1231). Although we have no direct evidence of his association with troubadour lyrics, Garland was a prolific Latin poet with an appreciation for rhythmic Latin lyric forms that coincided with the flourishing of similar forms in the Romance vernaculars. His *Poetria* provides a full description of a variety of lyrics with abundant examples. Garland's work, like Geoffrey of Vinsauf's better-known *Poetria Nova* (which "represents what is practically a treatise on rhetoric as applied to poetry"[9]) influenced European vernacular poetry as well as the Latin for which it was explicitly intended.[10]

Among sources which may have had a more direct influence on Chaucer's understanding of versification is Guilhelm Molinier's *Las Leys d'amors* (1356), "the climax of Provençal theorizing on grammar, rhetoric, poetics, and metrics."[11] This extensive codification of the sophisticated practices of the poets of Southern France emphasizes techniques of versification. Another and more certain source for Chaucer's versification was the work of the poet and musician Guillaume de Machaut (1290?-1377), who is credited with making the ballade and rondeau fashionable and with presenting Chaucer with the model for the English heroic couplet.[12] Machaut was also a major influence on Chaucer's acquaintance, the great French lyricist Eustache Deschamps, who proclaimed himself Machaut's pupil and codified their mutual view of poetic technique in the short treatise, *L'Art de Dictier* (1392).[13]

The ties between England and France from 1066 through the fourteenth century were very close. It would be a mistake to take the fourteenth-century French verse treatises as complete or sufficient descriptions of what English poets were attempting, but they are perhaps better guides at least to English courtly poetry than has generally been assumed. For one thing, most writers of English verse inherited a tradition of Anglo-Norman verse and verse forms in their own country. For another, the fourteenth-century English court and all literate English society spoke both French and English, if not French, English, and Latin. Most importantly, the English language of Chaucer's time incorporated many features from the French, including vocabulary and syntactic patterns. The polysyllabic words from French (and sometimes from Latin) combined with a relatively more fixed word order to make the heavy stresses of Old English give way to more variable and fluid patterns of relative stress in Middle English. This alteration in the language made French verse models more compatible with English poetry than would have been the case three hundred years before.[14] In the absence of authors who write about English verse, then, Molinier, Machaut, and Deschamps provide a useful outine of established verse practices contemporary with Chaucer and far from alien.

Molinier's emphasis is on a variety of strophes, in their patterning within a given poem, and in the decorous use of form to serve certain kinds of subject matter, mostly related to the general topic of love. His treatise also defines some of the most basic ingredients of verse: syllable, accent, rime, and the single line, among others. The "Seconde Partie" of *Las Leys d'amors*, for example, begins with a definition "des bordos (ou vers)": "Le *bordos* (ou vers) est une partie de rime, qui dôit compter douze syllabes, au plus, et au moins quatre, a moins qu'il ne soit *enté*, ou *brisé;* car alors il peut être non seulement de quatre, mais de trois et de moins, jusqu'à une syllabe."[15] The acceptable line of verse is thus measured by the number of syllables, which ordinarily may be no fewer than four nor more than twelve. These limits describe most European practice in the twelfth through fourteenth centuries, and beyond.

Precise syllable count was not a feature of Anglo-Saxon alliterative verse, and although English poetry borrowed rime, strophic forms, and a general sense of syllabic number as early as the twelfth century, most pre-Renaissance English poets resisted more stringent rules for syllabic number. As a result, one of the difficulties of describing medieval English versification lies in determining the extent to which the line's proper measure is seen as syllabic and the extent to which stressed syllables are heard as the primary metrical feature, with or without regular syllabification.

In lyric verse the lines tend to be short and there are fewer opportunities for rhythmic confusion. Additionally, the best of the lyrics carry a sense of their musical settings, whether or not precise accentuation or syllabification is present. We see this in the well-known *reverdie*, or celebration of spring, from the early thirteenth century:[16]

> Sing! cuccu, nu. Sing! cuccu.
> Sing! cuccu. Sing! cuccu, nu.

> Sumer is icumen in–
> Lhude sing! cuccu.
> Groweth sed and bloweth med
> And springeth the wude nu–
> Sing! cuccu.

> Awe bleteth after lomb,
> Lhouth after calve cu,
> Bulluc sterteth, bucke verteth,
> Murie sing! cuccu.
> Cuccu, cuccu,
> Well singes thu, cuccu–
> New swik thu never nu!

Natural Emphasis

The syllabification is imprecise in lines that should be analogous (as lines 2 and 4 of the first stanza) and the accent pattern is fairly complex (the refrain is divisible in several ways; the two stanzas are arranged 43432 and 4443233). Even so, most readers have no problem hearing a rhythm based on the accented syllables. The recurrent rime undoubtedly helps to underscore accentuation. End-rime always sounds the second syllable of "cuccu," and there is internal rime in the third line of each stanza.

Narrative poetry illustrates both the extent of the English debt to the French during the Middle Ages and the resistance of English verse to strict syllabification. Many of the earliest post-conquest narratives show clear French influence. Several are direct or indirect imitations of French verse *(e.g., The Owl and the Nightingale, Kyng Alisaunder, and Floris and Blauncheflour).*[17] As a rule, the English poems treat the syllabic range with greater flexibility than their French models. French octosyllabic poetry will allow for as many as nine or as few as seven syllables in the line, but the eight-syllable norm will usually obtain and there are definite rules for the seven- and nine-syllable versions of the line. In a similar English poem a variety of line lengths is quite common, although the octosyllabic norm is apparently assumed and more or less maintained. There are occasional six-syllable lines in this English narrative poetry and riming lines may not be of the same number of syllables (much more rare in good French verse).[18]

Kyng Alisaunder, for example, from the late twelfth or early thirteenth century, asserts a clear octosyllabic norm in the first few lines:

On a day sone after than
Com Candulek, a gentil man—
Candaces son, kyng of Brye—
With wel faire chyvalrye,
And wolde with Alisaunder speke,

But what its modern editors refer to as "forceful and lively verse" quickly shows disregard for strict syllable count.[19] Some lines have ten or more syllables, even allowing for elision:

> 'Sir, graunt mercy! Therwhiles I was fare
> On pilgrimages to Jerusalem and Yndare,
> The duk Hirtan, a tyraunt of Brye,

(ll. 55-57)

Others have nine syllables, permissible in French octosyllabic verse, but in many instances an accent falls on the ninth syllable, which is unacceptable in French practice, where the accent must fall on the eighth syllable:

>   /
> 'Telle on thi wronge,' quoth Tholomay,

>   /
> 'We shulle the helpe gif we may.'

(ll. 53-54)

What finally keeps the rhythm more surely than syllabification is a consistent four-accent norm, which will obtain across lines of unequal syllables:

>   /   /   /   /
> 'Sir, graunt mercy! Therwhiles I was fare

>   /   /   /   /
> On pilgrimages to Jerusalem and Yndare,

>   /   /   /   /
> The duk Hirtan, a tyraunt of Brye,

Natural Emphasis

/   /   / /
Com with grete chyvalrie,

/   /   /   /
Robbed my make Blasfame

/   /   / /
Also fair as was Dyane.

(ll. 55-60)

There is even more syllabic disarray in Layamon's *Brut*, which, like *Kyng Alisaunder*, occurs at about the time when French poetic practices were being integrated into English verse. In *Brut* the accentuation remains as inconsistent as the syllabics:

> Tha com ther in are tiden an oht mon riden,
> And brohte tidinge Arthure than kinge
> From Moddrede his suster sune; Arthure he wes wilcume:
> For he wende that he brohte boden swithe gode.
> Arthur lai alle longe niht and spac with thene yeonge cniht,
> Swa naver nulde he him sugge soth hu hit ferde.

(ll. 1-6)

The number of syllables tends to range from ten to fourteen, with no regular rime or alliterative pattern. The verse appears as a confusion of metrical possibilities, perhaps with a tendency toward a five-stress norm. But the stress pattern is not regular enough to be readily perceptible as an overall metrical intent. The number of accents in the first six lines ranges from four in line 1 to seven or eight in line 5. What *Brut* appears to assert is the metrical continuity of the hemistich or half-line for English verse. In lines 82-85, for example, the syllabic range is from twelve to fourteen, the accentual range from four to six, but the phrasing breaks around the middle to allow for what is some-times called "dipodic," or double-foot verse, but which is really a verse dependent upon rhythmic phrasing within each hemistich:

28

   /   /   /   /
Tha saet hit al stille || in Arthures halle.

   /   / /   /   /
Tha wes ther saerinaesse || mid sele than kinge.

   /   /   /   /   /   /
Tha weoren Bruttisce men || swithe unbalde vor thaen.

It is easy to exaggerate the English departure from French rules of versification, but it is also important to remember that Middle English, like Old English, remained a more heavily and consistently stressed language than French, with greater importance attached to the mid-line break, whether a formally metrical cesura or hemistich is apparent or not.[20] Another difference suggested by Molinier's treatise is the relative importance of rime and rime scheme to Romance versification as opposed to English. Complex strophic constructions were central to the techniques of Romance verse,[21] since many words rime naturally in the Romance languages. It is and was more difficult to sustain a long series of rimes in English. Rime is therefore especially suitable for patterning Romance verse, as alliteration was for the patterning of Old English verse, and theorists such as Molinier were as concerned with avoiding monotony as they were with suggesting rime schemes. One technique is "rime riche," or polysyllabic rime. Another is the design of complex and extended stanzaic forms, so that a more-than-ordinary virtuosity is required to extend appropriate rimes.[22]

The relatively greater difficulty of extended riming in English may largely account for the less complex stanza forms we tend to find in English as compared with Romance poetry. In discussing *las coblas* (literally, "couplets," but used to mean the joining of lines in stanza units of up to sixteen lines), Molinier examines the diverse combinations of line length, stanza length, and rime scheme available to the writer of Provençal poetry. Despite definite rules, the overall impression is of variety, abundance, and almost infinite possibility for stanzaic construction. Molinier does insist on decorum. The "couplet" must correspond to the period, or unit of thought; short *vers brisés* must not be allowed to break the flow of thought; the midline pause or *répos suspensif* should bear some relation to that flow as well as obeying traditional placement rules; and so forth. It is clear, however, that Molinier's delight is in formal variety and elaboration.[23] Almost any collection of Provençal lyrics will show that his discussion is descriptive of the practice from which it derives, while English forms are largely confined to lyric stanzas of from two to eight lines (with or without refrains) or to the octosyllabic verse of narrative poetry.[24]

By Chaucer's time, then, Latin and Provençal verse traditions had provided the theory as well as the model for sophisticated verse, but not all of it was fully appropriate to English. Machaut and Deschamps represent and codify practices more directly applicable to the writing of English verse, with observable impact on Chaucer.

Machaut is of great importance to the history of music as well as of poetry. He gives some account of his poetic theory in a "Prologue" to *Le Dit dou Vergier* (c. 1330; "Prologue" c. 1370) and "Intermèdes lyriques" to *Le Rémede de Fortune* (c. 1340). In these, Machaut insists upon the importance of the relation between words and music, and gives precedent for the simplification of the proliferating lyric forms of the troubadours and trouvères. While Molinier had suggested an almost infinite set of strophic possibilities, Machaut confines himself to forms that work effectively in musical settings. In particular, "the genres advocated by Machaut are . . . the chanson, the lai, the motet, the rondeau, the virelai, the ballade, and the complaint."[25] Machaut's influence on Chaucer is readily identifiable in the octosyllabic *Book of the Duchess*, which supports the assumption that Chaucer owed to Machaut the decasyllabic couplet as well.[26] He may also have owed to Machaut the simplification of courtly lyric forms, which allowed for the variousness of the rime royal stanzas of *Troilus and Criseyde* as well as the rich variety of Chaucer's *ballades*. Machaut in effect gave authority for a limited range of stanzaic types, most of which did not require the elaborate and extensive riming approved by Molinier.

Machaut's ideas have survived not only in his own verses but in the theory and practice of his "pupil" Deschamps. Much of Deschamps' *L'Art de Dictier* is devoted to a theoretical discussion of music and poetry. In the practical section of his treatise, he acknowledges a large variety of forms suitable to song, or "musique naturele," but he affirms that those forms most usual and appropriate to this natural music are "serventois de Nostre Dame, chançons royaulx, pastourelles, balades et roundeaulx."[27] With these limited lyric genres and strophic forms in mind, Deschamps discusses versification as "an acquirable verbal dexterity, a skill in rhythms and rimes," and offers a profusion of decasyllabic examples.[28]

There are three important areas in which the theory and practice of Chaucer's French contemporaries very likely had an influence on him and through him on the development of English versification as it moved from Middle to Modern English. First, by limiting both the number and complexity of strophic forms, Machaut and Deschamps provided a model for elegant lyricism accessible to the English language with its fewer available rimes. Second, by emphasizing the relationship between poetry and music, they confirmed that merely counting syllables does not produce effective versification. Deschamps further codified rules for rhythmic elision in an extension of Molinier's insistence on grace of language in a syllabic poetry. The effect of their work with language sounds is twofold: it confirms the importance of rhythm as well as meter, of the movement within the line as well as its measure; and it insists that elegant courtly poetry must reflect the sung or spoken voice. Deschamps makes it clear that literacy is not an excuse to ignore the sounds of language. Although his focus on elision as an element of rhythm is far more useful to French than to English poetry, Chaucer is analogously aware of the rhythms and sonorities proper to his own language. His is a more masterful, thoroughgoing, innovative, and influential use of the sounds of Middle English than had gone before. Third, Machaut's use of and Deschamps' apparent preference for the decasyllabic line is surely the major source for Chaucer's own longer line. Whatever the Italian

31

influences in the middle and later part of Chaucer's career, he already possessed knowledge of the French version of the *endecasillibo*. The Italian line may have reinforced Chaucer's interest in decasyllabics, but it did not begin it.

Up to Chaucer's time the octosyllabic line was the primary vehicle for narrative in English. Lyric verse, which had a rich tradition in English, was confined to lines of from four to nine syllables in stanzas of varying complexity. Until Chaucer, English had no line that could serve adequately as an English narrative line, and no line generally flexible enough for a variety of purposes. Chaucer's greatest achievement is in his adaptation of the decasyllabic line for many purposes, and in thereby establishing new meters proper for the fullest and most effective expression of the increasingly important London dialect.

Although the decasyllabic line had appeared in French poetry as early as the eleventh century, Chaucer was the first to employ it clearly and consistently in English. In the process, he both used and varied the Romance rhythmic model for the line, which posited accents on the fourth and tenth syllables and a pause after the fourth syllable.[29] His work led toward what we have come to call the accentual iambic pentameter line, although he did not invent the precise English pentameter on which Renaissance poets built many of their greatest works. However it is described, Chaucer's achievement with the decasyllabic line is a major feature of his wide-ranging genius.

The best approach to Chaucer's decasyllabic line is through his use of the more traditional octosyllabic line. His octosyllabic couplets in particular illustrate his metrical assumptions and rhythmic characteristics in a context that invites comparison both with earlier practice and with his own later use of decasyllabics. Those couplets are exemplified with great range and variety in *The Book of the Duchess*, Chaucer's earliest major poem (c. 1369), whose verse form is proper for the narrative elegy and dream-allegory genres it combines. Chaucer's debt to Machaut is evident not only in his choice of genres and in certain specific echoes, but in the greater care he gives the octosyllabic norm relative to the tradition of English octosyllabic narratives.

The opening lines of Chaucer's *Book of the Duchess* show syllabification more consistent than in such earlier English octosyllabic narratives as *Kyng Alisaunder:*[30]

> I have great wonder, be this lyght,
> How that I lyve, for day ne nyght
> I may nat slepe wel nygh noght;
> I have so many an ydel thoght,

(ll. 1-4)

The octosyllabic standard is seldom violated, with apparent violations usually within the bounds of recognizable French practice or common elision. In line 4, for example, "many an" is treated as two syllables, and lines 21-22 have feminine endings, which conventionally produce a ninth syllable:

> Withoute slep and be in sorwe.
> And I ne may, ne nyght ne morwe,

Finally, the major mid-line pause in most lines occurs after the fourth or occasionally the fifth syllable, according to French and rhythmic Latin rules for the cesura, and not simply at or near the middle of syllabically inconsistent lines, as in *Brut* and other earlier English verse. The first obvious features of Chaucer's versification as distinct from that of his predecessors are his greater consistency with the syllabic rules he is borrowing, and a continuing ear for the movement of half-lines.

Most of the lines from *The Book of the Duchess*[31] can be scanned as if they were iambic tetrameter on the post-Renaissance model, as:

$$x \; / \quad x \; / \quad x \; / \quad x \; /$$
I have | gret won | der, be | this lyght

$$x \quad / \; x \; / \quad x \; / \quad x \; /$$
How that | I lyve, | for day | ne nyght

Natural Emphasis

```
x  /   x  /  x  /  x    /
I may I nat slep I e wel I nygh noght

x  /   x  /   x  /  x  /
I have I so ma I ny  an y I del thoght
```

Despite the ease with which these lines will fit the artificial scansion, there is no solid sense of the accentual iambic norm that Surrey and Gascoigne were to establish for English verse. Some feet require a fairly arbitrary decision as to which syllable should be counted as accented (the first feet of lines 1 and 2; the last foot of line 3). In other instances the iambic pattern is simply irrelevant to a clearly perceivable rhythm, as in the first line:

```
x  x   \   /  x   x  \  /
I have gret wonder, be this lyght
```

or

```
x  x   /   /  x  \   x  /
I have gret wonder, be this lyght
```

However the line is scanned, the major accentuation must be on "wonder" and "light," with "gret" providing an accentual preface to the stress on the first syllable of "wonder." In short, the rhythmic emphasis is in the middle and at the end of the line, as we would expect from lines which depend for their rhythms on the movement of whole lines and hemistiches (or half-lines) rather than on the syllabic groups that evoke the foot meters of the Renaissance and after.[32]

In addition to the syllabic meter, then, we can discern patterns of accentuation that derive from the movement of half and whole lines. Overall, there is a definite tendency toward two or three strong stresses and one or two secondary stresses in each line, usually adding up to four.[33] The accents are not necessarily patterned iambically, although they may be.

34

Chaucer was a master of the various possibilities of this line, which he used in service to his narrative skill. Observe, for example, lines 153-65:

/ \ / /
This messager tok leve and wente

\ / / /
Upon hys wey, and never ne stente

\ / / /
Til he com to the derke valeye

/ / / /
That stant betwixen roches tweye

/ \ / /
Ther never yet grew corn ne gras,

Ne tre, ne [nothing] that ought was,

/ / / /
Beste, ne man, ne noght elles,

/ \ / /
Save ther were a fewe welles

/ \ / /
Came rennynge fro the clyves adoun

\ / / /
That made a dedly slepynge soun,

/ / / /
And ronnen doun ryght by a cave

\ / / /
That was under a rokke ygrave

/ / / /
Amydde the valey, wonder depe.

Natural Emphasis

Typically, Chaucer ends his tumultuous action, and the sentence, in the middle of a couplet. This structural linking of one section to another and downplay of rime as a formal device is also characteristic of *The Canterbury Tales* and, to a lesser extent (given the stanzaic structure involved), of *Troilus and Criseyde*. It contributes to Chaucer's dynamic narrative style, as opposed to the more static lyric styles of the Provençal poets, whose *coblas* were to coincide perfectly with units of thought or narrative.

The linking and variety of patterning that are characteristic of larger units of poetic structure are also features of line rhythm. Chaucer's lines show the received Romance pattern of an accented eighth syllable, but his second major accent is not necessarily at the fourth syllable just before the cesura, as the Romance model prescribed. His lines almost always have a third major accent, and often a fourth, which makes his verse clearly more emphatic and accentually various than Romance verse. Chaucer's octosyllabic lines will customarily have two accented syllables among the first four (that is, before the mid-line pause traditional to both English and Romance verse), and two among the last four or five. But frequently the line will have one primary accent among the first four syllables and two more among the last four or five, as

           /   \\   /   /
This messager tok leve and wente

    \\   /   /   /
Upon hys wey, and never ne stente

    \\ /   /   /
Til he com to the derke valeye

Patterns of three rather than four primary accents are common in action sequences in *The Book of the Duchess*, and when the action stops they are often resolved, as here, into the static balance of a four-accent pattern:

/   /   /   /

That stant betwixen roches tweye

At base, the metrical model for Chaucer's *Book of the Duchess* is octosyllabic with a primary stress on the eighth syllable and an allowable unaccented ninth syllable. There may be up to three further primary accents, but the norm is three primary and one secondary accent per line, patterned variously but usually in some relation to the mid-line pause.

This is a more general prescription for Chaucer's verse than, say, the Halle and Keyser model. Indeed an octosyllabic version of their model would account for the great majority of lines in *The Book of the Duchess*. But its focus on positions and kinds of syllables rather than on number of syllables and number of accented syllables would be deceptive. Chaucer's rhythms can be most effectively read according to the line and half-line, not according to conventions of syllabic pairing or grouping. He skillfully combines the Anglo-Saxon four-stress and cesura traditions with Romance syllabics.

If the danger for metrical accentual-syllabic verse is monotony, the danger for Chaucer's rhythmic accentual-syllabic verse is chaos. The meter in Chaucer is kept by the number of syllables and the number of accents per line, but there are no prescribed patterns. There are, of course, natural prose rhythms that will inform a line, and if a poet has a good ear both recurrence and variety will serve the sound and meaning of his poem. So it was for Chaucer. But there were dangers for his followers, particularly in their handling of the less familiar decasyllabic line, to which I now turn.

The accent pattern for the Romance decasyllabic line was similar to the octosyllabic: an accent on the tenth syllable (often – in Italian, inevitably – followed by one or two unaccented syllables), and a second accent or rise in pitch at the fourth syllable, just before the cesura. Beyond that, there might be as many as two more accents or pitch positions, at the sixth or eighth or second syllable, in that order of probability. Elision was common.[34] The rough outline of English iambic pentameter was

37

therefore implied by the Romance model, and especially by Italian practice.[35]

Chaucer's tendency in the English decasyllabic line was to keep the familiar four-accent meter of the English tradition, and of his own octosyllabic verse. Two conditions helped develop a fifth accent: the pressure of rime on a word's secondary stress, and the cesura tradition. In addition to fully stressed syllables that would clearly be counted as accented, a fifth, secondary stress often appeared at the end of the line or at or near the middle of the line. The production of a fifth accent can be observed in Chaucer's ballades and complaints, which show the general form and variety of their French models, although most French ballades are octosyllabic and all of Chaucer's extant ballades are decasyllabic. The two poems in the following discussion are both in three "rime royal" stanzas (ababbcc) with a concluding short stanza, or "envoy."[36]

The "Balade de Bon Conseyl," probably written sometime before 1390, illustrates the fifth accented syllable produced under pressure from the rime. The first stanza has one possible and two definite instances of this, in lines 1, 3, and 4:

```
   /         /         /         /        \
Flee fro the prees, and dwelle with sothfastnesse,

   /  \         /           /       /
Suffyce unto thy good, though it be smal;

   /         /         /            \
For hord hath hate, and climbing tikelnesse,

   /         /         /        /  \
Prees hath envye, and wel blent overal

   /         /         /       /      /
Savour no more than thee bihove shal;

      /        /        /     /       /
Reule wel thyself, that other folk canst rede;
```

$$/ \qquad / \quad / \quad \backslash \quad /$$

And trouthe thee shal delivere, it is no drede.

Each of the three lines in question has four definite accents derived from syllables that receive primary stress even in prose registers ("Flee," "prees," "dwelle," the first syllable of "sothfastnesse," and so forth). Lines 1 and 3 require a fifth accent not only because decasyllabic verse requires an accent on the tenth syllable but also to keep the rime. As a result, the secondarily stressed syllables of "sothfastnesse" and "tikelnesse" are, in W. K. Wimsatt's term, promoted to accent.[37] While there is no evidence that poets of Chaucer's time thought rimed syllables must inevitably be accented, Chaucer's practice is consistent in riming accented syllables, and there is no need to wrench the normal accent pattern of these words in order to accommodate the promoted syllable. In addition, the corresponding rime words throughout the remaining stanzas are clearly accented, as

$$/$$

Tempest thee noght al croked to redresse

The situation in line 4 is less clear, since there is insufficient evidence on the stress configuration of "overal." The word may or may not have had its primary stress on the last syllable. If it did not, then it must in any case be considered accented to keep the rimes with "smal" and "shal."

"The Complaint of Chaucer to his Purse" illustrates how the cesura tradition supports the production of a fifth metrical accent at or near the middle of the decasyllabic line. Form words which the context gives a more-than-usual emphasis follow the major pauses in lines 3 and 4, and possibly line 2 as well:

> To yow, my purse, and to noon other wight
> Complayne I, for ye be my lady dere!
> I am so sory, *now* that ye been lyght;
> For certes, *but* ye make me hevy chere,
> Me were as leef be layd upon my bere;
> For which unto your mercy thus I crye:
> Beth hevy ageyn, or elles mot I dye!

In line 3, the sixth syllable is promoted; in line 4, the fourth syllable. In line 5, both the fourth and sixth syllables are fully stressed and clearly accented. The effect is analogous to the resolution of a musical cadence. Indeed, the promotion of a syllable at or near the middle of a line is a more supple and interesting way of adding a fifth accent to a four-accent line than is the promotion of a secondary stress at the end of a line. As here, it can provide balance, contrast, and progression in the rhythms within and among lines, and a controlled but abundant variety of rhythm is a large part of Chaucer's genius. In addition, it tends to make decasyllabic lines resemble the iambic pentameter we are familiar with, which has the advantage of rendering the rhythms of Chaucer's verse accessible, or apparently accessible, to modern readers. It has the disadvantage of arousing expectations that Chaucer does not always fulfill.

Questions concerning Chaucer's use and development of the decasyllabic line have long been central to discussions of the development of English versification. The view from the seventeenth through most of the nineteenth century was that Chaucer wrote a rough verse in a primitive language, but he prepared the way for smoother Renaissance writers to develop a flexible and vital iambic pentameter line. Since the late nineteenth century, particularly after the work of Bernhard ten Brink, the assumption has been that Chaucer in fact invented an accentual iambic pentameter but a full understanding of what he was doing was lost until Surrey revived it some 130 years after Chaucer's death.[38]

In recent years Chaucer's decasyllabic verse has been the focus of several studies which represent two basic approaches.

The more traditional approach, a heritage from ten Brink and his followers, is offered differently by Paull F. Baum and by Halle and Keyser, who concur in affirming Chaucer's verse as some form of iambic pentameter.[39] This approach assumes the primacy of syllabic position for the metrical model, and the primacy of syllabic relationship for determining where accent falls in an actual line of verse. Its usefulness lies in its invitation to objective analysis. Its danger is the resulting tendency to read Chaucer as if he were a sixteenth-century versifier and (in the case of ten Brink) to distort natural emphases in order to accommodate an artificial metricality. The second approach, which avoids being a throwback to earlier theories only by praising the looseness such critics as Thomas Warton condemned, sees Chaucer as unconcerned about syllabic relationship and even about precise meters generally. James G. Southworth and Ian Robinson, especially, treat Chaucer's line rhythms according to phrasal units and by analogy with musical concepts.[40] In this view, the exact number of syllables or accents in a line is less important than a general rhythmic movement derivable from phrase patterns. Their work has been useful in focusing attention on contexts larger than the syllable or pairs of syllables and in including semantic and syntactic features, as well as syllabic and abstracted phonological features, in their discussions of rhythm. In practice, however, this approach tends to be characteristically impressionistic and to dismiss some of the established facts of Chaucer's language.[41]

Chaucer's decasyllabic verse, whether lyric or narrative, reads most easily as a five-accent verse with four strong stresses and a fifth somewhat weaker stress whose position is variable but is most often around the middle of a line (that is, on the fourth or sixth syllable). The fifth accent is sometimes as fully stressed as the other four, and levels of stress among accented syllables may vary considerably. Accents are derivable from the stress patterns of the prose registers of the language, with some accentuation a product of the need to promote a fifth syllable to accent or of the rhetorical emphasis of a given context. The pattern of accents is not necessarily iambic but Chaucer's syllabic regularity and the five-accent rule combine with natural speech patterns to produce a great deal of iambic patterning. In short, Chaucer's meters are more precise than Southworth and Robinson suggest, but less prescriptive than Halle and Keyser's model would suggest. Baum's system of iambic pentameter variations comes closest to the mark but seems excessively complicated.

Chaucer's versification in *The Canterbury Tales* is not something entirely new; it may be seen as a decasyllabic version of the same principles we find in the more readily accessible octosyllabic verse of *The Book of the Duchess*. Where the norm for the octosyllabic line is three stress-accented syllables and a fourth syllable promoted to accent, the norm for the decasyllabic line is five metrically-counted stresses, most often with four of them clear from the prosaic registers of the language and a fifth promoted in the context of the whole line. In *Troilus and Criseyde* the decasyllabic rule is carefully kept, and the lines often read as a graceful (though varied) iambic pentameter. In *The Canterbury Tales* the decasyllabic norm is not quite as firm, and in "The General Prologue" especially Chaucer's skill with accentuation is most to the forefront. Perhaps in service to a new distinctly English poetic style, syllabic number seems in itself less important than it was in the Italianate *Troilus*, and the elegancies reside much more in the emerging sense of artful English rhythms.[42] These elegancies were not directly prescribed by Chaucer's meter, and when such followers as John Lydgate and William Hoccleve began to produce more-or-less decasyllabic, more-or-less five-accent lines, the results were variable in the extreme.

"The General Prologue" provides many examples of Chaucer's effectiveness with his decasyllabic verse. Although it often moves in iambic patterns, equally often it does not, whether or not an accentual iambic abstraction is derivable according to a traditional or linguistic model. Syllabic relationship, which was to emerge as the most important determiner of accent from Surrey forward, was important to accentuation even in Chaucer's time; the more casual syllabic variousness of the Anglo-Saxon alliterative line had long since retreated under the pressure of French and medieval Latin syllabic verse. But syllabic relationship was less important a determiner of accent pattern for Chaucer than it was to become, in part on the model of classical feet, in the Renaissance. The rule for Chaucer's long line was ten syllables and five accents, with accent determined by the line's total context, including semantic and literary contexts as well as the phonological environment.

The familiar first eighteen lines will illustrate the basic principles, virtues, and difficulties of Chaucer's pentameter.[43]

<pre>
 /   /   \   /   /
Whan that Aprill with his shoures soote

    /   /   /   \   /
The droghte of March hath perced to the roote

   /   /   /   /   /
And bathed every veyne in swich licour

   /   /   /   \   /
Of which vertu engendred is the flour

    /   /   \   /   /
Whan Zephirus eek with his sweete breeth

  /   /   /   /   /
Inspired hath in every holt and heeth

    /   /   \   /   /
The tendre croppes and the yonge sonne

  /   /   \   /   /
Hath in the Ram his half cours yronne

     /   /   /   /   \
And smale foweles maken melodye

    /   /   /   /   /
That slepen al the nyght with open eye

    /   /   /   /   /
So priketh hem nature in hir corages
</pre>

43

Natural Emphasis

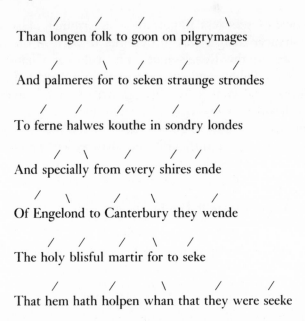

Than longen folk to goon on pilgrymages

And palmeres for to seken straunge strondes

To ferne halwes kouthe in sondry londes

And specially from every shires ende

Of Engelond to Canterbury they wende

The holy blisful martir for to seke

That hem hath holpen whan that they were seeke

Most of these lines could be read as four-accent verse, simply by dropping any emphasis on the syllables I have marked as secondarily-stressed (\). Many of them can be read according to phrasal rhythms derived from the hemistich, as:

Whan that Aprill || with his shoures soote
The droghte of March || hath perced to the roote
And bathed every veyne || in swich licour

and so forth. The effect is a rollicking rhythm appropriate to the good humored tone that introduces and dominates *The Canterbury Tales*. It serves well for an adventure on horseback, and is probably the effect perceived by such sixteenth-century readers as George Gascoigne, who referred to it as "ryding rhyme."[44] This rhythmic impressionism will only work up to a point, however. At least four lines call for five full accents: 3, 10, 11, and 14. Two other lines, 9 and 12, also appear to call for five metrical accents, since the weakest of five clearly-stressed syllables is the tenth syllable where the pressure of rime necessarily promotes to accent a secondary stress in a polysyllabic word. Other lines, such as 6, 8, and 18, have phonological or semantic environments that appear to require a fifth accent, though it may be less strongly stressed than the other four and could be suppressed if a four-accent line were more clearly the norm. In lines 2 and 13 the syllables whose promotion the five-accent norm requires are small words of no particular importance to the meaning and pace of the poem, but it does not inhibit either meaning or pace to consider them as accented. In only one instance does the five-accent norm produce what at first seems a genuine awkwardness. That is line 5, where the total context would suggest a fifth accent on "his" if a fifth accent must be found. The apparent awkwardness, however, serves the meaning of the poem. This line shifts attention from the effects of rain to the effects of "*his* sweete breeth," and the promotion of the pronoun is justified on the basis of that contrastive stress. Notice, however, that an insistence on iambic patterning in this line would make it very difficult to produce a fifth accent.

The evidence here confirms that Chaucer wrote a decasyllabic verse with four definite accents and a tendency always toward a fifth accent. That tendency is clearly enough pronounced in this opening passage to create an expectation that there will normally be five accented syllables in a line. Indeed, an interesting and artful pattern emerges here from the five-accent reading. The weakest accent occurs in the middle, as the third accent, in four of the eighteen lines (1, 5, 7, and 18), notably beginning and ending, with balanced lines, what is a clear and complete introductory verse paragraph. The second accent is the weakest in four lines (6, 13, 15, and 16) and the fourth is also the weakest accent in four lines (2, 4, 8, and 17). Four more lines contain five fully-stressed accents (3, 10, 11, and 14).[45] In only two lines (9 and 12) does the weakest accent occur as the fifth, in both cases under the influence of rime. Of five possible combinations, therefore, over the space of eighteen lines four of those possibilities are distributed over four lines and the fifth, the least interesting for purposes of variety and balance, appears in two lines.

Natural Emphasis

I am not suggesting that Chaucer deliberately aims at precisely balanced numerical accent patterning in these lines. What is clear is his ability to interweave various accentual rhythms on a five-accent pattern. The five-accent norm provides a useful guide to the verse rhythms that Chaucer elicited from the decasyllabic line. This is graceful and complex versification, most usefully described as decasyllabic pentameter, not necessarily iambic. It is the first verse to merge syllable and accent in a longer line than an octosyllabic line which does not, like the English alexandrine or fourteener, tend to break into ballad-like half-lines.[46]

Chaucerian pentameter went on to have a notoriously difficult time in England (though not in Scotland) until the sixteenth century. When we turn from Chaucer's versification to that of his most influential follower, John Lydgate, it is clear that syllabic relationship and patterning are more important to metrical accentuation in emerging Early Modern English than Chaucer's practice would have suggested. Lydgate wrote relentlessly and often pompously in a more-or-less decasyllabic line which he presumably borrowed, as he thought he was borrowing most of his style, from Chaucer.[47] Lydgate's difficulties apparently stem from his preference for some of Chaucer's less common accent patternings, one of which has come down to us as the "broken-backed" or "Lydgate" line, characterized by the yoking together of two accents, separated only (if at all) by an imprecise cesura or mid-line pause.

Line 8 from Chaucer's "General Prologue" appears to be a Lydgate line, but "half" should probably be emended to "halve," which in turn allows a weak syllable to separate the strong "hal-" and "cours," creating a neat iambic line.[48] Lydgate lines do appear in Chaucer, however, as in the portrait of the Somnour:

> And for to drynke strong wyn . reed as blood

(l. 635)

Even here, a contrastive stress on "strong" (as opposed to *weak* "wyn") has allowed modern readers to give this line a comfortable iambic flow. Nonetheless, since the juxtaposition of two stressed syllables was a central feature of Old English meter, its preservation up to and including Chaucer's time is not surprising. More surprising is the relative scarcity of such lines in Chaucer as compared with Lydgate and his followers. Its appearance in Chaucer and its persistence through the early sixteenth century suggest that neither Chaucer nor the later poets were writing with the post-Renaissance iambic pentameter in mind.

In summary: Chaucer did not, strictly speaking, invent iambic pentameter. He developed a pentameter, five-accent line that was usually rougher or less certainly patterned than Renaissance pentameter. Often, though by no means always, the accents in Chaucer's lines will appear: two toward the beginning of the line and two toward the end, leaving the less heavily stressed accent for the fifth. This floating accent may come at the middle of the line, following or replacing a cesura. When this happens the line will look like simple iambic pentameter, unless two accents are juxtaposed. The line's total context may direct that the fifth accent be placed elsewhere, however, and the iambic pentameter model is not a useful guide to the movement of many of Chaucer's lines. The reader of Chaucer in effect participates in the performance of the poem not only by deciding on levels of stress, as in most modern rhythmic readings, but also in many cases by deciding where the emphasis should be placed to elevate a syllable to the fifth metrical accent or (more rarely) to suppress an apparently-stressed syllable.

Chaucer's lines are usually accessible to the post-Renaissance reader because his accentual rhythmic movements are frequently iambic. It is far less damaging to read Chaucer's meter as iambic pentameter in the post-Renaissance sense, like Baum and Halle and Keyser, than to struggle with impressionistic rhythmic "cadences" loosely based on the hemistich tradition, like Southworth and Robinson. Still, the iambic pentameter reading remains achronological and will not finally account for

47

Natural Emphasis

Chaucer's influence on his immediate English followers. Despite Chaucer's apparently greater rhythmic regularity, he provides the model for many fifteenth-century variations from strict deca-syllabic patterns.

Lydgate and his followers, apparently less inclined to iam-bic movement in their sophisticated verse, impeded the develop-ment of the pentameter line as a flexible vehicle for English verse in the fifteenth century. Among their characteristic lines are the Lydgate line, which Joseph Schick calls "Type C" and defines as allowing "two accented syllables" to "clash together,"[49] and Schick's "Type B" line, which has an extra syllable at the cesura. Henry Bergen provides two good examples of "Type B" from his edition of Lydgate's *Troy Book*, Prologue lines 98 and 105:[50]

> The rotys vertu thus can the frute renewe
>
> Whyche me comaunded the drery pitus fate

Notice that in each of these instances the cesura occurs after the fifth syllable, precisely in the middle of what would be a deca-syllabic line without the extra syllable. This line is much more common than the "Type C" line in the verse of Lydgate's fol-lowers from William Hoccleve through such early sixteenth-cen-tury writers as Alexander Barclay and Stephen Hawes, and has implications for Sir Thomas Wyatt's practice. A second common fifteenth-century line is Schick's "Type D, the acephelous or headless line, in which the first syllable has been cut off, thus leaving a monosyllabic first measure."[51] Two of Schick's exam-ples from *The Temple of Glas*, lines 1311 and 1396, are perti-nent:[52]

> Of musike, ay dide his bisynes
>
> Unto hir & to hir excellence

48

An alternative reading to Chaucer's "General Prologue" line 5 would combine Types B and D:

$$/ \quad / \quad\quad / \quad\quad\quad\quad / \quad\quad /$$
(X) Whan Zephirus eek ‖ with his sweete breeth

The model of Lydgate has the effect of making both syl-labification and accentuation less clear and more variable than they had been in Chaucer's pentameter verse. The cesural pause after the fourth syllable, which Chaucer inherited from Romance decasyllabic verse and often employed, becomes more variable as well so that even the traditional movement of half-lines is less certain. It is fair to affirm the experience of most readers, that the poetry of such writers as Lydgate, Hoccleve, Barclay and Hawes is not as easy to read as Chaucer's, and sometimes it is awkward and ugly.

The apparent disarray of fifteenth-century pentameter has long been observed, and a great many explanations have been offered for it. George Saintsbury blames the changing nature of the English language itself for the chaos of fifteenth-century longer-lined verse, but this does not adequately take into account the richness of the fifteenth-century, shorter-lined lyric in England. Other critics have assumed either that the fifteenth-century narrative writers all had tin ears, or that some form of civil or linguistic flux made it difficult for Chaucer's followers to understand his iambic pentameter; usually the loss of final "-e" as a consistent syllable is cited.[53] More recently, Alain Renoir and Jerome Mitchell have portrayed Lydgate and Hoccleve as writers of a much varied Chaucerian iambic pentameter, and both critics have helped re-establish these poets as conscientious artists.[54] C. S. Lewis has argued persuasively that these writers were not writing iambic pentameter at all, but rather something he names "the fifteenth-century heroic line."[55] This he defines as an accentual line based on two half lines, each with at least two but no more than three accents. Lewis's argument is somewhat weakened by the inconsistency of the mid-line pause in this period, and by the ease with which the same definition could apply to Chaucer's lines, from which Lewis was attempting to differentiate fifteenth-century practice.

Most recently the tendency has been to see Lydgate's verse, and by implication the verse of his followers up to and including Sir Thomas Wyatt in the early sixteenth century, as centered in Chaucer's pentameter but with a liberty bordering on license where syllabification and accent-patterning are concerned. This is the view, for example, in Dudley Hascall's linguistic approach to Lydgate's verse:

> Lydgate differs from Chaucer exactly where we
> should expect – he overuses Chaucer's exceptional
> line types. What Chaucer used sparingly, his disciple
> uses regularly, having his precedent as justification,
> but not having his feeling as check.[56]

Hascall goes on to note several of the major exaggerations of Chaucerian practice common to Lydgate's verse, including the practice of riming on an unstressed syllable. While Chaucer regularly elevates a secondary accent in a word of three or more syllables, Lydgate commonly allows for a rime on what must be read as an unaccented syllable, most often because it is the unstressed syllable in a disyllabic word. Hascall finds this a pervasive enough practice to suggest a riming rule: "If unstressed syllables carry the rhyme, they are considered to have metrical stress."[57] In response to Hascall, Karen Lynn's computer-assisted study based on Halle and Keyser's theory of iambic pentameter observes that both Lydgate and Hoccleve rime on unstressed syllables and that this is "outside the boundaries of what Chaucer allowed himself."[58] Lynn's study posits that Chaucer was writing an iambic pentameter poetry, according to Halle and Keyser's model, but that Chaucer's followers were doing something else.

Those critics who have suggested that later poets simply made more frequent use of a rare license they happened to spot in Chaucer have offered an oversimple solution. The later poets didn't just use these variations more frequently; they expanded them beyond what seems to have been Chaucer's own preference, and went ahead to add new possibilities for which Chaucer's verse contained in fact no suggestion at all.[59]

The fact of the matter is that Chaucer's pentameter will not comfortably satisfy the requirements of a post-Renaissance iambic pentameter model, even one as sophisticated as Halle and Keyser's. As a result, Chaucer will often provide evidence of the sort of variations Hascall finds common in Lydgate. Lynn is right in noting that he will not provide for all the exceptions from an iambic pentameter norm that one finds in Lydgate, Hoccleve, and the other poets of her study, the Scots poet William Dunbar and the early Tudor John Skelton. They were not writing iambic pentameter. But neither was Chaucer. The reasons for his relative success and his followers' relative failure are probably a compound of all the suggestions that have been put forward. The language was changing, which may well have made it harder to focus on a single poetic voice to carry a narrative rhythm. Chaucer was unquestionably a genius, not only in his rhythms but in his use of all poetic and narrative techniques. There are no comparable suggestions of genius in his followers, and so they may indeed be perceived to have less trustworthy poetic ears. And finally, Chaucer's very success apparently spurred Lydgate, and Lydgate's followers, to a far more ambitious English poetry than had been attempted before.

What Lydgate missed in Chaucer was the latter's clear dependence on the spoken language.[60] Chaucer's narrative voices may be heard not only in *The Canterbury Tales*, where "oral" story-telling is crucial to the fiction, but in his other works as well. His poetry has the ease of speech rather than the self-consciousness of art. The Franklin may be too modest about his ability to use the colors of rhetoric, but both his denial and the narrator's

51

pose of simplicity reflect an important feature of Chaucer's style. He is a storyteller, not an artisan. Lydgate is the reverse; his voice is subordinate to artifice. Lydgate's poetry, therefore, was not less artful than Chaucer's, but relentlessly more so. He apparently pursued Chaucer's unquestionable achievement with bookish delight, and sought new heights for English eloquence just when the language itself was unsteady. Just as Lydgate overburdened his narrative with volumes of self-conscious rhetorical coloring, so, too, he overburdened the Chaucerian pentameter with endless elaboration of accent position and syllabic shading.

Walter Schirmer was the first to develop this view of Lydgate's excessive artifice:

> Chaucer varied his iambic scheme by approximation
> to narrative prose, as a consequence of which the
> verses read as though an experienced story-teller were
> reciting them orally. Lydgate, who does not excel in
> narrative, and whose verses, weighed down with
> "aureate Terms," lose more and more of the quick
> flow of the metre they are modelled [sic] upon, also
> gives the effect of artificiality in his verse variations,
> so that his work is by no means easy to read.[61]

Or, as Derek Pearsall has put it, Lydgate's "metre is not confused but excruciatingly rigid."[62] A few examples of Lydgate's influence through the early sixteenth century should confirm both the nature of the Chaucerian pentameter line and also its decline from satisfying the ear to appealing to an intellectual sense of variety.

Here is Lydgate himself in his pose of humble ineloquence:

> Thouh that I have lak off eloquence
> I shal procede in this translacioun,
> Fro me avoiding all presumpcioun

Lowli submyttyng everi hour & space
Mi reud language to my lordis grace.

(Fall of Princes, I, ll. 437-41)

Hoccleve uses similar patterning, including the haphazard reliance on the mid-line pause for rhythmic effect, in his *Ad Filium*:[63]

> I am the wownde of al . thy grevance;
> I am the cause of thyn occisioun,
> And of thy deeth dessert of thy vengeance
> I am also verray flagicioun;
> I causid thee thy grevous passioun;
> Of thy torment I am solicitous
> Thow Goddes sone our Lord & Sauveour.

(ll. 8-14)

Although the "Scottish Chaucerians" (Gavin Douglas, Thomas Henryson, and William Dunbar) are beyond the scope of this study, one must mention that they are generally conceded to have been better imitators of Chaucer than their English contemporaries. Writing in the second half of the fifteenth century for a court that appreciated poetry, and where it was probably read aloud, they tend toward more consistent syllabification and the more readable narrative rhythms we associate with Chaucer. Still, we do find examples of Lydgate's influence, as in the broken-backed second line of this passage from Dunbar:[64]

> Quhen Merche wes with variand windis past
> And Appryll had . with hir silver schouris
> Tane leif at Nature with ane orient blast.

("The Thrissill and the Rois," ll. 1-3)

Natural Emphasis

Both Lydgate and Hoccleve make ample use of the promotion of a secondary word accent at the end of a line. Dunbar is more sparing in this practice, but he does make use of it (as in the lyric beginning "Blyth Aberdeane, thow beriall of all tounis"). Other of the more awkward devices, such as inconsistent syllabification and unstressed rimes, appear in fifteenth-century lyrics as well as in narrative, but the shorter-lined poetry seems better able to accommodate such practices without total rhythmic disruption. Thus, for example, the second stanza of John Audelay's carol, "In his utter wretchedness":[65]

> Fore blindness is a hevy thing,
>
>   /
> And to be def therwith only:
>
>   /
> To lese my light and my hering–
> Passio Christi conforta me.

(ll. 5-8)

Lydgate's influence can scarcely be overestimated throughout the fifteenth century and into the sixteenth. As late as Stephen Hawes's *Pastime of Pleasure* (1509), a lengthy allegory on the seven liberal arts, "the monke of Bury" is the acknowledged master for artful English verse:

> Your noble grace/ and excellent hyenes
> For to accept/ I beseche ryght humbly
> This lytell boke/ opprest with rudenes
> Without rethorycke/ or colour crafty
> Nothynge I am/ experte in poetry
> As the monke of Bury/ floure of eloquence
> Whiche was in tyme/ of grete excellence.

(ll. 22-28; 1509 edition)

54

It would be kind to take such sentiments at face value, but the humility expressed here takes its model from Lydgate, just as the "artful" rhythms go stumbling after their master. Although Hawes's rhythms are awkward, it is worth noting that he keeps the decasyllabic standard except when he refers to Lydgate; the second to the last line has eleven syllables, and the last line has nine. This may well be in tribute to the artful variety of the model Hawes is invoking.

It is one thing to acknowledge the pervasive and even self-conscious rhythmic awkwardness of Lydgate and his followers; it is another thing to account for its popularity. I think it likely that the pleasures of reading Lydgate were the pleasures of the eye rather than the ear, roughly the equivalent of an appreciation for eye-rime or for some kinds of concrete poetry.[66] Chaucer was, in a sense, too natural for the more academic of his followers. It has been usual to blame the often boring rigidity of mid-sixteenth-century versification on Humanism and its focus on the ideal models of the classics. The love of Lydgatian artifice may in fact be a product of the first blush of what was called the "New Learning" in England. In the early sixteenth century John Skelton, more a follower of Lydgate than a precursor of Surrey, was immensely proud of being a "Laureate" of two universities, a title that Petrarch had revived on the steps of the Roman Senate some 150 years earlier.

Whatever the reason or reasons, it is the model of Lydgate that dominates the developing poetry of the London dialect, though Chaucer is the acknowledged first-begetter of a legitimate English verse. And it is the model of Lydgate with which the new poets of the Tudor courts will ultimately have to contend.

While Chaucerian pentameter was suffering from the bookish variety of Lydgate and his followers, heard poetry flourished through the fifteenth century. The euphony of most shorter-lined verse helps confirm the deliberate aberrance of Lydgate and proves that whatever the language changes of this period, English continued to be speakable and singable in pleasant ways. The richness of English lyrics, both "plain" and "eloquent" (according to Douglas Peterson's definitions),[67] is a subject in itself and not central to this book. It will accompany discussion throughout, but for now it is enough to affirm the continuing vitality of the lyric from the introduction of strophic verse to England in the eleventh and twelfth centuries through the fifteenth century.[68]

Before turning to the early sixteenth century, a period crucial for the direction of English verse generally, a few words should be said about the "neo-alliterative revival" and the great, mostly Northern, fourteenth and fifteenth-century poems based on much earlier native English techniques.

Alliteration continued to be an important feature of English verse after the decline of the Anglo-Saxon alliterative line, but as an ornamental rather than a metrical feature. Rime replaced it as the metrically-prescribed device of phonetic harmony. About the same time as Chaucer was importing the decasyllabic line, a series of poems were being written that apparently reincorporated alliteration on the metrical level, though not in the same form as in Old English verse, nor in as regular or predictable a manner. They nonetheless illustrate both the richness of alliterative ornament available to English and also the fluidity of English meter in the fourteenth and fifteenth centuries.

"Neo-alliterative verse" refers to works written in the North of England during the fourteenth and earlier fifteenth centuries.[69] Although their subsequent influence is not large, the works themselves are sometimes of very high artistic merit. The alliterative lyric has the clearest tradition and is pervasive in the popular poetry of this period, although its prominence is challenged by the more European courtly poetry of London and it is the latter that survives past the fifteenth century.[70] The variety of neo-alliterative verse is best illustrated not from the lyric but from some of the very fine dramatic and narrative poetry of the period.[71] The best known of the dramatic alliterative works are the Townley and Wakefield cycles of Mystery plays, where the neo-alliterative material is interspersed with other lyric forms. The best known of the narrative works are William Langland's *Piers Plowman* and the two works by the Gawain poet, *Pearl* and

Sir Gawain and the Green Knight. J. A. W. Bennett describes the verse of *Piers Plowman* as consisting of two half-lines with each half-line containing "two or more strong syllables, two being the original and normal number. More than two are often found in the first half-line, but less frequently in the second."[72] This is similar to Lewis's description of the "fifteenth-century heroic line," and suggests affinities with the fifteenth-century version of Chaucerian pentameter as much as with the remote Anglo-Saxon tradition.[73]

Pearl is a neat octosyllabic version of rimed alliterative narrative, and would fit comfortably in the octosyllabic narrative tradition inherited from France, though with the less careful syllabification common to English versions of that line and with the question of syllabification made more difficult by the uncertainty over final "-e."[74] *Sir Gawain and the Green Knight*, like *Pearl* written before 1400, uses the "bob and wheel" form of long-lined stanzas concluded by a shorter-lined coda of verses. The longer lines are usually around twelve syllables but may range from fourteen to ten or less, and in any given passage syllabification is variable.[75] Together *Pearl* and *Gawain* make it clear that a talented author could choose careful syllabification or not. In one instance this author apparently decided to follow the tradition of octosyllabic narrative, in another he followed the native Northern stanzaic tradition. The differences are substantial, but in the hands of this poet each form is effective. The only formal feature that remains the same is patterned alliteration, which in both cases sometimes seems more ornamental than metrical since the alliterative patterns are not consistent enough to announce the precise formal control they signaled in Old English verse.

Although alliteration is sometimes ornamental even in this heavily alliterated verse, the heavy accentuation we associate with Old English verse is present throughout. Marie Borroff refers to "chief syllables" as controlling the movement of *Pearl*, for example, with certain general rules of "intermediate syllables."[76] She resists referring to this neo-alliterative verse in terms of foot meter. The precise nature of its versification remains elusive, as does its origins. Geoffrey Shepherd sees it as an artistic expression of a Northern popular tradition, with an unbroken if often strained line back to Old English verse.[77] Norman Blake, on the other hand, considers it to be the literary product of experiments with alliterative prose.[78] Whatever its origins, and however it may be described, it contributes to the main development of English versification only by illustrating certain general tendencies of English versification.

The first is the tendency toward metrically-counted accentuation. Whether the patterning of *Pearl* depends on "chief syllables" or what we would call primary accents, it clearly perpetuates the emphatic quality native to virtually all forms of English verse. A second tendency is for accentuation or line rhythm to depend in part on the presence of a mid-line pause, whether considered as an absolute metrical feature in the classical and Romance traditions of the cesura or more loosely, as in Chaucer's verse. A third tendency is to lengthen the line for serious narrative. The neo-alliterative line serves as an alternative to the shorter-lined Northern verse of the period. Finally, there will remain in even the English verse of London a tendency to use alliteration as a prominent ornament.

Like Chaucer's achievement and the experiments of his followers, the rise of neo-alliterative verse illustrates the continuing tension between the Germanic origins of English and its (largely French) Romance models. Accentuation remains crucial; alliteration remains common; complex rime schemes remain more difficult for English than for Romance languages; but rime and careful syllabification have, by the end of the fifteenth century, established themselves as principal if not exclusive elements of English meter.

It was the Tudor poets who developed the accentual-syllabic analogue to classical verse models, and so formalized the sometimes uneasy union of accent and syllable count that only Chaucer appeared to sustain beyond the length of a lyric poem. This process, although it does not produce any written guides to English verse until Elizabethan times, begins in the reign of Henry VIII.

NOTES

1. For a standard view, see Albert C. Baugh, *A Literary History of England* (New York: Appleton-Century-Crofts, 1948), 263: "Others had translated and adapted French works before, but nobody else, either in his own day or before or after his day, so completely transferred to English the whole spirit of polite literature in Europe." See also Derek Pearsall, *Old English and Middle English Poetry* (London: Routledge and Kegan Paul, 1977), 197-204; Charles Muscatine, *Chaucer and the French Tradition* (Berkeley and Los Angeles: Univ. of Calif. Press, 1960), 4-12, 124-32; and A. Lytton Sells, *The Italian Influence in English Poetry* (Bloomington, Ind.: Univ. of Indiana Press, 1955), 19-59.

2. *Liber Bedae de Schemate & Tropo* (Milan, 1473) is the earliest printed version of this treatise, with *Eiusdem vero ars de metris incipit feliciter* beginning B2v. My source is the Huntington Library copy. Aldhelm's *Epistola ad Acircium de Metris* is a standard treatise on Latin meter, dedicated to Aldrid, King of Northumbria. See also M. L. W. Laistner, *Thought and Letters in Western Europe, 500-900*, rev. ed. (London: Methuen, 1957), 153-56.

3. Warner Forrest Patterson, *Three Centuries of French Poetic Theory (1328-1630)*, 2 vols. (Ann Arbor: Univ. of Michigan Press, 1935), 1:14. For a general discussion of Bede's relation to European literary criticism, see J. W. H. Atkins, *English Literary Criticism: The Medieval Phase* (London: Methuen, 1952), ch. 3. Throughout this book I refer to end-rime as "rime" to distinguish it from the "rhythmic" verse usually referred to as "rhyme" or "ryme" in the Renaissance. See chapter 6.

4. For distinctions pertinent to this discussion, see chapter 1, n. 5.

5. Dag Norberg, *Introduction de l'étude de la versification latine médiévale* (Stockholm: Almqvist & Wiksell, 1958), 88.

6. Pearsall states, "Anglo-Saxon versification is based on a two-stress half-line with a variable number of syllables; half-lines are bound into full lines by alliteration, which is borne always by the first stress of the second half-line and by either or both of the stresses of the first half-line. Alliteration thus holds one formal unit, the long line, in tension against another formal unit, the verse paragraph composed of an indefinite number of half-lines freely run on. It is a favourite device of Anglo-Saxon poetry to heighten this tension by placing major syntactical breaks at the medial caesura" (15). For a summary of the conservative view of this meter and some of its poetic effects, see Barbara C. Raw, *The Art and Background of Old English Poetry* (New York: St. Martin's Press, 1978), 97-122.

7. Patterson, 1:16-17.

8. *The Parisiana Poetria of John of Garland*, ed. Traugott Lawler (New Haven: Yale Univ. Press, 1974). Lawler's description of Garland and his text, xi-xxv, is succinct and useful.

9. Atkins, 97.

10. Patterson, 1:19; Atkins, 112.

11. Patterson, 1:35. For the text of *Las leys d'amors*, with a modern French translation, see M. Gatien-Arnoult, *Monumens de la littérature romane*, 4 vols., (Paris, 1841-49).

12. Patterson, 1:76-77.

13. Eustache Deschamps, *Oeuvres complètes*, ed. Auguste Queux de Saint-Hiliare (1-6) and Gaston Raynaud (7-11), 11 vols. (Paris: Firmin Didot & Cie., 1878-1903; rpt. New York, 1966), 9:266-92.

14. For a general history of this aspect of the English language see Albert C. Baugh, *A History of the English Language* (Englewood Cliffs, N.J.: Prentice-Hall, 1957), chs. 5 and 6, and Thomas Pyles, *The Origins and Development of the English Language*, second ed. (New York: Harcourt, Brace, 1971), 152-80, 324-28. For the effect of this alteration on medieval poetry, see *Early Middle English Verse and Prose*, ed. J. A. W. Bennett and G. V. Smithers (Oxford: Oxford Univ. Press, 1968, 2nd ed.), xi-xix and xlix-liv; and *Fourteenth Century Verse and Prose*, ed. Kenneth Sisam (Oxford: Clarendon Press, 1921), ix-xvi. The pervasive Anglo-Norman culture is documented by M. Dominica Legge, *Anglo-Norman Literature and Its Background* (Oxford: Oxford Univ. Press, 1963).

15. Gatien-Arnoult, 1:101.

16. *Medieval English Lyrics*, ed. R. T. Davies (London: Faber and Faber, 1963), 52.

17. Bennett and Smithers, 1-51.

18. As for example in *Floris and Blauncheflour*, ll. 147-48:

>Nou thou might wel ethe
>Arede me fram the dethe.

Here and throughout, I modernize usage of *u*, *v*, *i*, and *j*, and translate archaic orthography, such as *th* for ʒ and ð and *gh* or *y* for ʒ.

19. Bennett and Smithers, 29.

20. Urban T. Holmes, *A History of Old French Literature* (New York: F. S. Crofts & Co., 1962), 7-10. See also L. E. Kastner, *A History of French Versification* (Oxford: Clarendon Press, 1903), 1-2.

21. Holmes, 9-10. See Molinier's emphasis on rime, in Gatien-Arnoult, 1:141-97.

22. "The true genius of the Provençeaux was expressed not so much in rhetoric as in the elaboration of the rhyme. The choice and disposition of the rhymes was considered of prime importance." Maurice Valency, *In Praise of Love* (New York: Macmillan, 1961), 121; see also 122.

23. Gatien-Arnoult, 1:201-209, especially 201, 203.

24. Compare any general collection of French lyrics with any of English lyrics in this period. *E.g.*, *Lyrics of the Troubadours and Trouvères*, ed. Frederick Golden (Garden City, N.J.: Doubleday, 1973), and *Medieval English Lyrics*, ed. Davies. English verse stanzas as printed in modern texts may appear more complex than they are, since it is usual to combine sets of ballad stanzas (4a3b4c3b), and refrains are common. But even in the longer and more complex English strophic forms (as in thirteenth and fourteenth-century hymns, often derived from Latin rhythmic hymns) rime schemes are only seldom extended throughout the poem. In the complex stanzas of Romance verse, however, rime schemes are usually extended.

25. Patterson, 1:82. For his summary of the importance of Machaut and Deschamps to the evolution of French poetics, see 1:95-96.

26. See F. N. Robinson, *The Works of Geoffrey Chaucer* (Boston: Houghton Mifflin, 1957, 2nd ed.), 266-67, for several echoes of Machaut in *The Book of the Duchess*. See also C. H. Conrad Wright, *A History of French Literature* (New York: Oxford Univ. Press, 1912), 112-13: "He was directly imitated by Chaucer among others whose *Boke of the Duchesse* takes hints from his *Dit de la Fontaine Amoreuse*, and he gave to English literature the heroic couplet."

27. Deschamps, 7:271.

28. Patterson, 1:90.

29. Michel Burger, *Récherches sur le structure et l'origine des vers romans* (Geneva: E. Droz, 1957), 20.

30. In Bennett and Smithers, 28-39.

31. The text is from Robinson, 267 ff.

Natural Emphasis

32. There were earlier examples of rigid syllabification, but they tended to be monotonous, as if they had borrowed the principle of syllabic number but had not incorporated the rules for rhythmic variety. The most notorious example is the *Ormulum* (c.1200).

33. An analysis of these lines according to Halle and Keyser's system would confirm a derivable iambic tetrameter, but would also show that there are few "stress maxima," or stressed syllables in strong positions surrounded by unstressed syllables in weak positions. "Stressed" and "unstressed" here refer to the ordinary values of these syllables in the prose registers of language.

> I have gret wonder, by this lyght,
> W S   W S W   S W S
>
> How that I lyve, for *day* ne nyght
> W   S W S   W S   W S
>
> I may nat *slepe* wel nygh noght
> W S   W   SW S W   S
>
> I have so *ma*ny an *y*del thoght.
> W S   W S   W SW   S

I have underscored the syllables that would be considered "stress maxima" according to the pentameter theory outlined in Morris Halle and S. Jay Keyser, *English Stress: Its Form, Its Growth, and Its Role in Verse* (New York: Harper and Row, 1971), 169.

34. This sort of accentual overlay of the octosyllabic line is the origin of rhythmic patterns that C. S. Lewis attributes to the "Fifteenth-Century Heroic Line," *Essays and Studies*, 24(1938):28-41.

35. See Dante:

>   /   /
> Era venuta nella mente mia

Petrarch:

>   /   /   /
> Li angeli eletti e l'anime beate

(Oxford Book of Italian Verse, ed. St. John Lucas and C. Dionisotti [Oxford: Oxford Univ. Press, 1952], 67, 105). See also Deschamps' ballade to Chaucer:

       /   /   \   /
O Socrates plains de philosophie

(Oxford Book of French Verse, ed. St. John Lucas and P. Mansell Jones Oxford: Oxford Univ. Press, 1957], 22).

36. See Robinson, 522-23, 536, 539, for dating and texts.

37. *Style in Language*, ed. Thomas A. Sebeok (Cambridge, Mass.: MIT Press, 1960), 202.

38. For a standard late eighteenth-century view, see Thomas Warton, *A History of English Poetry*, 3 vols. (London, 1774-81), vol. 2; Bernhard ten Brink, *The Language and Metre of Chaucer*, 2d ed., rev. by Frederick Kluge, tr. M. Bentinck Smith (London: Macmillan, 1901). For a review of studies of Chaucer's versification from ten Brink to the present, see Tauno F. Mustanoja, "Chaucer's Prosody," in *Companion to Chaucer Studies*, ed. Beryl Rowland, rev. ed. (New York: Oxford Univ. Press, 1979), 65-94.

39. Paull F. Baum, *Chaucer's Verse* (Durham, N.C.: Duke Univ. Press, 1961), 13-79; Halle and Keyser, 179-80.

40. James G. Southworth, *The Prosody of Chaucer and His Followers* (Oxford: Basil Blackwell, 1962); Ian Robinson, *Chaucer's Prosody* (Cambridge: Cambridge Univ. Press, 1971).

41. Ian Robinson, for example, follows Southworth in disputing the scholarly consensus on syllabification of final "-e" in Chaucer's poetry, and so treats as irrelevant what is probably a systematic feature of Chaucer's versification. (M. L. Samuels, "Chaucerian Final '-e'," *Notes & Queries*, 217(1972):445-48, responds to Robinson on this topic.) In addition, his textual evidence for Chaucer's rhythmic units is based on the virgules (or comma-like punctuation) that appear in manuscripts and early printings of *The Canterbury Tales*. Virgule placement is inconsistent among these texts, however. The Ellesmere and Hengwrt manuscripts disagree nine times among the first twenty lines of the "General Prologue." Further, even within a given text the placement of a virgule seems sometimes to be grammatical (like a modern comma) and sometimes prosodic, marking a cesura. This inconsistency is apparent from a comparison of manuscript and early printed versions in Frederick Fur-

Natural Emphasis

nivall's *A Six-Text Print of Chaucer's Canterbury Tales* (London: EETS, 1872). I have compared Furnivall's transcription of the Ellesmere Manuscript "General Prologue" with the original in the Huntington Library and his transcriptions of the 1526 Pynson and 1532 and 1561 Thynne editions with the copies at the Huntington, and he appears accurate in his recording of virgule placement (commas in the 1561 edition). It is clear that in these early, generally good editions of *The Canterbury Tales*, there is a great deal of consistency, and most of the differences are not arbitrary. But they do indicate different readers of Chaucer working with the standard assumption of a cesura after the fourth syllable and/or with other ideas about where a pause (often grammatical) ought to go. They are not to be dismissed as guides to line rhythm, but they are not useful for describing meter, except insofar as they illustrate the assumption that a cesura is expected somewhere toward or at the middle of the line. Finally, Robinson admits a difficulty in seeing the relevance of metrical models to poetry, and so presents us with a study that deals largely with phrasal rhythms, sometimes persuasively and sometimes not. He is unpersuasive when he dismisses linguistic studies of Chaucer's phonology in order to rely on his own ear. Despite some continuing controversy, there is more agreement on Chaucer's phonology than Robinson suggests. For the generally-accepted summary, see Samuel Moore and Albert H. Marckwardt, *Historical Outline of English Sounds and Inflections* (Ann Arbor, Mich.: George Wahr, 1951), 36-63. For an example of recent controversy, see W. Bruce Finnie, "On Chaucer's Stressed Vowel Phonemes," *The Chaucer Review*, 9(1975):337-41.

42. In the verse from the *Hous of Fame* that serves as an epigraph for this chapter, Chaucer shows his consciousness of syllabic versification, and acknowledges that his syllabic verse did not always follow syllabic rules: ". . . som vers faile in a sillable" (3.8).

43. *The Text of the Canterbury Tales*, ed. John M. Manly and Edith Rickert, 8 vols. (Chicago: Univ. of Chicago Press, 1940), 3:3. A more accepted reading for line 8 is:

Hath in the Ram his *halve* cours yronne

F. N. Robinson prints "halve." For the importance of this distinction for metrical purposes, see 46.

44. George Gascoigne, "Certayne Notes of Instruction Concerning the Making of Verse or Ryme in English," *Posies of George Gascoigne*, 1575.

45. If line 8 is read with the disyllabic "halve," we add another line of five fully-stressed accents, bolstering the case for a pentameter expectation and barely altering the artful pattern I am describing.

46. Cf. Surrey's fourteeners in Tottel's *Miscellany* (1557), especially those beginning with "Such waiward waies hath love, that most part in discord," and Wyatt's trimeter quatrains "Although I had chek" and "Though I regarded not." Wyatt's trimeter quatrains function like broken alexandrines.

47. Pearsall, 228-29.

48. Grammatically, "halve" is the form for a weak adjective following a possessive, as in this line. It is possible the scribal sources for Manly and Rickert's edition simply perpetuated a common mistake. It is also remotely possible that they were reflecting an actual pronunciation, though not Chaucer's poetic use of final "-e."

49. *Lydgate's Temple of Glas*, ed. Joseph Schick (London: EETS, 1891), liv-lix.

50. *Lydgate's Troy Book*, ed. Henry Bergen (London: EETS, 1906), xi-xvi. See also Bergen's expanded discussion of Lydgate's meter in his edition of *Fall of Princes*, 3 vols. (London: EETS, 1924), 1:xxviii-xlvi.

51. *Temple of Glas*, lix.

52. Chaucer has a number of these as well, beginning with "Whan that Aprill with his shoures soote," but they are more usually balanced by a feminine ending and generally keep the decasyllabic norm.

53. This was the prevailing theory from Warton through the nineteenth century. See George Saintsbury, *A History of English Prosody*, 3 vols. (London: Macmillan, 1906-10), 1:292-93, and W. J. Courthope, *A History of English Poetry*, 6 vols. (London: Macmillan, 1895), 1:326-40.

54. Alain Renoir, *The Poetry of John Lydgate* (Cambridge, Mass.: Harvard Univ. Press, 1967); Jerome Mitchell, *Thomas Hoccleve: A Study in Early Fifteenth-Century Poetic* (Urbana, Ill.: Univ. of Illinois Press, 1968), ch. 5.

55. Lewis bases his suggestion on a very real feature of the English lyric: the common alternation of two- and three-accent lines.

56. Dudley Hascall, "The Prosody of John Lydgate," *Language and Style*, 3(1970):144.

57. Hascall, 141.

58. Karen Lynn, "Chaucer's Decasyllabic Line: The Myth of the Hundred-Year Hibernation," *Chaucer Review*, 13(1978):116-27.

59. Lynn, 119.

60. It is this vocal quality that the "Scottish Chaucerians" did perceive, and which makes their verse seem to constitute something of an iambic pentameter Chaucerian tradition.

61. Walter Schirmer, *John Lydgate: A Study in the Culture of the XVth Century*, tr. Ann E. Keep (Berkeley and Los Angeles: Univ. of Calif. Press, 1961; from the 1952 German edition), 71.

62. Pearsall, 229.

63. Huntington Library holograph manuscript HM 111.

64. *The Poems of William Dunbar*, ed. James Kinsley (Oxford: Oxford Univ. Press, 1979).

65. Davies ed., no. 81.

66. There is a parallel development in fifteenth-century France, where the *grands rhetoriqueurs*, including Jean Marot, delighted in elaboration and formal complexity virtually for their own sakes. See Grahame Castor, *Pleiade Poetics* (Cambridge: Cambridge Univ. Press, 1964), 6-7.

67. Douglas Peterson, *The English Lyric from Wyatt to Donne* (Princeton: Princeton Univ. Press, 1967), ch. 1.

68. For the history of the secular lyric, see Peter Dronke, *Medieval Latin and the Rise of the European Love Lyric*, 2nd ed., 2 vols. (Oxford: Clarendon Press, 1968), vol. 1; and Peter Dronke, *The Medieval Lyric* (London: Hutchinson, 1968). For the religious lyric, see Rosemary Woolf, *The English Religious Lyric in the Middle Ages* (Oxford: Clarendon Press, 1968). See also John Speirs, *Medieval English Poetry: The Non-Chaucerian Tradition* (London: Faber and Faber, 1957), 50-51.

69. For a summary of this tradition, see J. P. Oakden and E. R. Jones, *Alliterative Poetry in Middle English*, 2 vols., (Manchester: Manchester Univ. Press, 1930 and 1935), and Thorlac Turville-Petre, *The Alliterative Revival* (Cambridge: D. S. Brewer, 1977).

70. Richard H. Osberg, "Alliterative Lyrics in Tottel's Miscellany: The Persistence of a Medieval Style," *Studies in Philology*, 76(1979):334-52, traces the alliterative lyric, particularly from the school of Richard Rolle in the fourteenth century, and notes the closeness of Rolle's own lyrics to alliterative prose. He suggests that the decline from regular pattern to irregular alliteration may have been a function of the popularity and influence of Rolle's prose-like lyrics, citing the irregularity of alliterative drama in particular, and attributes the alliterative lyrics in Tottel (1557) to the conservative bent of its editor, suggesting they are

probably smooth versions of older lyrics rather than recent alliterative composition.

71. Alliterative verse appears in a great many Northern works of this period. A summary of its characteristics and effects has been most fully presented by Marie Boroff in *Sir Gawain and the Green Knight: A Stylistic and Metrical Study* (New Haven: Yale Univ. Press, 1962), "Part Two: Meter," 133-210.

72. *Langland, Piers Plowman*, ed. J. A. W. Bennett (Oxford: Clarendon Press, 1972).

73. *Piers Plowman* begins (Bennett ed.):

> In a somer seson whan soft was the sonne
> I shrope me in shroudes as I a shepe were;
> In habite as an heremite unholy of workes
> Went wyde in this world wondres to here.

74. *Pearl* begins:

> Perle, plesaunte to prynces paye
> To clanly clos in golde so clere,
> Oute of oryent, I hardyly saye,
> Ne proved I never her precios pere.

E. V. Gordon, ed. (Oxford: Clarendon Press, 1953).

75. See, for example, *Sir Gawain and the Green Knight*, ed. J. R. R. Tolkein, E. V. Gordon, and Norman Davis (Oxford: Clarendon Press, 1967), lines 1-7:

> Sithen the sege and the assaut watz sesed at Troye,
> The borgh brittened and brent to brondez and askez,
> The tulk that the trammes of tresoun ther wroght
> Watz tried for his tricherie, the trewest on erthe:
> Hit watz Ennias the athel, and his highe kynde,
> That sithen depreced provinces, and patrounes bicome
> Welneghe of al the wele in the west iles.

76. Boroff, *Sir Gawain*, 144-45; see also Marie Borroff, *Pearl: A New Verse Translation* (New York: Norton, 1977), 32-39.

77. Geoffrey Shepherd, "The Nature of Alliterative Poetry in Late Medieval England," *Proceedings of the British Academy*, 56(1970):57-76.

78. Norman Blake, remarks made in an unpublished talk given at the University of Southern California, April, 1980. See also, Norman Blake, "Middle English Alliterative Revival," *Review*, 1(1979):205-214.

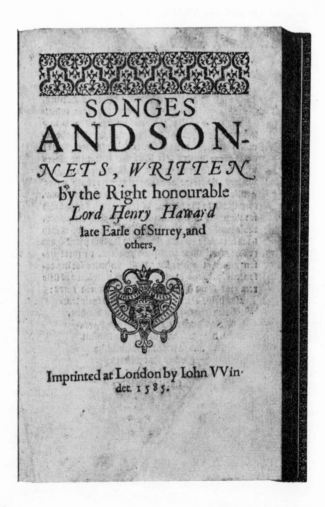

Chapter Three

Wyatt and Surrey

Our naturall tong is rude,
And hard to be enneude
With pullysshed termes lusty:
Our language is so rusty,
So cankered, and so full
Of frowardes, and so dull,
That if I wolde apply
To wryte ornatly,
I wot not where to fynd
Termes to serve my mynde.

Skelton, "Phyllyp Sparowe"

Early sixteenth-century poetry, with the exception of the longstanding traditions of popular and courtly lyric, is at first the heritage of Lydgate. The development of verse in modern English centers around the transformation of Chaucer's pentameter line from its rough and awkward decadence in Skelton, Barclay, and Hawes, through the often confusing practice of Wyatt, to the smooth measures of Surrey. After Surrey, much early Elizabethan poetry fell into a tedious regularity, but by the end of the sixteenth century English verse had flourished into elegant and powerful variety on a clear-cut accentual iambic pentameter base.[1] The broad outlines of this development have not been seriously challenged, although evaluations of each stage of it have varied.[2] So, too, have theories on how a sure iambic pentameter

69

was accomplished and on how its apparent mid-century fettering was released into the achievements of Spenser, Sidney, Shakespeare, and the great tradition of writers of English pentameter verse through the nineteenth century.[3]

John Skelton (c.1460-1529) is the most interesting of the old order of poets, but his characteristic verse form – the riming runs of short lines now known as Skeltonics – was not an important influence on the direction of English verse.[4] Although he must be considered one of the supreme specialists in shorter-lined English verse and an important figure in early Tudor poetry, insofar as he is in the poetic mainstream it is with conservative Lydgatian pentameter verse, as in the allegorical *Bowge of Court* or in much of his interlude, *Magnificence*. While his longer lines are more fluid than those of Barclay, Hawes, or Lydgate, Skelton achieves neither the relaxed conversational quality of Chaucer nor the smoother, more certain syllabification that was to follow him.

Sir Thomas Wyatt the Elder (1503-42), on the other hand, has long been recognized as a pivotal though problematic figure in the development of English verse.[5] He introduced into English the sonnet, the epigram, the Horatian epistle, and was an early psalm translator, as well as a contributor to the rich tradition of the English lyric. He may therefore be seen as the first true Humanist poet with borrowings and reflections not only of Martial and Horace but also of the continental classicists, most notably Petrarch.

Wyatt's skills with lyric verse have been generally admired in this century. He was a musician in the musical court of Henry VIII and his shorter-lined verses, apparently written to be sung, have a consistent and excellent plainness, and readily accessible rhythms. They extend the lyric tradition that originated with the models of Latin rhythmic verse and French and Provençal lyrics as early as 400 years earlier. Wyatt also writes in a regular poulters measure, which may be a variation of the English ballad (the similar fourteeners conflate the four-line ballad into couplet form) and so part of the general lyric tradition.

But Wyatt's more-or-less decasyllabic verse, particularly

the verse of his sonnets, has posed serious difficulties from at least the time of Thomas Warton forward.[6] Those difficulties were summarized in an anonymous London *Times Literary Supplement* review of E. M. W. Tillyard's 1929 edition and discussion of Wyatt. "The mystery of Wyatt," the reviewer comments,

> is simply whether he knew what he was doing or
> whether he did not. . . . At one moment he is the
> equal of the greatest in his command of rhythm and
> metre; at another he seems to be laboriously counting
> syllables on his fingers – and getting them wrong
> sometimes – and at a third he is, like some of his
> predecessors, floundering about for a foothold on
> stresses that may happen anywhere in the bog. It is
> more than an academic question. The doubt
> interferes with the reader's enjoyment of the poetry.

Among the many twentieth-century attempts to unravel "the mystery of Wyatt" or explain (and in most cases defend) his "harsh and unmelodious" lines is Alan Swallow's discussion of both Wyatt and Skelton.[7] He suggests, for example, that both Skelton and Wyatt used more Romance accentuation than was common in the speech of the day, which would allow a number of otherwise awkward lines to read more iambically, as in these lines from the introduction to Skelton's *Bowge of Court:*

> Me thoughte I sawe a shyppe, goodly of sayle,
> Come saylyng forth into that haven brood,
>
> /
> Her takelynge ryche and of hye apparayle;
>
> (ll. 36-38)

Swallow's argument that Skelton and Wyatt were both moving toward iambic pentameter in their decasyllabic lines provides a

71

good example of the twentieth-century effort to regularize "irregular" poets, beginning with Chaucer (where the attempt has been largely successful) and then Lydgate.[8] Lydgate's heritage is particularly strong in the early sixteenth century and imitations of his awkward versifying are common in the longer-lined verse of the period.[9] After Surrey and the great reformers of the Elizabethan period it is easy to dismiss that model as confusing and artificial, pretentious and "unmelodious," but Lydgate was unquestionably important to the period itself.[10]

Yet the mystery of Wyatt is not solved if we see him in terms of Lydgate, for Wyatt has from the beginning, and with considerable justice, been paired not with the older poets such as Skelton, but with his younger contemporary and admirer, Henry Howard, Earl of Surrey (1517-47). The earliest pairings of Wyatt and Surrey give them mutual and comparable credit for refining English verse.[11] From the eighteenth century forward the tendency has been to see Wyatt as a pioneer and Surrey as a refiner of versification in Early Modern English, with Surrey given precedence until this century when the freeing of forms has allowed Wyatt's ascendency. Although the relative historical positions of the two have in the main been rightly perceived, the polemical attitudes necessary for asserting the preeminence of one or the other poet have obscured or distorted most critical perceptions of what each poet contributed to the development of English verse.[12] It is more useful to assume the differing excellences of these poets and simply to describe what each contributed to English versification.

Wyatt was an experimenter, Surrey an inventor. The evidence suggests that Wyatt was not attempting to found a secure meter for English verse; his poetic interests lay elsewhere. Surrey did make such an attempt, and did in fact succeed.

Most of the difficulties that critics have encountered in Wyatt's more-or-less decasyllabic verse may be resolved if we posit that he was experimenting with both accentual and syllabic lines, but, unlike Surrey, was not comfortable producing a consistent accentual-syllabic line. Wyatt's experimentation is not precisely a working with "native" and "foreign" traditions, as

Tillyard claims, since by Wyatt's time both accentual and syllabic verse are native to English. However there does appear to be genuine uncertainty over how accents and syllables are to be artfully varied in pentameter verse, the verse of "literature" (on Lydgate's model) as opposed to the verse of song or popular romance. Wyatt's many notable successes with a more-or-less pentameter verse may be attributed to his excellent ear and mimetic sense. His difficulties in finding a sure base for accentual-syllabic patterning can be attributed to certain problems inherent in the Lydgate tradition and to Wyatt's ear for complex rhythms that convey an impassioned voice or imitate the poem's subject.

A key problem in the tradition is a lingering uncertainty over where to place a cesura in a decasyllabic English poem. By Wyatt's time the prosodic regularity of a sure cesural position, if it had existed at all since Anglo-Saxon verse, had developed into a general sense that there should be a pause somewhere at or toward the middle of a line. Even in Chaucer's decasyllabics, a prosodic pause (that is, one that furthers the rhythm and is perceived phonologically, but is not necessarily required by the syntax) may or may not follow the fourth syllable, as French and Italian practice would have it. Further, in Chaucer's verse accentuation always occurred at more than the two positions (fourth and tenth syllables) required by Romance practice. This combination, of a tradition of mid-line pause and the association of pause and accent in the Romance model, would not likely bother the bookish writers such as Lydgate and Hawes nearly so much as the lyricist Wyatt. It was apparently difficult for him to make Lydgatian artifice produce the elegant verbal phrasing of which he was capable. In a probable attempt to make the artificial decasyllabic structure more regular, Wyatt often places the pause after the fifth syllable, perhaps on the native model of the mid-line cesura in octosyllabic and accentual tetrameter verses. This practice mitigates against an easy iambic movement. Wyatt's verse in general provides no model for where the cesura should fall in English decasyllabic verse and whether it should or should not have a bearing on the pattern of accentuation.[13]

73

Natural Emphasis

When Wyatt assumes the artificiality of the mid-line pause and puts it after the fifth syllable, he loses the disyllabic pattern necessary for iambics, but he often finds other ways of producing effective rhythms. His most successful response to the theoretical confusion about English meter is his mastery of rhythms mimetic of voice or content, evident when we look at specific examples of both his successful and less successful experimentation.

Wyatt's well-known translation of Petrarch's *Rime* 140, "Amor che nel penser mio vive e regna," illustrates metrical problems that may be associated in part with confusion over the cesura.[14]

> The longe love that in my thought doeth harbar
> and in myn hert doeth kepe his residence
> into my face preseth with bold pretence
> and therin campeth spreding his baner
> She that me lerneth to love & suffre
> and will that my trust & lust negligence
> be rayned by reason shame & reverence
> with his hardines taketh displeasur
> Wherewithall unto the hertes forrest he fleith
> leving his entreprise with payn & cry
> and ther him hideth & not appereth
> What may I do when my maister fereth
> but in the feld with him to lyve & dye
> for goode is the liff ending faithfully

This is perfect decasyllabic poetry (line 9 is conventionally hendecasyllabic), but it follows the further rules for the Romance model sporadically. Lines 1 and 4, for example, are accented on the ninth rather than the tenth syllable (the Lydgatian bad habit of riming on a final unaccented syllable), and only four of the lines may be perceived to have their major pause after the fourth syllable (lines 2, 3, 12, and 13). There are two instances of the pause after the third syllable (lines 1 and 9) and one after the sixth syllable (line 10), but pauses occur most often after the fifth syllable (lines 4 to 8, 11, and 14).

74

All scansions of the more difficult Wyatt poems are problematic, but I suggest the following accent patterning for this poem:

$$/ \quad / \quad \backslash \quad / \quad /$$
The longe love ‖ that in my thought doeth harbar

$$/ \quad / \quad / \quad / \quad \backslash$$
and in myn hert ‖ doeth kepe his residence

$$/ \quad / \quad / \quad / \quad /$$
into my face ‖ preseth with bold pretence

$$/ \quad / \quad / \quad \backslash \quad /$$
and therin campeth ‖ spreding his baner

$$/ \quad \backslash \quad / \quad / \quad /$$
She that me lerneth ‖ to love & suffre

$$/ \quad / \quad / \quad / \quad \backslash$$
and will that my trust ‖ & lust negligence

$$/ \quad / \quad / \quad / \quad \backslash$$
be rayned by reason ‖ shame & reverence

$$/ \quad / \quad \backslash \quad / \quad /$$
with his hardines ‖ taketh displeasur

$$/ \quad \backslash \quad / \quad / \quad / \quad /$$
Wherewithall ‖ unto the hertes forrest he fleith

$$/ \quad / \quad \backslash \quad / \quad /$$
leving his entreprise ‖ with payn & cry

$$/ \quad / \quad \backslash \quad / \quad /$$
and ther him hideth ‖ & not appereth

$$/ \quad / \quad / \quad / \quad /$$
What may I do ‖ when my maister fereth

$$/ \quad / \quad / \quad / \quad /$$
but in the feld ‖ with him to lyve & dye

75

Natural Emphasis

$$\text{for goode is the liff} \ || \ \text{ending faithfully}$$

<small>(with stress marks: / over "goode", / / over "liff ending", / over "faith", \ over "fully")</small>

Two of the four lines with major pauses after the fourth syllable may be read as conventional iambic pentameter (2 and 13) and a third (3) may be read as iambic pentameter with trochaic substitutions in the first and third feet. Line 7, where the pause falls after the fifth syllable, is regular iambic pentameter and line 10, with the pause after the sixth syllable, is regular with an initial trochee. Five of the fourteen lines, therefore, fit neatly into our expectations for English pentameter poetry. The remaining nine lines can only be considered properly iambic by questionable addition (by pronouncing the final "e" of "longe"), modern labeling conventions (calling line 12 "headless iambic pentameter with a feminine ending" instead of "trochaic tetrameter"), or unacceptable wrenchings of stress patterns (*e.g.*, "baner" in line 4).

Not only is the accent pattern uncertain, it is difficult to be sure of the intended number of accents. Although the majority of lines have five accents, lines 4 and 5 can only gracefully be read with four accents and line 11 reads better with four than with a fifth on "&." In short, the only regular metrical element of this poem is syllable-count. Neither cesural position nor accent number will provide a predictable rhythmic base for the poem. The rhythm here depends entirely on the phrasal movement established by line endings and major mid-line pauses. This is similar to the movement of many of Chaucer's lines, and is the only principle that obtains throughout the body of Wyatt's poetry. When the syllabic meter is kept, the pause after the fifth syllable often provides the normative pivot around which Wyatt attempts various phrasal rhythms. Although that cesural position mitigates against a consistent iambic movement, it does not always eliminate it (as it does not in line 7), and it will sometimes allow for interesting effects, as in "and therin campeth || spreding his baner."[15]

Other of Wyatt's sonnets may have less regular syllabification than "The longe love," sometimes with more regular accentuation. An example is "ffarewell Love and all thy lawes for ever" (Harrier no. 13), a Lydgatian pentameter poem occasionally awkward in its rhythms but apparently intended to have five accents per line (with the possible exception of lines 7 and 13).

ffarewell Love and all thy lawes for ever
    thy bayted hookes shall tangill me no more
    Senec and Plato call me from thy lore
    to perfaict welth my wit for to endever
In blynde errour when I did persever
    thy sherpe repulce that priketh ay so sore
    hath taught me to sett in tryfels no store
    and scape fourth syns libertie is lever
Therefore farewell goo trouble yonger hertes
    and in me clayme no more authoritie
    with idill yeuth goo use thy propertie
    And theron spend thy many britill dertes
    for hetherto though I have lost all my tyme
    me lusteth no lenger rotten boughes to clyme

Most of the lines are decasyllabic, or may be considered so with some common elisions, but there are three hendecasyllabic lines (4, 13, and 14) and only one of these (4) follows the Romance rule of accentuation on the tenth syllable. The unconventional eleven-syllable lines of the couplet are accented on the eleventh syllable, a clear departure from Romance syllabic verse, though in keeping with an English five-accent norm. Wyatt's invention of the concluding couplet has endured as the most typical feature of all varieties of the English sonnet.

    Wyatt's rhythmic units do not always move over a syllabic metrical base even this secure. An example of variable syllabification is his translation of that catalog of Petrarchan oxymorons, "Pace non trovo e non da far guerra" (*Rime* 134; Harrier no. 26):

Natural Emphasis

> I fynde no peace and all my warr is done
> I fere & hope I burn & freise like yse
> I fley above the wynde yet can I not arrise
> and noght I have & all the worold I seson
> That loseth nor locketh holdeth me in prison
> and holdeth me not yet can I scape no wise
> nor letteth me lyve nor dye at my devise
> and yet of deth it gyveth me occasion
> Withoute Iyen I se & withoute tong I plain
> Idesire to perisshe and yet I aske helthe
> I love an othre and thus I hate my self
> I fede me in sorrowe & laught in all my pain
> likewise displeaseth me boeth lyff & deth
> and my delite is causer of this stryff

The poem is framed by four decasyllabic lines (1 and 2, 13 and 14) with regular iambic movement. The rest of the lines are of eleven or twelve syllables (4, 7, 10, 11; 3, 5, 6, 8, 9, and 12). All the lines but two are accentual pentameter; lines 3 and 9 are hexameter. The rhythmic movement throughout the poem is what used to be called "rising" – that is, either iambic or anapestic. Here, although there is a five-accent norm, the rhythm is maintained more by our involvement with accent pattern (loosely iambic) than by accent number. This poem is rhythmically analogous to Wyatt's poulters measure or to his "smooth" tetrameter songs, which may have varying line lengths but which keep the steady beat suggested by musical rhythm, as in Harrier no. 34:

> Madame withouten many wordes
> ons I ame sure ye will or no
> and if ye will then leve your bordes
> and use your wit and shew it so
> And with a beck ye shall me call
> and if of oon that burneth alwaye
> ye have any pitie at all
> aunswer him faire with & . or nay
> Yf it be & . I shalbe fayne
> if it be nay frendes as before

ye shall an othre man obtain
and I myn owne and your no more

Wyatt's meters are roughly syllabic throughout. He uses,
but does not depend on, the five-accent norm in his decasyllabic
poetry. He experiments with cesural placement, and appears to
pursue a variety of rhythms within single poems. Sometimes,
however, a poem is kept more by the single rhythmic pattern
than by either syllable-count or accent. This is not usually the
case in his decasyllabic poetry, however, and there is no evidence that he is interested in producing a pentameter line any
more consistent than the fifteenth-century accentual pentameter
of Lydgate, Hoccleve, and ultimately Barclay, Hawes, and Skelton. He is more adventuresome in trying out various patterns
within a given poem or poetic genre (sonnets most notably, but
epigrams and psalms as well) and he has an excellent ear which
he sometimes allows to dictate the rhythmic movement of a
poem and sometimes does not.

Since Wyatt's problematic poetry is usually more-or-less
decasyllabic, it might seem expedient simply to label it as such
and rely on the insights of those who have suggested ways in
which conventions of syllabification could be used to rectify the
problem lines.[16] This would in many cases force his poems into
metrical regularity without sufficiently acknowledging the great
variety, and often difficulty, most readers encounter. If we see
Wyatt as an experimenter, we approach the mystery by allowing
that some of Wyatt's experiments were more successful than
others.[17]

An important difference in Wyatt's poetry is between
verses intended to be read or spoken, and verses apparently
intended to be sung (as, for example, the well-known octosyllabic tetrameter, "My Lute Awake," or the tetrameter/dimeter
stanzas of "Forget not yet"). Wyatt did not need musical settings
to keep him from awkward rhythms, but he may have thought
of songs differently from his other poetry. If any single impulse
governs his spoken poetry, it is the impulse to create imitative

79

forms. Success or failure in that area often defines the success or failure of a given pentameter poem.

Two examples will illustrate Wyatt's efforts at mimetic rhythms. The first, "Eche man me telleth I chaunge moost my devise" (Harrier no. 10), is not considered among his successful poems. The second, "They fle from me that sometyme did me seke" (Harrier no. 37), is his most discussed and often most admired lyric. The first tries too hard to imitate the content by the form; the second limits the mimetic impulse to the drama of the speaker's voice.

The first poem barely approximates a syllabic meter. Most of the lines are decasyllabic, but 1, 7, 13, and 14 are rather arbitrarily hendecasyllabic, line 6 has twelve syllables, and line 9 has nine. The meter is kept by a five-accent norm which is only rarely iambic:

> Eche man me telleth I chaunge moost my devise
> and on my faith me thinck it goode reason
> to chaunge propose like after the season
> ffor in every cas to kepe still oon gyse
> ys mytt for theim that would be taken wyse
> and I ame not of suche maner condition
> but treted after a dyvers fasshion
> and therupon my dyvernes doeth rise
> but you that blame this dyvernes moost
> chaunge you no more but still after oon rate
> trete ye me well & kepe ye in thesame state
> And while with me doeth dwell this weried goost
> my word nor I shall not be variable
> but alwaies oon your owne boeth ferme & stable

The clue to the poem's movement is in the two pronunciations of "dyvernes" in lines 8 and 9. In line 8 both the first and third syllables must be accented to keep the five-accent norm, and also to allow any phrasal balance to the line. In line 9 the third syllable should *not* be accented, in order to avoid a wrenching awkwardness with "moost." Occurring as it does at the turn from octave to sestet, this rhythmic trick underscores the mimetic intention of the poem's structure. The lover has been accused of changing his "devise," of being variable and unpredictable in his behavior and presumably in his affections as well. The rhythms of the octave are equally variable. But in line 7 he attributes his own manner to being "treted after dyvers fasshion" himself, and offers in the sestet to respond consistently to consistent treatment. The sestet is considerably more regular in its rhythms than the octave, and concludes with an elegantly perfect hendecasyllabic couplet, with accentuation that is clearly regular whether or not Wyatt consciously intended iambic patterning.

This poem shows Wyatt aware of his own rhythmic variety, and purposeful even in his most awkward lines (such as 3, "to chaunge propose like after the season"). It also illustrates the artistic limits of dogged imitative form. The wit of the poem is simply not worth the distractions of its rhythmic "dyvernes." In this poem it is variability itself that is being imitated, and the impression is one of rhythmic chaos.[18]

Wyatt is usually more successful when his mimetic rhythms serve the tone of the speaker's voice than when he tries to create schematic reinforcement of theme. His ability to hear the rhetoric of the spoken voice and his excellent dramatic sense allow for a variety of phrasal rhythms centered by the voice of a single character and laid over an approximate decasyllabic base. The most famous example is "They fle from me," a rime royal dramatic monologue and meditation on the realities of courtly love:

> They fle from me / that sometyme did me seke
>   with naked fote stalking in my chambre
>   I have sene theim gentill tame and meke
>   that nowe are wyld and do not remembre
>   that sometyme they put theimself in daunger
>   to take bred at my hand & nowe they raunge
>   besely seking with a continuell chaunge
> Thancked be fortune it hath ben othrewise
>   twenty tymes better but ons in speciall

      in thyn arraye after a pleasaunt gyse
      when her lose gowne from her shoulders did fall
      and she me caught in her armes long & small
      therewithall swetely did me kysse
      and softely saide dere hert howe like you this
It was no dreme I lay brode waking
      but all is torned thorough my gentilnes
      into a straunge fasshion of forsaking
      and I have leve to goo of her goodenes
      and she also to use new fangilnes
      but syns that I so kyndely ame served
I would fain knowe what she hath deserved

The syllabification is variable. There is one line of eight syllables (line 13), four of nine syllables (3, 15, 20, and 21), three of eleven syllables (7, 8, and 9), and the remaining thirteen lines are decasyllabic. Most of the lines have five clear accents, but line 15 may be read with anywhere from four to six, and lines 3, 7, and 13 may be read with either four or five.

This was one of the most heavily edited of Wyatt's poems in Tottel's *Miscellany*, and the extensive treatment it has received is partly a response to the interesting comparisons the two versions allow.[19] Without question the editor of Tottel succeeded in smoothing out the rougher rhythms so the poem reads like an elegant courtly lyric, with the lyric impulse and the subtle ironies that the Elizabethans preferred. But what is gained in lyricism is lost in emphasis and a sense of the speaker's individual personality. This is so even in the simpler changes, as in the Tottel version of line 3:

Once have I sene them gentill tame and meke

The contrast between past and present that Wyatt's own version achieves with the accent on "have" is lost in the Tottel version. Similarly,

That nowe are wild and do not once remember

breaks up the force of their wildness and their errant memories by placing the major emphasis in the line on the distracting "once."

The real damage to the poem comes in line 15 and in the last two lines. Instead of "It was no dreme I lay brode waking," Tottel has

It was no dreame: for I lay brode awakyng.

The thoroughgoing denial of the dream convention is lost in the Tottel version, along with the sense of conviction about what the speaker has experienced. Tottel's version is almost apologetic compared with the certainty of Wyatt's own. Perhaps Tottel's editor was trying to recover the poem's strength (as well as refine its meters) when he replaced "straunge" in line 17 with "bitter." But that also directly distorts the poem's meaning. "Straunge" means "foreign" (as in Chaucer's "straunge strondes"), implying that good English girls have been behaving according to flighty continental (probably French) standards of courtly love. Further, the sense that somehow all of this behavior is alien, not according to the English kind, permeates the poem and helps to inform the ironic power of the conclusion.

Throughout the poem Wyatt has used animal metaphors. The women who were tame are now wild. In a particularly effective reversal of the Petrarchan metaphor, the lady is the hunter and the lover the "dere hert." Tottel's editor obviously understood most of the import of these allusions when he changed the couplet to flow smoothly as

But syns that I unkyndly so ame served
How like you this, what hath she now deserved.

This suggests that women are not animal kind, after all. If they will not behave according to human kind, to the codes appropriate to courtly ladies, the editor of Tottel implies, then they deserve no better than unkindly treatment from their lovers. Presumably lovers behave according to kind when they are, for example, faithful and discreet, but they may feel free to behave unkindly toward these equally unkind ladies. The modern sense of "unkindly" as meanly or unpleasantly may also apply here.

Several of my colleagues have expressed a distinct prefer- ence for Tottel, admiring in particular the elegance of the rhe- torical question at the end. It does knit up the poem with a clo- sure the Wyatt version lacks. But it does not have the ironic force of Wyatt's own version, which insists that the speaker has been served according to kind. On the level of simple irony, we may of course understand that he means precisely the reverse. But if we look again at the predatory imagery he has developed in the poem, it becomes clear that there is another level of irony. If she is of the predatory "kynde," and if he is the *"dere hert,"* then he *has* been "kyndely" treated – that is, pursued and in some sense destroyed by the predator. The concluding question therefore makes a much stronger statement than in the Tottel version. The speaker would like to know what predators deserve. His readers, familiar with the problem of predatory invasions of deer parks, can readily supply the answer: destroy them.

Not only is the double irony lost in Tottel's more civilized version, so too is the deliberately prosaic force of the couplet's rhythms. As in "It was no dreme I lay brode waking" the speaker is appealing beyond the fictive environment to an intense and personal sense of reality. "They fle from me" may not have highly regular rhythms, but they are for the most part lyrical enough – until line 15. From there, and especially in the last three lines, the dream-like quality of rhythm as well as of image is abandoned to the cold morning light. It is a very strong poem, in large part because we are convinced of a real voice first stating a real grievance, then lapsing into dreamy recollection, and then returning bitterly to the recent present and his own immediate question about justice in the painful world of courtly love.

Wyatt's command of irregular rhythms for mimetic pur- poses is not confined to the harsher tones of the speaking voice. The renunciation of "Who so list to hounte I know where is an hynde" (Harrier no. 7) is effected with a tension between nostalgic resignation and lingering desire. In particular the run-on lines of the poem's second stanza are as effective an imitation of the speaker's own longing and sense of futility as anything written decades later.

> yet may I by no meanes my weried mynde
> drawe from the Diere but as she fleeth afore
> faynting I folowe I leve of therefor
> sethens in a nett I seke to hold the wynde

The mystery of Wyatt will never be solved in a way that will satisfy all of his readers. That he was a superb lyricist and, if a minor poet, one of the best English minor poets, has been increasingly affirmed. The decasyllabic poetry, while overall his strongest in terms of idea and rhetorical strategy, does contain bad lines and some unfortunate effects. Yet it is mostly very good, and the closer it has been examined the better and more generally consistent it looks. It is not a certain or secure iambic pentameter. It is a more-or-less decasyllabic poetry that shows the poet's restless determination to try every sort of variation on the pentameter model of the fifteenth century. The rhythms are usually (though not always) more easily read in terms of the mid-line pause than in terms of syllable-groups or the whole line. Wyatt's phrases are those of the heightened speaking voice and of the developing Humanist appreciation for elegant rhetoric, though his lyrics remain tied to the personal rather than the public voice.

Surrey's poetry is from the outset more public in tone, even though several of his poems have a more explicit autobiographical reference than anything of Wyatt's. His appreciation for the conventions of a public voice may be partly what enables him to design a meter less dependent on the specific skills or idiosyncracies of the individual poet.[20] Whatever the reason, Surrey clearly and I think consciously invented what we have come to call the English iambic pentameter line. Surrey accomplished his invention of iambic pentameter by solving the problem of where to place the cesura in a decasyllabic line and this invention solved the problem of a heroic line for English verse.

Surrey's sonnet translations tend to lack the dramatic immediacy of Wyatt's verse, but they do not make the Lydgatian mistake of excessive artificial complexity. Surrey constructs a sonnet form which accommodates the facts of the English language and then writes consistently and for the most part simply in that form. His inventive genius apparently went into the creation of the form itself, not into the tortuous pursuit of artful variety that is typical of the Lydgate tradition.

On turning from Wyatt's sonnets to Surrey's, one is immediately struck not only by the relative "smoothness," but by a particular element of that quality: the consistent placement of the mid-line pause.[21] There is a distinct pattern of a rhythmically and/or syntactically-directed pause after the fourth syllable of most and sometimes all the lines of a sonnet, as in Surrey's version of Petrarch's "Amor che nel penser" *(Rime* 140):[22]

> Love that doth raine II and live within my thought,
> And buylt his seat II within my captyve brest,
> Clad in the armes II wherin with me he fowght
> Oft in my face II he doth his banner rest.
> But she that tawght me love and suffre paine,
> My doubtfull hope II and eke my hote desire
> With shamfast looke II to shadoo and refrayne,
> Her smyling face II convertyth streight to yre.
> And cowarde love II than to the hert apace
> Taketh his flight II where he doth lorke and playne
> His purpose lost, II and dare not show his face.
> For my lordes gylt II thus fawtless byde I payine;,
>   Yet from my lorde II shall not my foote remove.
>   Sweet is the death II that taketh end by love.

Although this cesural pattern may be attributed in part to the Italian model he is translating (though Petrarch's version is far less regular than this), it is equally consistent in poems and sonnets that are Surrey's own invention. A famous example is his sonnet/*reverdie*:

The soote season, ‖ that bud and blome furth bringes,
With grene hath clad ‖ the hill and eke the vale;
The nightingale ‖ with fethers new she singes;
The turtle to her make hath tolde her tale.
Somer is come, ‖ for every spray nowe springes;
The hart hath hong ‖ his olde hed on the pale;
The buck in brake ‖ his winter cote he flinges;
The fishes flote ‖ with newe repaired scale;
The adder all ‖ her sloughe aweye she slinges;
The swift swalow ‖ pursueth the flyes smale;
The busy bee ‖ her honye now she minges;
Winter is worne ‖ that was the flowers bale.
   And thus I see ‖ among these pleasant thinges
   Eche care decayes, ‖ and yet my sorow springes.

It is interesting to see how Surrey uses alliteration for this more traditional and domesticated topic. Line 9, "The adder all her sloughe aweye she slinges," appears to have a prosodic though not a grammatical pause after the fourth syllable largely because of the alliterative pattern of the preceding lines. If after "hart hath hong," "buck in brake" and "fishes flote" we find a logical pause, we will tend to impose one after "adder all." The same pattern continues for the next three lines as well.

The very relentlessness of the cesural pattern, though it can tend toward monotony, has the positive effect of emphasizing disyllabic stress relationships. Since the two sections of the decasyllabic line thus produced, the first with four and the second with six syllables, are each divisible by two, and since English stress is and apparently was based on phonological context, the result is a tendency to derive stress patterns from pairs of syllables. Chaucer's syllabic consistency and frequent use of Italianate cesural patterns promoted iambic rhythms. Surrey takes it a step farther. His syllabicism is invariable, and instead of superimposing accentuation over a more-or-less decasyllabic base, as Wyatt had done, he accommodates accentuation to the syllabic and cesural pattern. The result is accentual-syllabic iambic pentameter.

There is of course no way to prove that Surrey con-

87

sciously invented what was to be called iambic pentameter. He left no record of his poetic intention. But his sonnets attest to a formal genius that understood certain facts of English phonology. Surrey not only provides the first clear-cut iambic pentameter, he also created what has since come to be known as the "English" or "Shakespearean" sonnet form: three quatrains and a couplet. The couplet, and hence the basic epigrammatic quality of the English sonnet, was Wyatt's invention, but the break with the octave/sestet vision of sonnet form is Surrey's. The English sonnet can accommodate that division; it will also readily support rhetorical organizations of four/four/four/two, eight/four/two, and twelve/two. Equally important, Surrey's form frees the English sonnet from the tyranny of difficult riming. Elizabethan poets could and did carry three and four rimes through whole sonnets (as in the Spenserian sonnet) but the model of Surrey is the base from which Sidney ranges, and of course it served Shakespeare very well.

Surrey's feeling for formal clarity is evident in his tetrameter as well as his pentameter verse. Although Martial's epigram 47 (Book X) was to be frequently translated through the Renaissance, Surrey's version may well be the best:[23]

> Marshall, the thinges for to attayne
> The happy life be thes, I fynde:
> The riches left, not got with payne;
> The frutfull ground; the quyet mynde;
> The equall frend; no grudge, nor stryf;
> No charge of rule nor governance;
> Without disease the helthfull life;
> The howshold of contynuance:
> The meane dyet, no delicate fare;
> Wisdom joyned with simplicitye;
> The night discharged of all care,
> Where wyne may beare no soverainty;
> The chast wife wyse, without debate;
> Such sleapes as may begyle the night;
> Contented with thyne owne estate,
> Neyther wisshe death, nor fear his might.

Surrey's classicism, whether a reflection of his own temperament or a product of his Humanist education, or both, shows in the grace and balance of this translation, which captures the tone as well as the meaning of the original.

Although Surrey's regularity provided the model for a great quantity of highly regular and sometimes equally tedious mid-century verse, the model for an effective and flexible English versification had at last been found.[24] Surrey's second major contribution to English versification, English iambic pentameter blank verse, was eventually to be recognized as the great English heroic line, illustrating in various contexts the strength and flexibility of the new English pentameter.

The more successful blank verse efforts of Marlowe, Shakespeare, and Milton have obscured the impact of Surrey's revolutionary achievement. It is true he had the model of an Italian unrimed decasyllabic line, the *verso sciolto* used in the *Aeneid* translations of Liburnio (1534) and de Molza (1539).[25] But there was no particular reason, beyond his excellent formal sense, to borrow the idea. He had no compunction in transforming the Italian sonnet. He also had other verse models for the *Aeneid* beside Liburnio and de Molza. Virgil's original was in quantitative hexameters, while Surrey's main non-Virgilian source, the *Eneados* of Gavin Douglas, was written in quite decent Chaucerian pentameter couplets.[26] Surrey's choice of decasyllabic blank verse was not only brilliant in itself, it had a solidifying effect on the iambic pattern of decasyllabic verse generally. In blank verse it is the rhythm of syllabic accentuation rather than the feature of rime which must keep the meter in such verse.

Surrey's blank verse makes clear that even if his pentameter model contributed to mid-century metrical monotony, it also anticipated the variety and elegance of which the iambic pentameter line would shortly be capable. While Surrey's sonnets maintain an appropriate lyrical consistency through the inevitable cesura and other patterns of rhythmic parallelism (as in "The Soote Season"), and his poulters measure poems maintain the heavy accentuation which most likely derived from their balladic background, his *Aeneid* aims for variety and subtlety within the line, and a forward-moving narrative. The nearest thing to it rhythmically is the *Canterbury Tales*, though it is unlikely Surrey considered Chaucer a model for his *Aeneid*. It may well be that the influence of the Chaucerian, Douglas, allowed for an indirect receptivity to the master's rhythmic felicities. Further, although deliberate artfulness is a feature of the Lydgate tradition, Surrey derives his aesthetic artistry not from Lydgate but from the inspiration of Virgil and probably from his own sonnet experiments. The result is an iambic pentameter blank verse that uses techniques of variety that were to dominate English versification until the Romantic period: trochaic substitution and variety in the levels of stress among accented syllables in a given line.

Thus, for example, the second book begins with the usual Surreyan pattern of a cesura after the fourth syllable, but proceeds to introduce more and more various pause patterns than can be found in any of his sonnets:[27]

> They whisted all, with fixed face attent,
> when prince Aeneas from the royal seat
> thus gan to speak. O Quene, it is thy wil,
> I shold renew a woe can not be told:
> How that the Grekes did spoile, and overthrow
> The Phrygian wealth, and wailful realm of Troy,
> Those ruthfull things that I my self beheld,
> And wherof no small part fell to my share.

(ll. 1-8)

These are shortly followed by lines far more rhythmically various than we find in the sonnets, but without the awkwardness of the Lydgate tradition:

>   / x   x /   / x   \   x / x
>   By the divine science of minerva

(l. 22)

```
 /    x  x   /    x   /   / x  x   /
In the dark bulk they closde bodies of men
     4  2      1
```

```
   / x    x / x    / x   /    x  /
Chosen by lot, and did enstuff by stealth
```

```
   x / x    /     x  / x  / x /.
The hollow womb with armed soldiars.
   4   2 3    1     3  2  4   1  4 3
```

(ll. 26-28)

If these do not achieve the rhythmical interest and variety of the later Elizabethans, they are nonetheless forward-looking in outline. Unfortunately, the early Elizabethan translators did not follow Surrey's lead, persisting instead in an attempt to make fourteeners and poulters measure serve as English heroic lines. Ironically, it may have been Surrey's own relative success with poulters measure in the popular Tottel's *Miscellany* that obscured his blank verse model for a generation.[28]

In any case, it was Surrey's rimed verse that had the immediate impact. A lyric example will serve to summarize the range of his formal genius, and suggest a paradigm for the relation between formally consistent verse and the poet's choice of a public voice, even in a poem of personal importance. Among Surrey's more complex lyrics is the lament of a lady bewailing the absence of her beloved, beginning "O happy dames, that may embrace." Reminiscent in tone of Dorigen's lament for Arveragus in Chaucer's "Franklin's Tale," this lyric and a similar one in poulters measure very likely derived from the denial of Surrey's petition to have Lady Surrey join him in France.[29] The occasion is personal, but the expression is formal and stylized, even to the extent of presenting the complaint in the woman's voice rather than in the more directly personal voice of her husband. The stanza form supports a tension between private occasion and public expression. It is idiosyncratic, suggesting the personal or individual, but it is made up of familiar materials:

> O happy dames, that may embrace
> The frute of your delight,
> Help to bewaile the wofull case
> And eke the heavy plight
> Of me, that wonted to rejoyce
> The fortune of my pleasant choyce:
> Good Ladies, help to fill my moorning voyce.

(ll. 1-7)

The first four lines are "common meter," the ballad-like 4a3b4a3b that probably underlies fourteeners. The last three lines provide a somewhat unusual tag; a concluding couplet is a usual enough ballade device, but the seventh, pentameter line, alters the expectation by refusing a common closure. Not only does a seventh line extend the stanza, but its added syllables offer first surprise and then flexibility for expressing the continuing lament of the speaker. The effect is not unlike the alexandrine in Spenser's *Faerie Queene* stanza, though here in a lyric rather than narrative context.

The meter throughout this poem is usually regular, typically coinciding metrical pattern with the prose rhythms of the informing language – except in certain key places. The surprising seventh line, for example, remains decasyllabic throughout the poem, but in three of its six instances is unmetrical as accentual-syllabic verse:

> . . . that is his sail
> Toward me, the swete port of his avail.

(ll. 13-14)

> Lo, what a mariner love hath made me!

(l. 28)

Now he comes, will he come? alas, no no!

(l. 42)

These lines come in contrast to steady iambic movement else-where, including the other three seventh lines. Overall, the poem shows the control and accessibility of the formal public voice, while expressing the personal tension of the lament. It is precisely in contrast to the public formality that such expression gains its poignancy:

```
     x  x    /   x  /   /  x  \ x  /
Toward me, the swete port of his avail
```

```
 /    x x  / x x  /   x    x   /
Lo, what a mariner love hath made me
```

```
 /   x  /   /  x  /   x/   x  /
Now he comes, will he come? alas, no, no!
```

Each of these is an example of the modern notion of sprung rhythm. The first has five accents, but they are wrenched from iambic pattern (and the third syllable, a stressed syllable in a weak position surrounded by two unstressed syllables in strong positions, renders the line unmetrical in Halle and Keyser's terms as well). The second instance offers only four accents across ten syllables (whether one stresses "me" as rime and the emphatic pronouncement suggest, or "made," as ordinary phrasal rhythms might insist). The third requires six accents across ten syllables. In each case something chaotic and unpredictable breaks through the formal ease, allowing Surrey a modicum of imitative form made especially powerful because of its highly regular context. Surrey also uses enjambment rather more in this poem than he does elsewhere, notably in the second stanza:

93

Natural Emphasis

In ship, freight with rememberance
Of thoughtes and pleasures past,
He sails that hath in governance
My life, while it wil last;
With scalding sighes, for lack of gale,
Furdering his hope, that is his sail
Toward me, the swete port of his avail.

Even with this infusion of variety, the poem's tone and force depend on the heightening and generalizing effect of the complex strophic construction and the regular iambic rhythms. Its tone is public, and the predictable evenness of its rhythms provides not only a backdrop against which the irregularity of passion may be set, but the common currency of expectation which poet and reader share. Wyatt, Sidney, and Donne often aim for the personal voice, and their common formal device (though very differently expressed) is idiosyncratic rhythms. The reader is forced to engage in performance choices. Surrey, Spenser, and Jonson, on the other hand, assume the distancing and heightening of the more regular formal base, and work from there either to establish emotion by subtle contrasts or to generalize and make memorable essentially public statements. Despite the attempt to smooth Wyatt's verse in Tottel's *Miscellany*, it is easy to see how Wyatt and Surrey provided for their century the paradigms of private and public verse. The formal essence of that distinction lies in the choice of metrical styles. Though all such generalizations are born to be disproved, by and large smooth verse achieves a more public tone than verse perceived as rough, as challenging or breaking rules, whether those rules are external or perceptibly inherent.

The enormous impact of Wyatt and Surrey on succeeding poets derived from their appearance in "the epoch-making book correctly known as *Songs and Sonnets* but popularly . . . as Tottel's Miscellany," that first appeared and was well received during Mary's reign and went on to have a vigorous popularity under Elizabeth.[30] The unknown editor's predilection for smooth pentameters did not drown Wyatt's idiosyncracies altogether, but it did establish a popular, conventional, and essentially public fashion of courtly lyric, based primarily on Surrey's model. It also went a long way toward encouraging mid-century iambic monotony and establishing what we may now call the Surreyan decasyllabic: a line consistently syllabic, with relative stress on the even syllables and a cesura almost always after the fourth syllable.[31] This is the line that appears in the better poems of the narrative *Mirror for Magistrates*, and it is the line George Gascoigne codified and developed into a vehicle for sure and subtle authorial control. In its most regular form, this line and the strangely popular poulters measure and fourteeners were undoubtedly behind the scholarly rejection of "rhyme."

NOTES

1. For the traditional description of this process, see George Saintsbury, *A History of English Prosody*, 3 vols. (London: Macmillan, 1906-10), 1:292-306; Saintsbury, *Historical Manual of English Prosody* (London: Macmillan, 1910), 1-58; John Thompson, *The Founding of English Metre* (New York: Columbia Univ. Press, 1961). This summary of English versification's progress in the sixteenth century is standard and pervasive, and may be found in a wide range of works on poetry and on the period. See, for example, Tucker Brooke, in *A Literary History of England*, ed. Albert C. Baugh (New York: Appleton-Century-Crofts, 1948), 339-45.

2. There is currently disagreement, for example, over the highly regular mid-century poets. C. S. Lewis offers the traditional view (neatly if reductively expressed in his "drab" vs. "golden" distinction) that Gascoigne is the best of a boring and bad lot of over-regular poets. Yvor Winters, on the other hand, posits a "School of Gascoigne" that produced superb aphoristic poetry in the plain style, and prefers it to the more ornamental school of "Petrarchists," led by Sidney and Spenser. (C. S. Lewis, *English Literature in the Sixteenth Century* [Oxford: Oxford Univ. Press, 1954], Bk. II, Ch. II, "Drab Age Verse"; Yvor Winters, "The English Lyric in the Sixteenth Century," *Poetry*, 1939; rpt. in *Elizabethan Poetry: Modern Essays in Criticism*, ed. Paul J. Alpers [New York: Oxford Univ. Press, 1967], 93-125.)

3. Lewis thinks the only explanation is in the individual genius of the Elizabethan poets; Thompson sees variety following naturally from the new, if emphatic, regularity of the mid-century poets; Catherine Ing, in *The Elizabethan Lyric* (London: Chatto and Windus, 1951), suggests the

influence of song; and Douglas Peterson, *The English Lyric from Wyatt to Donne* (Princeton: Princeton Univ. Press, 1967), follows Winters in admiring the plain style, and suggests that the richness of Elizabethan poetry proceeds from the interaction of courtly and didactic verse traditions.

4. His most recent editor describes the skeltonic as "readily identified by its mono-rhyme leashes that extend for 12-14 lines at times and are internally distinguished by 2-3 accents per line" (*John Skelton: Poems*, ed. Robert Kinsman [Oxford: Clarendon Press, 1969], xviii). William Nelson, *John Skelton: Laureate* (New York: Columbia Univ. Press, 1939), describes the probable origins of the Skeltonic in medieval verse traditions and riming prose, notes how early Skelton was (often disparagingly) associated with his short-lined verse, and acknowledges that it "never merged with the general stock of English verse patterns" (83). See also Stanley Fish, *John Skelton's Poetry* (New Haven: Yale Univ. Press, 1965), 250-57, on the effects and the limits of skeltonics.

5. Saintsbury, *A History of English Prosody*, 1:305-07; Harold H. Child, in *The Cambridge History of English Poetry*, ed. A. W. Ward and A. R. Waller, 15 vols. (New York: G. P. Putnam's Sons, 1907-1933), 3:168-74; Tucker Brooke, in *A Literary History of England*, ed. Baugh, 339-42. Saintsbury and Child admire Wyatt's importations but Brooke, following E. M. W. Tillyard, admires the shorter-lined lyrics, and considers Wyatt's sonnets "in the main hard reading" and "disfigured" by Wyatt's "'not keeping of accent'" (342).

6. Thomas Warton, *The History of English Poetry*, 4 vols. (London: T. Tegg, 1814), 3:314-15:

> Wyat cooperated with Surrey, in having corrected
> the roughness of our poetic style. But Wyat,
> although sufficiently distinguished from the common
> versifiers of his age, is confessedly inferior to Surrey
> in harmony of numbers, perspecuity of expression,
> and facility of phraseology. . . . He has too much art
> as a lover, and too little as a poet. His gallantries are
> labored, and his versification negligent.

Or as his first good editor, G. F. Nott, put it more than 100 years earlier than the *TLS* article:

The versification of Wyatt's sonnets is uniformly
harsh and unmelodious. The lines are cumbered with
heavy monosyllables, and are deformed with
antiquated words and ungraceful contractions; so that
though the thoughts may be pleasing in themselves,
they are so expressed as to destroy the effect they
might have otherwise produced.

(The Works of Henry Howard, Earl of Surrey and Thomas Wyatt the Elder,
ed. G. F. Nott, 2 vols. [London: T. Bensley, 1815-16], 2:cxviii).

7. Alan Swallow, "The Pentameter Lines in Skelton and Wyatt," *Modern Philology*, 48(1950):1-11.

8. See chapter 2. The mystery of Wyatt has prompted a number of proposed solutions over the course of this century. Saintsbury attributed Wyatt's pentameter to a misreading of Chaucer. A. K. Foxwell and F. M. Padelford saw it as iambic pentameter with a consistent scheme of variations, much as Schick and Bergen had described Lydgate's versification. Tillyard thought Wyatt's was an awkward pioneer effort to combine two metrical traditions, "the native and the foreign," and attributed the roughness of some of the sonnets to the efforts of translation. Lewis thought Wyatt's verse a version of the "fifteenth-century heroic line" that he also saw in Lydgate (i.e., a line composed of two half-lines, each with two or three stresses, resulting in anywhere from four to six, but usually four or five stresses, in an approximately decasyllabic line). Swallow thought Wyatt's longer line was a combination of old and new pentameters. D. W. Harding saw the line as phrasal or pausing, and prototypic of twentieth-century verse. Sergio Baldi argued for Wyatt's sophisticated understanding and use of Italian prosodic principles, notably of elision. John Thompson saw it as based on rhetorical speech stress with only secondary concern for meter as such. Elias Schwartz claimed that at least some of Wyatt's pentameter poems were based on the Old English four-accent tradition. Saintsbury, *A History of English Prosody, 1:305-06,* and *Historical Manual of English Prosody,* 57-58; A. K. Foxwell, *The Poems of Sir Thomas Wiat,* 2 vols. (London: Univ. of London Press, 1913), 1:viii; F. M. Padelford, "The Scansion of Wyatt's Early Sonnets," *Studies in Philology,* 30(1923):138; C. S. Lewis, "The Fifteenth-Century Heroic Line," *Essays and Studies,* 24(1938):28-41; E. M. W. Tillyard, *The Poetry of Sir Thomas Wyatt* (London: Scholartis, 1929), 13; Swallow; D. W. Harding, "The Rhythmical Intention in Wyatt's Poetry," *Scrutiny,* 14(1946):96; Sergio Baldi, *La Poesia di Sir Thomas Wyatt* (Florence: F.

Natural Emphasis

Le Monnier, 1953); Thompson, 29; Schwartz, "The Meter of Some Poems of Wyatt," *Studies in Philology*, 60(1963):155-65.

9. The traditional belief that a misreading of Chaucer, particularly his syllabic final "-e," contributed to early sixteenth-century confusion remains probable, but it does not account for Lydgate's practice, and he was admired and imitated at least as much as his master.

10. The earliest English printers, William Caxton and Wynken de Worde, published numerous volumes by or attributed to Lydgate, and their successors through the mid-sixteenth century kept up the practice at a vigorous pace. Caxton first printed Lydgate's *Temple of Glas* in 1477, and by 1529 it had gone through five more editions by three other printers. The *Fall of Princes* was printed at least four times between 1494 and 1555, including a 1554 Tottel edition.

11. This begins with their first publication, appearing together posthumously in Richard Tottel's *Songs and Sonnets* (1557). In his preface Tottel ascribes to them the honor of doing for the English vernacular what certain Italians (presumably the Florentines) had done for the Italian: rendered it worthy of literature comparable to that of Classical Rome.

> That to have written well in verse, yea & in small
> parcelles, deserveth great praise, the workes of divers
> Latines, Italians, and other, doe prove sufficiently.
> That our tong is able in that kynde to do as
> praiseworthely as the rest, the honorable stile of the
> noble earle of Surrey, and the weightinesse of the
> depewitted Sir Thomas Wyat the elders verse . . .
> doe show abundantly.

George Puttenham's 1589 *Arte of English Poesie* more particularly pairs the two as great reformers of English versification:

> In the latter end of the same kings raigne [i.e., Henry
> VIII] sprong up a new company of courtly makers,
> of whom Sir *Thomas Wyat* th'elder & *Henry* Earle of
> Surrey were the two chieftaines, who having
> travailed into Italie, and there tasted the sweete and
> stately measures and stile of Italian Poesie, as novices
> newly crept out of the schooles of *Dante, Arioste,* and

98

Petrarch, they greatly pollished our rude & homely
maner of vulgar Poesie from that it had bene before,
and for that cause may justly be sayd the first
reformers of our English meetre and stile.

Book I, ch. xxxi; see *Elizabethan Critical Essays*, ed. G. Gregory Smith,
2 vols. (Oxford: Oxford Univ. Press, 1904), 2:62-63. All quotations
from Puttenham and other Elizabethan critics are taken from this edition unless otherwise noted.

12. On Surrey's earlier precedence, see Warton, Courthope, and
Saintsbury; for the recent admiration of Wyatt, see Foxwell, Muir,
Southall, and Thompson.

13. Throughout this discussion I refer to "major mid-line pause" or
"the pause" in a given line as roughly a synonym for the more precise
concept of the metrical cesura. The distinction between "pause" and
"cesura" will be re-established with Surrey and, especially, Gascoigne.

Metrical conventions remain the ones used for Chaucer in
Chapter 2: / = fully stressed and accented; \ = relatively stressed in the
context, and counted as accented; x = unaccented. In addition, I use
the double bar (‖) to indicate the major mid-line pause.

14. The text is Harrier no. 4, 101; all Wyatt's texts will be from this
edition of the Egerton Manuscript. A more complete and somewhat
modernized version of Wyatt's poems is the edition by Kenneth Muir
and Patricia Thomson, generally considered standard: *Collected Poems of
Sir Thomas Wyatt* (Liverpool: Liverpool Univ. Press, 1969). It is not
entirely reliable in its punctuation or even its syllabification (see "lyms"
vs. "lymmis" in l. 5 of LXXX as printed on pages xxvi and 60).
Through no. 74 Harrier and Muir-Thomson offer parallel numbering.

Surrey also translates this poem (*Henry Howard, Earl of Surrey,
Poems* ed. Emrys Jones [Oxford: Clarendon Press, 1964], 3), which has
made the pair of translations a standard test exercise in the differences
between the two poets. Hallett Smith uses the poems in an enlightening discussion of "The Art of Sir Thomas Wyatt," *Huntington Library
Quarterly*, 9(1946):323-55. Among other things, he shows that Wyatt's
revisions were not necessarily in the direction of metrical smoothness,
which eliminates the longstanding assumption that Wyatt eventually
figured out iambic pentameter and wrote his smooth verse later, or that
his smoother poems were the ones he had a chance to revise.

15. See Appendix A for further discussion of this subject.

16. See Baldi and also Robert O. Evans, "Some Aspects of Wyatt's

Natural Emphasis

Metrical Technique," *Journal of English and German Philology*, 53(1954):197-213.

17. Saintsbury and Tillyard assumed that Wyatt's sonnet translations were among his roughest poems because he was more concerned with accurately rendering Petrarch than with polishing his versification. Smith, however, shows that Wyatt revised this verse very carefully though apparently without an eye to making it smoother. Harrier's edition of the Egerton MS supports Smith. The exigencies of translation still cannot be dismissed as one possible obstacle to elegant versification.

18. Other poems use rhythms to imitate the speaker's unsettled situation with more success. "My galy charged with forgetfulnes" (Harrier no. 28), for example, uses an underlying ocean rhythm (strongly iambic) to support such effectively variant movements as "thorrough sharpe sees in wynter nyghtes doeth pas / twene Rock and Rock & eke myn ennemy Alas" (ll. 2-3). In this instance the poem has the virtue of being readable over what is to us a familiar iambic base. Another successful poem with deliberately varying rhythms is "Unstable dreme according to the place" (Harrier no. 81). Here it is the rhythms and syllabification both that are variable, as in "my body in tempest her succour to enbrace" (l. 8) and "retorning to lepe into the fire" (l. 12). In this poem the variations are themselves notable and effective enough to sustain interest. They are closely interwoven with the whole statement of the poem, rather than standing as a scheme for the subject (as in "Eche man me telleth").

   Wyatt's impulse toward imitative forms is not confined to the spoken poetry, though it is less common or at least less pronounced in the songs. Still, a song such as "Helpe me to seke for I lost it there" (Harrier no. 17), with its sexual references abruptly resolved by the designation of the speaker's "hert" as the thing lost, uses as much rhythmic variety as any of the sonnets, and is as difficult to read as "Eche man me telleth." Deliberate rhythmic variety in imitation of the poem's topic, or the voice of the speaker, is clearly a conscious and pervasive characteristic throughout the body of Wyatt's verse.

19. For example Leonard E. Nathan, "Tradition and Newfangleness in Wyatt's 'They Fle from Me,'" *English Literary History*, 22(1965):1-16; Donald M. Friedman, "The Mind in the Poem: Wyatt's 'They Fle from Me,'" *Studies in English Literature*, 7(1967):1-13; and Carolyn Chiapelli, "A Late Gothic Vein in Wyatt's 'They Fle from Me,'" *Renaissance & Reformation*, 1(1977):95-102.

20. Of all the Henricans, Surrey most resembled Castiglione's perfect courtier. Heir to the dukedom of Norfolk, he was given a solid classi-

cal education first by the great Catholic Humanist, John Clerke, and then at Windsor in the company of the King's natural son, Henry, Earl of Richmond. In this latter context, as he tells us in the autobiographical "So crewell prison," he developed the courtier's skills of love, music and dance, horsemanship, and friendship. See the biography by Edwin Casady, *Henry Howard, Earl of Surrey* (New York: Columbia Univ. Press, 1938). Emrys Jones reminds us that the great mid-century Humanists, including John Cheke and Roger Ascham, were Surrey's contemporaries *(Henry Howard, Earl of Surrey, Poems,* xxv).

21. I have heard it suggested that Surrey's iambic regularity, like Wyatt's in Tottel, is the product of somewhat later editors and that he may have had no better understanding of the accentual patterning of his decasyllabic lines than Wyatt did. While it is true that almost all of Surrey's poetry was published after his death, manuscript evidence shows his poetry to be unquestionably smoother than Wyatt's, and at least one iambic pentameter poem was printed during his lifetime. This is the moving epitaph on Wyatt which begins with a hexameter line and then moves to pentameter throughout the rest of the poem:

> Wyat resteth here, that quicke coulde never rest.
> Whose hevenly gifts, encreased by disdayn
> And vertue sanke the deper in his brest
> Such profit he, of envy could optayne.

This version is from the (probably 1542) pamphlet *An excellent Epitaffe of syr Thomas Wyat.* Jones cites a 1544 reference to establish its latest possible date.

22. Unless otherwise indicated, all Surrey texts are from the Jones edition. I have added the cesura punctuation (‖).

23. Later versions include those by John Davies, Sir Henry Wotton, and Ben Jonson (see chapter 7).

24. Many of the poems in Tottel are monotonously regular, and the rigidity of mid-century English verse has often been noted. A typical comment is Saintsbury's in *The Historical Character of the English Lyric* (London: British Academy Proceedings, 1911-12, 1914):

> It should only be for a moment . . . surprising that
> the famous reform of Wyatt and Surrey produced at

101

> first effects which were, if improving from one point
> of view and in the long run, positively impoverishing
> for the time and from another point. . . . It was at
> this time that there first established itself the
> deplorable heresy that there was in English only "a
> foot of two syllables" – from which it almost
> necessarily followed that lyric must be crippled or at
> least fettered. In Wyatt and Surrey themselves, and
> in the generation that followed, such cripplement or
> fettering did in fact follow.

25. *The Aeneid of Henry Howard Earl of Surrey*, ed. Florence H. Ridley
(Berkeley and Los Angeles: Univ. of California Studies, 1963), 3-4.

26. Ridley argues strongly for Douglas's influence (13-30), and Jones
accepts it (xiv). Douglas's *Eneados* was completed in 1513, and although
it was not printed until 1553, it was commonly circulated in manuscript.

27. Citations from Surrey's *Aeneid* are from Ridley's edition.

28. At least nine of the poulters measure poems in Tottel are certainly
by Surrey, and they all come toward the beginning of the 1557 volume. These are the poems beginning "Such waiward waies hath love,"
"When sommer took in hand," "In winters just returne," "Good Ladies:
ye that have," "To dearely had I bought," "Wrapt in my carelesse
cloke," "Gyrt in my giltlesse gowne," "If care do cause men cry," and
"Layd in my quiet bed."

29. Jones (118) accepts Casady's assessment of the poems' contexts
(Casady, 163).

30. *Tottel's Miscellany (1557-1587)*, ed. Hyder E. Rollins, 2 vols. rev.
ed. (Cambridge, Mass.: Harvard Univ. Press, 1965), 2:vii. The work
went through three editions in 1557, and at least six others appeared
during Elizabeth's reign (1559, 1565, 1567, 1574, 1585, and 1587). See
Rollins, 2:107-24, for a summary of its immediate influence and general
approbation through the nineteenth century.

31. A typical pentameter model for midcentury monotony is the anonymous forty-two-line poem in Tottel, "Comparison of life and death,"
written in what George Gascoigne was to describe as "ballade" stanzas
(ababcc). The poem begins:

The life is long that lothsomly doth last:
The dolefull days draw slowly to their date:
The present panges, and painfull plages forepast
Weld griefe aye grene to stablish this estate.
So that I feele, in this great storme, and strife,
The death is swete that endeth such a life.

Compare the last line with Wyatt and Surrey's translations of
Petrarch's *Rime* 140, and compare the rhythmic movement, the use of
alliteration, and the moral tone to the poem by Lord Vaux from the
1576 *Paradise of Dainty Devices* (see chapter 4).

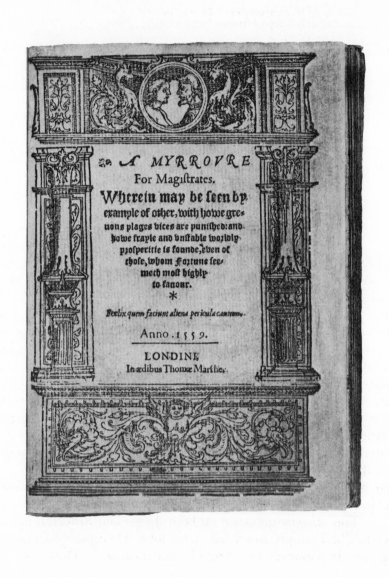

A MYRROVRE
For Magiſtrates.
Wherein may be ſeen by
example of other, with howe grecuons plages vices are puniſhed: and
howe frayle and vnſtable worldly
proſperitie is founde, even of
thoſe, whom Fortune ſeemeth moſt highly
to fauour.
*
Fœlix quem faciunt aliena pericula cautum.
Anno. 1559.
LONDINI.
In ædibus Thomæ Marſhe.

Chapter Four

Mid-Century Theory and Practice:
The Mirror for Magistrates, Gascoigne, and "Rhyme"

This poetic license is a shrewd fellow,
and covereth many faults in a verse.

Gascoigne, "Certayne Notes of Instruction"

The Mirror for Magistrates, which might be subtitled
"Lydgate's Last Gasp," was an explicit and very popular attempt
to provide a sequel to *The Fall of Princes*. After Tottel it is this
work and the singular and influential activities of George Gascoigne that established the direction for English versification. The
Mirror shows the developed and developing solidity and range of
the mid-century iambic pentameter line, while Gascoigne, in his
theory and practice, codified English accentual-syllabic verse and
illustrated some of the aesthetic and mimetic possibilities that the
new security allowed. At the same time, Humanist intellectuals
were actively questioning those possibilities, and advocating a
classical quantitative model to replace what they called the
system of "rhyme." Together, the *Mirror*, Gascoigne's work,
and the rhyme controversy illustrate the metrical situation in the
first half of Elizabeth's reign and suggest some of the directions
the interplay between meter and prose rhythms would take.

The *Mirror*'s influence on both drama and historical narrative has been amply discussed, with John Thompson document-
ing its importance for English versification.[1] Much of its

versification remains little more than a smoother presentation of Lydgate's rime royal stanzas, often bordering on what appears to be a monotonous imitation of Surrey's model decasyllabic regularity. It does, however, illustrate the security of iambic rhythms in a mostly conservative and sometimes even regressive verse context.

The first extant edition of the *Mirror* (1559) prints nineteen "tragedies," many by men who had been of Edward Seymour, Duke of Somerset's party early in the reign of Edward VI.[2] These include the principal author and editor of the work, William Baldwin, whose *Treatise of Moral Philosophy* (1547) was dedicated to Edward, Earl of Hertford, the son of Lord Protector Somerset. The medieval and moral tone of Baldwin's *Treatise* along with his alliance with the Seymour family suggests alienation from the rival Howard family and, by extension, .from Surrey and the courtly lyrics he wrote and represented in this period. Other professional courtiers associated with Somerset and longtime colleagues of Baldwin include George Ferrars (1500?-1579), who wrote "Tresilian," the first tragedy of the *Mirror*, and "Thomas of Woodstock," the third; Thomas Chaloner (1521-1565), who wrote the story of "Richard II"; and Thomas Phaer (1510?-1560), who probably wrote the "Owen Glendower" and also published separately a translation of seven books of Virgil's *Aeneid* in 1558 and nine books in 1562.[3]

These four men established the tone and formal outlines of the *Mirror*. Both are intentionally reminiscent of Lydgate's *Fall of Princes*, although the prose connections give the whole a new coherence. Some of the "tragedies" were in fact written at the end of the fourteenth or beginning of the fifteenth century (Skelton's version of the story of Edward IV is a notable example) and even the verifiably more recent tragedies show the conservative bent. They are all in rime royal or variations of it; although more syllabically regular than fifteenth-century verse, they retain the pattern of at least four accents among ten or eleven syllables and variable placement of the cesura. Some of them also retain regular alliteration to help carry the accent pattern. Thus, for example, Ferrars' "tragedy" on "Thomas, Duke of Gloucester" begins:

> Whose state is stablisht in semyng most sure,
> And so far from daunger of Fortunes blast,
> As by the compas of mans conjecture,
> No brasen pyller maye be fyxte more fast:
> Yet wantyng the staye of prudent forecast,
> Whan frowarde Fortune lyst for to frowne,
> Maye in a moment tourne upsyde downe.

(ll. 1-7)

The last line shows the general tendency in this first edition for the authors to seek sophistication through rhythms mimetic of statement. The whole stanza illustrates the slightly clumsy use of the decasyllabic line. It is most easily read as rhythmic four-accent verse which uses ornamental alliteration as an aid to determining accent.

Baldwin himself is a somewhat more graceful versifier, as in the clearly iambic pentameter tragedy of "Lord Mowbray," which begins:

> Though sorowe and shame abash me to reherce
> My lothsum lyfe and death of due deserved,
> Yet that the paynes thereof may other perce,
> To leave the lyke, least they be lykely served,
> Ah Baldwin marke, I wil shew thee how I swarved:
> Dyssemblyng, Envy, and Flattery, bane that be
> Of all their hostes, have shewed their power on me.

(ll. 1-7)

This is relatively more forward-looking than Ferrars insofar as it is at least perceptibly more like Surrey. Elisions in the first, fifth, and sixth lines will render it metrical iambic pentameter, though not without some effort. Its combination of roughness and regularity, however, makes it an unsophisticated version of Surrey's new meter. Additionally, although alliteration is not the regular feature it is for Ferrars, it remains a chief ornament of the verse. The accentuation in the lines has more balance

107

than in Ferrars' lines, but the balance is seldom varied except for mimetic effects which are relatively crude, as in the wrenched rhythm and run-on of the second of lines 57-63:

> Beholde in me due proofe of everye parte:
> For pryde fyrst forced me my prince to flatter
> So muche, that what so ever pleased his harte,
> Were it never so evyll, I thought a lawfull matter,
> Whiche caused the lordes afresh against him clatter,
> Because he had his holdes beyond sea solde,
> And seen his souldiers of theyr wages polde.

The two authors whose contributions to the *Mirror* have received the most critical praise are Thomas Sackville, Earl of Dorset (1536-1608), who wrote the meditation on fortune called "The Induction" and its accompanying tragedy of the "Duke of Buckingham," and Thomas Churchyard (1520-1604) who wrote the touching tragedy of "Jane Shore." Their works appear for the first time in the second (1563) edition of the *Mirror*. Interestingly, both men were associated at least indirectly with Surrey. Sackville's father, Sir Richard Sackville, was a first cousin of Anne Boleyn as was Surrey himself from the other side of the family, and Churchyard was at one time in service to Surrey and contributed to Tottel's *Miscellany*. He was also an admirer of Skelton and contributed prefatory verses to the 1568 Thomas Marshe edition of Skelton's poems.

Sackville's "Induction" begins with an alliterated setting of place that is conservative only in its outline. The authority of the smoother decasyllabic line underlies the medieval appearance, and there is an energy that has made Sackville a favorite for critics seeing in the *Mirror* a prototype for the development of Elizabethan drama:

> The wrathfull winter prochinge on a pace,
> With blustring blastes had al ybared the treen
> And olde Saturnus with his frosty face

With chilling colde had pearst the tender green:
The mantels rent, wherein enwrapped been
The gladsom groves that nowe laye overthrowen,
The tapets torne, and every blome downe blowen.

(ll. 1-7)

Sackville, who co-authored the blank verse tragedy *Gorboduc* (see chapter 8), is a relatively sophisticated poet whose rhythms anticipate Elizabethan drama here as well as in his directly dramatic effort. When he portrays heightened emotion, particularly in dialogue, he is able to make conventional schematic language sound natural across the iambic base. When Sorrow guides the narrator of "The Induction" to the vision of Fortune, for example, her voice is convincingly chilling:

Cum, cum, (quod she) and see what I shall shewe,
Cum heare the playning and the bitter bale
Of worthy men, by Fortune overthrowe.
Cum thou and see them rewing al in rowe.
They were but shades that erst in minde thou rolde.
Cum, cum with me, thine iyes shall them beholde.

(ll. 148-54)

Churchyard's skills are similar. He has an ease with the decasyllabic line that Ferrars and even Baldwin do not, although his assured regularity does not carry with it the subtle variations and compelling intensity of Sackville's verse. Sackville anticipates the later Elizabethans; Churchyard is in the mainstream, with verse that is most like what we see in Gascoigne and his followers. Churchyard relies still on alliteration but with a variety that Ferrars and Baldwin do not have. His poetry is more descriptive and explanatory than Sackville's, but more compelling than the poetry of most other contributors, not least because of Churchyard's skillful management of even the cruder effects of his versification. The moral told against forced marriage is particularly effective when presented with varied repetition, as in the constructions beginning with "what":

> Note wel what stryfe this forced maryage makes,
> What lothed lyves do come where love doth lacke,
> What scatring bryers do growe upon such brakes,

(ll. 120-22)

Regardless of the degree of iambic smoothness (or monotony) we may be able to attribute to the various authors of the *Mirror*, certain elements of the verse of Sackville and Churchyard have rightly set them apart for most modern readers. Those elements may be summarized as assurance, sophistication, and above all a willingness to look beyond the simple mimetic variation to patterns of rhetorical presentation whose effects may sometimes be mimetic of voice but which may as often be simply various, elegant, and pleasing in the aesthetic sense. Building on the possibilities suggested by the lyric verse of Tottel's *Miscellany*, these authors are able to extend the use of the Surreyan pentameter into the narrative mode, and do it with sufficient skill, variety, and poetic interest to provide a legitimate model for the general expansion of the new decasyllabic line into a great many verse genres. They help establish a model which competes with the narrative poulters measure and fourteeners, and their success may well have helped with the unlamented languishing of their sing-song competitors.

Gascoigne's work, however, most securely establishes both the mimetic and aesthetic potential of the new accentual-syllabic verse. George Gascoigne (1542-1577) was the spokesman for the early Elizabethan poets and the first person to describe English metrical practice. Courtier, soldier, and perpetual litigant, he was not a financial success in anything he undertook, but he was the acknowledged master of English poetry for his generation and he helped define the courtier-poet in the Elizabethan age. His acquaintance with Sir Walter Ralegh gave him a direct importance to the development of the high Reniassance lyric in England and his theory and practice had apparent influence on Edmund Spenser.[4] The difference between Gascoigne and the tradition represented by the *Mirror* is striking from Gascoigne's own attempt at a poem in the mirror tradition, *The Steele Glas* (1576). It is one of only a few works in iambic pentameter blank verse between Surrey and Marlowe. It also adopts a regular cesura (marked in print by a comma) after the fourth syllable of each line. *The Steele Glas* therefore illustrates in practice the impress of both Surrey's cesura and his blank verse solution to the problem of a flexible line for serious English verse, but it is Gascoigne's treatise on verse making and his lyric practice that were to codify and extend Surrey's reforms.

Gascoigne published his "Certayne Notes of Instruction Concerning the Making of Verse or Ryme in English" in 1575. Although they are too brief to be more than an outline of certain assumptions about verse making and a warning against common inartistic pitfalls, they are tremendously valuable for observing the development of the actual practice of versification. Unlike most other Renaissance discussions of meter, they are strictly practical and make no claim to serve larger philosophical or rhetorical purposes. They also illustrate the tremendous range of their author, who was not only the pre-eminent poet of his generation, but also a pioneer in drama and prose fiction.[5]

The complete title of the treatise is instructive. It assumes the distinction between classical measures and English "ryme," and says no more about it. The versification he then describes is a clear heritage of the European tradition, primarily the French and Latin rhythmic traditions, with the modifications proper to the development of an English accentual verse using the analogue, but not the actual model, of classical feet.

According to Gascoigne, syllabic regularity and consistency of verse type are the first bases of English versification. He advises the aspiring poet to "hold the just measure wherwith you begin your verse." In addition to affirming a regular syllabic base for English poetry, this appears to require that strophic patterns be maintained within a given poem, to reject the more-

111

or-less decasyllabic tradition of the Lydgate heritage, and possibly, as Gabriel Harvey thought, to show a preference for stanzas composed of lines of equal length.[6] Even "master" Chaucer is only barely excused from breaking the syllabic rule; Gascoigne acknowledges Chaucer's unequal syllabification, but argues for the lines' synchronicity: "who so ever do peruse and well consider his workes, he shall find that although his lines are not alwayes of one selfe number of Syllables, yet, beyng redde by one that hath understanding, the longest verse, and that which hath most Syllables in it, will fall (to the eare) correspondent unto that which hath fewest sillables in it."[7] Gascoigne associates this synchronicity with "the same libertie in feete and measures that the Latinists do use," but he does not claim that Chaucer was writing quantitative verse. When lines are neither syllabically regular nor isochronic, they produce what Gascoigne (and others) called "ryding ryme," perceived as the meter of *The Canterbury Tales* and "divers other delectable and light enterprises."[8]

Neither rime nor accurate syllabic composition were felt in this period to be enough for elegant English verse. Roger Ascham, for example, in his argument for importing classical meters into English, denounced not only the rough accentuation he associated with the barbarism of rime but simple syllabics as well. Ascham claimed that if true English versifiers using classical models would come forth, "surelie than rash ignorant heads which now can easely recken up fourten sillabes, and easelie stumble on every Ryme, either durst not . . . or els would not . . . be so busie as everywhere they be; and shoppes in London should not be so full of lewd and rude rymes, as commonlie they are."[9] While Gascoigne's treatise is a cheerful description of how to write the despised "ryme," he nonetheless recognizes the metrical implications of mere syllabics or inharmonious accentuation, and gives a good deal of consideration to stress patterns and kinds of accent. He insists that words fulfill metrical feet based on "accent," with his discussion of this topic both revealing and misleading.

Gascoigne mentions but in effect dismisses "length" and "shortness" as features of accent suitable for English feet. He goes on to discuss "elevation or depression of sillables," positing "three maner of accents" for English: *gravis*, or long(/); *levis*, or light (\\); and *circumflexa*, or "indifferent" (^). In practice, the circumflex becomes long or short as the requirements of the meter dictate, confirming an early recognition of relative stress. Monosyllabic words, of which English has many, are for Gascoigne frequently "indifferent," since they depend upon context for their emphasis. They "will more easily fall to be shorte or long as occasion requireth" than will polysyllabic words.[10] Although Gascoigne in this instance uses "long" and "short" to describe what we would call stressed and unstressed, he apparently has in mind the Romance and not the Latin model for English. In classical quantitative meters short syllables can become long by position, with comparatively simple rules. Most commonly, a short vowel becomes long if it is followed by two consonants, even across a word boundary. Although Gascoigne suggests the usefulness of monosyllabic words for English verse, which would presumably allow for more flexible positioning in this classical sense, he is not trying to follow the classical model. He assumes, rather, that stress-accent is relative in English, and may be more easily manipulated among monosyllables than with the fixed accentuation of polysyllabics.[11] Gascoigne's phonological (if not terminological) emphasis on "gravis" and "levis," or heavy and light, suggest distinctions appropriate to French versification.[12]

Altogether, Gascoigne's discussion reveals actual English practice by suggesting how English poets could use the models of both Romance versification and Latin versification for stress-accent verse, particularly by borrowing the analogy of classical feet to describe accent-patterning. It is important to remember, however, that Gascoigne disallowed the kinds of substitutions that would vary the syllabification of lines ("hold the just measure wherwith you begin your verse"). Gascoigne's treatise is therefore the first clear statement of how English versification had evolved in the sixteenth century.

His terminology is misleading, however, not only in his inconsistent use of "short" and "long," but also in perpetuating

113

the confusion between Romance and English accentuation; English accent is not, strictly speaking, pitch-accent in the French and Italian senses, and Gascoigne's terminology codifies a misconception about English accent that persists into the twentieth century: that pitch and stress are coincident, which they are not.[13] Nonetheless, the overall impression of his treatise is of a practical, sensible description of a versification that has only just emerged fully but which has had a long and logical development at least from the time of Chaucer. Gascoigne's injunctions carry the authority of simple assurance and serve to establish the importance of words placed according to their "natural *Emphasis* or sound," and the primacy of the accentual iamb in English.

Gascoigne's description of the verse appropriate to various poetic genres is reminiscent of Deschamps, though with a decidedly English cast. In addition to Chaucer's merry "ryding ryme," Gascoigne describes a number of different verse and stanza forms along with their appropriate topics and tones. He considers "Rythme royall" a stately verse "serving best for grave discourses," and the "Ballade" as "beste of matters of love." Gascoigne is the first to define the "ballade" stanza as an octosyllabic or decasyllabic sizain, riming ababcc. Chaucer's ballades were in rime royal, and the Romance ballade stanza usually varied from six to ten lines.[14] More conventionally, "Rondlettes" are "moste apt for the beating or handlyng of an adage or common proverbe"; "Sonets" interestingly "serve as well in matters of love as of discourse," which suggests the development of the English epigrammatic sonnet; "Dizaynes" and "Sixaines" – what we would think of as ten- and six-line epigrams – serve "for shorte Fantazies"; "Verlayes," decasyllabic stanzas riming abab, serve "for an effectual proposition"; and "the long verse of twelve and fourtene sillables" would "serve best for Psalmes and Himpnes," even though "it be now adayes used in all Theames."[15] Gascoigne's attitude toward the "long verse" of poulters measure is particularly perceptive. It indirectly notes the verse's probable origin in ballad or common meter and directly projects it back to the popular lyric. Its propriety for hymnody had been reinforced by Sternhold and Hopkins, who used it for their popular

114

(though unsophisticated) psalm translations (ten editions were printed between 1549 and 1561). Those translations were even more widely disseminated by inclusion in the Elizabethan *Book of Common Prayer* beginning in 1562, which may help to explain the meter's pervasiveness; it probably does explain Gascoigne's recommending it for hymns.

Poulters measure may have achieved its improbable ubiquity among literary poets from the conflicting impulses of English Humanism. A line like the stately Latin hexameter continued to elude English writers, who had not yet seen the implications of Surrey's translation of Virgil. Poulters measure provided native long lines, appealing to English patriotism, and at least the pretense of syllabic variety characteristic of dactylic hexameters. In the classical line syllabic variety could be achieved through substituting trochees for dactyls, and in poulters measure not all lines were exactly the same length. That they were only of two lengths, and predictably alternate, may have seemed less important than the appearance of variety-in-regularity. In any case, the classical influence behind poulters measure and the more regular fourteeners is evident from the mid-century translations. Thomas Phaer's *Aeneid* (1558) and Arthur Golding's *Metamorphoses* (1567) were both written in fourteeners. It is difficult now for us to understand the attraction of such meters, as in the opening of Golding's translation of Ovid:[16]

> Of shapes transformde to bodies straunge, I purpose to entreat;
> Ye gods vouchsafe (for you are they that wrought this wondrous feate)
> To further this mine enterprise. And from the world begunne,
> Graunt that my verse may to my time, his course directly runne.

Fourteeners may be considered Latin hexameters "transformde to bodies straunge."

The attempt to make this essentially lyric native meter carry so many kinds of poetic discourse hastened its decline for virtually all serious verse. Gascoigne's insight into the best use of these meters testifies to his sense of verse decorum. It is almost solely in the "common meter" quatrains of hymnody (actual or, as in Emily Dickinson's verse, variant) that fourteeners and poulters measure survive today.

Gascoigne himself followed the fad, however, and a good portion of his surviving verse is in poulters measure. His practice somewhat follows his observations; although he manages to write effective poems on a variety of topics in this meter, most of them carry a penitential or moral message. "The Divorce of a Lover," for example, is a moving statement (though, typically, not without humor) about the decline of love and life and the renunciation of both. The poem concludes with the speaker addressing death in terms equally appropriate to Cupid:

> Wherefore thy sentence say, devorce me from them both,
> Since only thou mayst right my wronges, good death nowe be not loath.
> But cast thy pearcing dart, into my panting brest,
> That I may leave both love and life, & thereby purchase rest.

The characteristic problem here is the echo of the native ballad tradition. The precise cesura, which made the iambic pentameter line possible, here has the effect of dividing long lines into rhythmic halves, and the more one insists upon keeping the whole line as a rhythmic unit, the more one is likely to fall into sing-song. The only way to avoid that sing-song effect is to run syntactic pauses counter to the cesural pause, and this is hard to sustain without the lines breaking down altogether.

Although Gascoigne himself wrote some of the best poulters measure extant, the majority of his own poetry is written in decasyllabic or octosyllabic lines where the subtle interactions between metrical prescription and language rhythm are not as easily overwhelmed by the new regularity. In these shorter lines, Gascoigne's practice proves that mid-century poetry is not necessarily the unrelieved monotony that has sometimes been suggested.

The Posies of George Gascoigne (1575) represents his most

careful effort to collect and edit his verses, despite a few readings arguably inferior to the anonymously printed *A Hundreth Sundrie Flowers* (1573). Though some of the changes probably reflect some readers' moral outrage over the earlier work (especially the rollicking prose *Adventures of Master F. J.*), the later work bears the imprint of authorial concern, particularly for structural coherence. Although it never achieved the popularity of Tottel's *Miscellany* or *The Mirror for Magistrates*, it would be one of the major volumes in the development of English versification in the Renaissance even if it had not included (as it does) the "Certayne Notes."

 The Posies contains an unusually large number and variety of verse forms. Of 111 non-dramatic poems (including two introductory), sixty-three are in iambic pentameter (including twenty sonnets or sonnet-based poems), thirty-five are in poulters measure or fourteeners, eleven are tetrameter (mostly in Gascoigne's six-line ballade stanzas), and there is one in hexameter ballade stanzas. This does not suggest the range and interweaving of various stanza forms nor the structural coherence Gascoigne gives whole sections by means of either prose connectives, obvious sequencing, or both. Included, for example, are the verses from the prose novella, *The Adventures of Master F. J.*, the long sequence on "Dan Bartholmew of Bath" and the short one on "The Green Knyght."

 The structure of the whole is notable. Although it by no means achieves the coherence of *The Shepheardes Calendar* or *Astrophil and Stella*, it has considerably more order than collections which preceded it.[17] Gascoigne divides the book into three sections, ostensibly to appease those who would object to light or amorous verses on moral grounds. "Flowers" are pleasant poems of no great moral value but inventive and surely of no offense; "Hearbes" are positively moral; and "Weedes" may be read as examples of how not to behave and what not to write.[18] Overall, his handling of iambic pentameter shows a superb ear for effective subtlety and illustrates a clear sense of what metrical substitutions could be considered standard and how variations in stress patterns may effect both aesthetic and mimetic rhythms.

117

Natural Emphasis

Gascoigne's success can best be measured in contrast to the monotonous or awkward use of regular meters by many of his contemporaries. The poems found in *The Paradise of Dainty Devices* (1576), the most popular Elizabethan miscellany, may be considered typical of the period. This volume went through at least ten editions between 1576 and 1606. A large portion of the poems are in poulters measure or variations on it, but there are also a good many pentameter poems. Lord Vaux's "In his extreame sycknesse" is one of the better ones:[19]

> What greeves my bones and makes my body faint?
> What prickes my flesh and teares my head in twayne?
> Why doo I wake, when rest should me attaynt?
> When others laugh, why doo I live in paine?
> I *toss* I *turne*, I *change* from side to side,
> And *stretche* me oft, in sorowes linkes betyde.
>
> I *tosse*, as one betost in waves of care,
> I *turne*, to flee the woes of lothsome life:
> I *change* to spie, yf death this corps might spare,
> I stretche to heaven, to ridde me of this strife.
> Thus doo I *stretche* and *change* and *tosse* and *turne*,
> Whyle I in hope of heaven my life doo burne.
>
> Then holde thee still, let be thy heavinesse,
> Abolishe care, forgeat thy pining woe:
> For by this meanes soone shalt thou find redresse,
> When oft betost, hence thou to heaven must goe.
> Then *tosse* and turne, and *tumble* franke and free.
> I happy thryse when thou in heaven shalt be.

There are many excellences here, including a clear and mostly well-handled rhetorical structure and the transformation of "toss and turn" in the last stanza. But this poem also illustrates some of the problems of the new regularity. Its rhythm is relentlessly regular, with heavy correspondence between the iambic metrical model and the fulfilling language – between accent and stress. Some phrases seem labored to fit the meter (as in line 12) and when tensions are felt between the meter and the informing language (as in the last line) the result is distortion rather than variation, clumsiness rather than sophistication. The poem works best when meter and language rhythm coincide, as if the poet had no sense of what variations were possible.

Gascoigne's verse, though almost as regular in the coincidence of language with metrical pattern, is a different matter. He varies rarely but effectively, with assurance and control. Two examples, "Gascoigne's Lullabie" and "Gascoigne's Woodmanship," illustrate his achievement with both mimetic and aesthetic rhythms, and show him to be a literary poet with a sure ear for the sounds of speech. Although these are among his best-known poems, there are others equally effective, such as the several "Memories" poems.

"Gascoigne's Lullabie" makes emphatic use of the new iambic rhythms in the context of traditional octosyllabic verse. What is new is not the smoothness of such verse, which (as we have seen) had a far longer and less problematic history than the decasyllabic. Rather it is the heavy iambic movement, on the model of the newly solidified pentameter, and the ways in which Gascoigne uses that iambic regularity for controlled emphasis and variation. The steady rhythm is announced at the outset by the cesura after the fourth syllable which is supported by the unwavering iambics of the rest of the stanza:

> Sing lullaby, as women doe,
> Wherewith they bring their babes to rest,
> And lullaby can I sing to,
> As womanly as can the best.
> With lullaby they still the childe,
> And if I be not much beguild,
> Full many wanton babes have I,
> Which must be stild with lullabie.

> (ll. 1-8)

The second stanza starts by continuing the deliberately soporific regularity of the first, but the second and fourth lines provide

119

sufficient disruption in the rhythm's steadiness to give the reader
pause. The fifth line immediately reestablishes the rocking iambics, however, and leads the reader to the sleep referred to in the
last line of the stanza:

> First lullaby my youthfull yeares,
> It is now time to go to bed
> For croocked age and hoary heares
> have wone the haven with in my head:
> With Lullaby then youth be still,
> With Lullaby content thy will,
> Since courage quayles, and commes behind,
> Go sleepe, and so beguile thy minde.

(ll. 9-16)

This stanza has established the rhythmic techniques of the poem.
The steady rhythms, reminiscent of a rocking cradle and therefore mimetic of subject matter on the metrical level, continue
throughout without any familiar trochaic substitutions. But there
is variation in levels of stress among accented syllables, with
particularly effective use of the rare 4-3-2-1 iambic stress-level
pattern, as in the penultimate line of the third stanza:

> Lette no fayre face, nor beautie brighte,
>   4   3   2   1
> Entice you efte with vayne delighte.

(ll. 23-24)

The other key element of variety is his use of the trisyllabic,
"Lullaby," in a poem that has a very large proportion of monosyllables. Besides the word "lullaby" itself, whose repetition and
placement is crucial to the poem's rhythmic movement, there are
only two other words longer than two syllables, both of them
trisyllabic as well: "womanly" in line 4 and "Remember" in the

120

last line of the poem. They make a substantial impact on so
steady a poem, with closure effected by the almost startling
occurrence of two trisyllabic words in the last line:

> And when you rise with waking eye,
> Remember then this Lullabye.

(Posies, 1575, A4v-A5v)

Throughout the poem the variations are few and subtle,
but crucial to the poem's sustained interest. In a reversal of what
was to become the usual pattern for the relation between aesthetic and mimetic in meter and rhythm, the meter is mimetic (of
the cradle and the hypnotic quality of a good lullaby) while the
rhythms, insofar as they vary the metrical prescription, are
aesthetic; that is, they do not serve particularly either to emphasize the speaker's quality of voice or his subject, but they
unquestionably serve to make the poem pleasing.

"Gascoigne's Woodmanship" uses meter itself more conventionally, as an aesthetically pleasing backdrop with no obvious mimetic functions in its iambic prescription.[20] It also provides more variations on the iambic pattern, although, as in all
Gascoigne's poetry, there is a high coincidence between meter
and rhythm. It provides good examples of the kinds of metrical
and rhythmic variations that were to be the mainstay of pentameter versification for many years to come, and although these
variations remain largely aesthetic, they also show a clear eye for
the kind of mimetic rhythms that would scarcely be possible
without the new security of Surreyan iambic pentameter.

The poem begins with as much coincidence between meter
and language rhythm as any model could describe:

> My woorthy Lord, I pray you wonder not,
> W   S W   S W S   W   S W S
>
> To see your woodman shoote so ofte awrie
> W S W   S   W   S   W S W S

121

Natural Emphasis

These variations would hardly be noticeable in late Elizabethan poetry, when variations had become fully integral to the rhythms overlaying the accentual iambic pentameter model. But they were scarcely possible in pentameter poetry before Surrey, where they were overwhelmed by Lydgatian metrical variety, with or without the often concommitant rhythmic confusion. Lines 41-48 exhibit a particularly effective example of both mimetic and aesthetic rhythms orchestrated across this regular pentameter. Continuing his third person description of how he "shotte to catch a courtly grace" and, as usual, "shotte awrie, / Wanting the feathers of discretion," he explains his bad judgment in terms of his impressionable naivete. He was deceived by the flashy appearance of the court,

> Yet more than them, the marks of dignitie,
> He much mistooke and shot the wronger way,
> Thinking the purse of prodigalitie,
> Had bene best meane to purchase such a pray.
> He thought the flattring face which fleareth still,
> Had bene full frought with all fidelitie,
> And that such wordes as courtiers use at will,
> Could not have varied from the veritie.

His foolish prodigality is emphasized not only by the prodigal use of accents on that unusual polysyllabic word in the third line of this passage, but also by the excess "f" alliteration in the fifth and sixth lines. The 4-3-2-1 rhythm of "Had bene full frought" completes the emphatic mouthful of the alliterated words, imitating the moral excesses of phony flattery, with the resulting moral casualness tossed off in the quicker-pace of the polysyllabic "fidelity." In the last line the weak accent on "from" has the effect of further emphasizing the irony and word play of "varied" and "veritie."

The prodigal use of accents in "prodigalitie" is mimetic of statement. Later in the poem, when Gascoigne's memories of his many failures have shocked him into a perception of his ill for-

122

tune, an unusual trochaic substitution is mimetic of the speaker's voice, specifically imitating its surprise:

> My minde is rapte in contemplation,
> Wherein my dazeled eyes *onely* beholde,
> The blacke houre of my constellation,
> Which framed mee so lucklesse on the molde:

> (ll. 93-96)

In general, trochaic substitutions, even initial trochees, are rare in Gascoigne. So too are the polysyllabic words that tend to vary the degree of accentuation within a line. But he uses these rhythmic devices, along with careful accent patterning, alliteration, control of rime and of mid-line pause, to produce mimetic and aesthetic elegance in a verse that is almost completely end-stopped and emphatic. Perhaps the full force of his control, and its derivation from the new regularity, is clearest from the one couplet that comes closest to providing a run-on line (albeit the enjambment is slight):

> And Tullie taught me somewhat to discerne
> Between sweete speeche and barbarous rudenesse.

Here the word "discerne" imitates its own meaning by separating the two lines, which might otherwise run together syntactically. The second of these lines is a perfect example of rhythmic discernment. The rime on the wrenched accent of "rudenesse" is the only such unnatural emphasis in the poem; its preceding rime-word, the more civilized "comelynesse," has the now-standard and acceptable secondary accent to allow for the rime.

These two poems illustrate something of the subtlety and complexity Gascoigne was able to achieve across the clear march of new accentual iambics. Despite the persistent tendency to read Gascoigne as if he were as rigid as some of the lesser poetic lights of Queen Elizabeth's earlier reign, he was inventive as well as craftsmanlike. He is not the only poet to use successfully such things as pause patterns, trochaic substitution, and variably stressed accents in highly regular verse. Yvor Winters performed a great service when he directed attention to the schematic felicities of the highly regular mid-century plain style poetry, including the work of Barnabe Googe and George Turberville.[21] But Gascoigne is the most consistently inventive of the poets of the new regularity, and his various successes with strict iambic meters surely contributed not only to the solidification of the accentual iambic base for English meters, but also to its adoption, exploration, and verification by the great poets of the later Elizabethan period.

Many influential theorists, however, were not convinced that accentual-syllabic meters offered any hope for a civilized English art of verse. The controversy over what they called rhyme is more than a short-lived though productive sidelight in the inexorable march of English accentual syllabics. It is the first debate to enunciate certain assumptions about verse generally and English verse particularly. It is also a splendid illustration of conflicting Humanist impulses: admiration of the classics and the attempt to "overgo" foreign models, on the one hand, and patriotism on the other. Roger Ascham, whose *Scholemaster* (1570) conveniently summarizes a point of view from which Spenser, Sidney, Gabriel Harvey, and other experimenters took their impulse, resolved the apparent conflict by urging English poets to produce a heightened English culture based on the classical rather than the popular continental model. His advocacy of rimeless quantitative verse is one aspect of that argument: "surely to follow rather the Gothes in rhyming than the Greekes in trew versifying were even to eate ackornes with swyne, when we may freely eate wheate bread emonges men."[22] So Gabriel Harvey in a letter to Spenser praises the quantitative verse experiments of Sidney, Dyer, and Spenser "for the Exchanging of Barbarous and Balductum Rymes with Artificial Verses, the one being in the manner of pure and fine Goulde, the other but counterfet and base ylfavoured Copper" (1:101). Spenser, too, in this correspondence with Harvey, makes the distinction between "English Versifying" and "Rhyming," the latter the common system of English versemaking, the former a new attempt to gain control over syllabic quantity and the rhythm within the line. In his *Apology for Poetry* Sidney distinguishes between the two kinds of verse without demeaning either: "Now, of versifying there are two sorts, the one Auncient, the other Moderne: the Auncient marked the quantitie of each silable, and according to that framed his verse; the Moderne observing only number (with some regarde of the accent), the chiefe life of it standeth on the lyke sounding of the words, which we call rhyme" (1:204).

Much confusion attended the discussion of English rhyme. The sources of that confusion were both historical and polemical. Just as English poetry was finding its own feet, so to speak, Renaissance Humanists were praising Augustan Latin and belittling the international living language that had until Petrarch been the common tongue of all educated Europeans. Sixteenth-century English poets were therefore confronted with two foreign models: the quantitative foot meter of Greek and Latin verse, and the syllabics of contemporary continental languages, especially French and Italian. Although the Italian of Petrarch and Castiglione was generally admired, and such figures as Baïf, Du Bellay, and Ronsard were important models for the development of vernacular quantitative verse, the association of rhyme with Latin rhythmic verse and its Romance imitations debased its status and muddied the issues. Rhyme was not perceived simply as the feature of rime, but rather as the whole system of syllabic verse.

Latin rhythmic verse, it will be recalled, was characteristically syllabic, "observing only number" rather than syllabic quantity. It did not permit the syllabic equivalences that allowed lines in the same meters to have various numbers of syllables. The great classical dactylic hexameter, Virgil's heroic line, for example, may have anywhere from thirteen to seventeen syllables without calling into play any conventions of elision, syncope, acope, or other devices for altering apparent syllable count. Of the six feet, the first four may be either trisyllabic dactyls (one long followed by two short) or the "equivalent" disyllabic spondee (two long). The fifth and sixth feet are conventionally a dactyl and spondee respectively.[23]

Latin rhythmic verse and its vernacular imitators, on the other hand, consisted of lines and stanzas made up of predictable syllabic number, with the "chiefe life" in variety and complexity of rime patterns. So Molinier's treatise devotes considerable space to varieties of strophic forms and kinds of rime, and Machaut and Deschamps try to reassert the importance of intralinear rhythm (see chapter 2). But the continental model is confused by English practice, and Ascham and others apparently included awkward Lydgatian accentuation as well as simple syllabics when they attacked rhyme.

Ascham is referring to the monotony of poulters measure and fourteeners when he refers to those "rash ignorant heads, which now can easely recken up fourten sillabes, and easelie stumble on every Ryme" (1:31). On the other hand, when he refers to "rude beggerly ryming" and "barbarous and rude Ryming" (1:29, 31) he seems to include the earlier Tudor poets of the school of Lydgate.[24] The only characteristic the two have in common (as opposed to the rigid syllabics and simple accentuation on the one hand and the more variable syllabification and complex, often awkward accentuation on the other) is the feature of rime itself. It is easy to see why rime was attacked as rhyme (or ryme), the feature seen as the metrical principle behind a confused and confusing system which was at once simple-mindedly regular and barbarously rough and cacophonous.

English did not, however, have the complex system of riming common to the Romance languages. In English the feature of rime was never the major rhythmic principle it was for Italian and French. Accentuation rather than syllabic regularity *per se* had always been, and remained, most important for euphony in English verse. Insofar as careful syllabics promoted more predictable accentuation, English tended toward syllabic regularity. This is what Chaucer understood, and what Surrey finally insisted upon. This is the ultimate origin of English accentual-syllabic verse, which Sidney would acknowledge and praise in his own description of rhyme: "Nowe, for the ryme, though wee doe not observe quantity, yet wee observe the accent very precisely: which other languages eyther cannot doe or will not do so absolutely" (1:205). Such verse was until the eighteenth century principally iambic and largely disyllabic in its patterns. Since rhyme, seen in part as syllabic verse, won out over what was sometimes called "meter," seen in terms of Latin quantitative feet and syllabic equivalence, it is not until the revival of classical experiments (by Coleridge, among others) that anapestic substitution becomes common in iambic poems.

From the nineteenth century forward a chief issue in discussing Renaissance verse, especially Milton's verse, has been the question of whether or not "extra syllables" were allowed in English syllabic lines; whether, in fact, a trisyllabic foot could be substituted for a disyllabic foot. There is no question that some strophic constructions in the seventeenth century included trisyllabic feet; clearly they did. (See the discussions of the Sidney/Pembroke psalms in chapter 5, and Jonson's lyricism in chapter 7). The issue is whether three syllables could be seen as a legitimate equivalent for two in the meter of a line. Apparently they could not. Not only does the distinction between "Moderne" rhyme and "Auncient" quantity affirm a theoretical syllabics, in practice, too, English poets varied their syllable count by using continental rules for syllabification rather than classical rules of quantity. Thus the disyllabic trochee is a legitimate substitution for an iambic foot (though until Donne most poets were sparing of trochees except in the initial position) while an anapest is not. English verse has long recognized, however, certain conventional elisions.

Elision has been central to the question of whether Milton and others allowed for trisyllabic substitutions.[25] Are two syllables to be counted as one to keep the syllabic meter in line 141 of Milton's "L'Allegro," which is in tetrameter couplets?

To many a youth and many a maid

Natural Emphasis

Or is the line to be read as iambic tetrameter with anapests substituted for iambs in the second and fourth feet?

x / x x / x / x x /
To ma | ny a youth | and ma | ny a maid

The question is largely academic, since most of us will read the syllables involved as a synalepha, or slurring, however we end up describing the line metrically. But historically it is of some importance to know whether seventeenth-century poets and readers thought in terms of free substitution, or if they stayed close to the prescriptions of syllabic verse. The outcome of the rhyme controversy makes it clear that they were probably more inclined to keep their syllabic number, and that the elegancies that the later Elizabethan poets brought to English versification came in response to the need to develop variety over that apparently rigid model.[26]

The English poets admired the intralinear flexibility and complexity of the classical model, but they could not, finally, discover systematic enough analogues to develop an English quantitative meter. Their response was to develop skill with rhythms: with the apparent tensions, confluences, and divergencies that the language produces when it informs the abstract patterns, iambic and otherwise, in English accentual-syllabic meter.

The discussion of quantitative meters itself focused attention on new ways to make English verse interesting and effective. Gabriel Harvey's marginal comments in his edition of Gascoigne's "Certayne Notes" illustrate what the quantitative experimenters were primarily looking for: more poetic variety and greater flexibility than Gascoigne's precepts and mid-century practice seemed to offer (1:359-62). Harvey reads Gascoigne's injunction to "hold the just measure wherwith you begin your verse," for example, to exclude stanzas constructed of varying line lengths, and counters it with the comment that "the difference of the last verse from the rest in every stanza" is "a grace in the Faerie Queene." It is clear that Harvey is looking for accentual analogues to classical versification; in what appears to be our earliest extant reference to the English decasyllabic line as "pentameter," he glosses Gascoigne's description of rime royal as "The Inglish Pentameter." Harvey, like Sidney, apparently recognized that accent was natural to English sound patterns and, by extension, appropriate for the development of English meters on the classical model. Harvey has "Prosodie" written above *Emphasis* in Gascoigne's phrase, "place every worde in his natural *Emphasis* or sound."[27]

Harvey was an influential Humanist scholar engaged in the discussion and writing of English meters on the classical model, who perceived the potential for artful variety in English verse while at the same time recognizing the difference between English and classical prosodies. Whatever pedantries he may be accused of (his reputation has suffered mightily from his published controversy with the wittier Thomas Nashe), his approach in this matter is relatively sensible.[28] Derek Attridge has amply and usefully surveyed the issues, participants, and effects of the English controversy over quantitative verse, and several times makes the point that experimentation stemmed from the Humanist belief in the civilizing qualities of an artifice more complex than native meters supplied. He further confirms that this apparent preference for art over nature tended to promote metrical schemes that were complex, intellectual, and visual, rather than simple, emotional, and aural.[29] We are, therefore, confronted with the Lydgatian impulse to search for sophisticated literary verse at the expense of the euphonies or mimetic possibilities of vocal rhythms. It is no wonder that the results were often flat and rigid. Even Spenser falls into prosaic mud in his efforts, as in these lines from a letter to Harvey:

> See yee the blindfoulded pretie God, that feathered Archer,
> Of Lovers Miseries which maketh his bloodie Game?
> Wote ye why his Moother with a Veale hath coovered his Face?
> Trust me, least he my Loove, happely chaunce to beholde.

(1:99)

Natural Emphasis

Neither Spenser nor Harvey treats English quantity as an entirely intellectual feature, however. Like Sidney, they make the effort to find rules for English quantity which least wrench accent. Thus in Harvey's system the "penultimate rule," which ascribes quantity in certain situations on the basis of where the accent falls in a polysyllabic word, should take precedence over length by "position." His example is "carpenter," where according to classical rules of position the second syllable would be considered long: the short vowel is followed by two consonants. In English such a lengthening would distort the proper accentuation and so presumably the syllable should be taken as short (1:117-19). Of the poets who attempted to write English quantitative meters, Sidney is usually considered the best, largely because he takes care to make accent and quantity coincide, although he does not confuse the two.[30] Like Campion after him, Sidney associated quantitative verse with music. "The Auncient (no doubt)," says Sidney, is "more fit" than the modern versification "for Musick, both words and tune observing quantity, and more fit lively to express divers passions, by the low and lofty sounde of the well-weyed sillable" (1:204). Both Sidney and Spenser were to make their influence most profoundly felt, however, by the gracefulness of their accentual-syllabic verse.

NOTES

1. Text and history of the *Mirror*'s importance are given in *The Mirror for Magistrates*, ed. Lily Bess Campbell (Cambridge: Cambridge Univ. Press, 1938). The *Mirror* is central to Thompson's statistical study of the smoothing out of English accentual-syllabic meters in the sixteenth century. John Thompson, *The Founding of English Metre* (New York: Columbia Univ. Press, 1961), 37: "These tragedies form an extraordinary museum of metre. The oldest kind of verse in the *Mirror* looks back to middle English, while the newest kind allows a look forward to the practices of metre for centuries to come."

2. Campbell, 5-12. Information about printing history is taken from Campbell's Introduction (5-58).

3. These are in relentless fourteeners, and represent a failure to see the heroic potential of Surrey's blank verse.
   The moral vs. courtly distinction in English poetry extends back

into the middle ages, as Douglas Peterson summarizes the traditions in the first chapter of *The English Lyric from Wyatt to Donne* (Princeton: Princeton Univ. Press, 1967).

4. C. T. Prouty, *George Gascoigne, Elizabethan Courtier, Soldier, and Poet* (New York: Columbia Univ. Press, 1942), documents Gascoigne's activities particularly in relation to the development of Elizabethan poetry. Ralegh contributed a dedicatory poem to Gascoigne's satire, *The Steele Glas* (1576), and also took the older man's personal motto, *Tam Marti Quam Mercurio*, after Gascoigne's death. Although there is no direct evidence that Spenser and Gascoigne met, "E. K." acknowledged Gascoigne to be "a wittie gentleman, and the very chefe of our late rymers" (glosse of the "November Eclogue" of the *Shepheardes Calendar*, 1579), and Lord Grey of Wilton was patron to both Gascoigne and Spenser.

5. Gascoigne's translations from Seneca and Ariosto, *Jocasta* and *Supposes*, gave important impetus to the newly developing Elizabethan drama; his *Adventures of Master F. J.* is arguably the first psychological novel in English. See Prouty, 159-72, 189-212.

6. George Gascoigne, "Certayne Notes of Instruction Concerning the Making of Verse or Ryme in English," in *The Posies of George Gascoigne* (1575), in *Elizabethan Critical Essays*, ed. G. Gregory Smith, 2 vols. (Oxford: Oxford Univ. Press, 1904), 1:49. Harvey, in Smith, 1:359.

7. Smith, 1:50.

8. Smith, 1:56.

9. *The Scholemaster* (1570), in Smith, 1:31.

10. Smith, 1:49, 51.

11. Compare his insistence on English syntax: "use your verse after thenglishe phrase, and not after the maner of other languages" (Smith, 1:53).

12. This terminology reflects Latin and perhaps French practice. Gascoigne does not appear to have the theoretical work of Du Bellay and the Pléiade in mind. He may have known Jaques Sebillet's *Art Poétique François*, first published in 1548, which, from chapter 3 forward, is in roughly the same order as Gascoigne's shorter treatise: it moves from the concept of "invention," to the techniques of versification, to descriptions of various kinds of verse and their decorous uses.

13. See Chapter 1. Gascoigne is also inconsistent in his use of symbols. His "gravis" accent is first presented as falling from left to right; thereafter it falls from right to left, like French *accent aigu*.

14. See Helen Louise Cohen, *The Ballade* (New York: Columbia Univ. Press, 1915), 228-32.

15. Smith, 1:56-57.

16. The first four books of this popular work were published in 1565. The complete translation went through at least seven editions between 1567 and 1612, and was therefore the standard English Ovid until well into the Jacobean period. It was finally replaced by George Sandys' version (1623 and 1625), a still highly readable work in iambic pentameter couplets.

17. Among the notable mid-century collections by single authors are Barnabe Googe's *Eglogs Epytaphes, and Sonettes* (1563), George Turberville's *Epitaphes, Epigrams, Songs and Sonets* (1567), and Thomas Howell's *An Arbor of Amitie* (1568).

18. Fol. x x 4:

> I tearme some Floures, bycause being indeed
> invented upon a verie light occasion, they have yet in
> them (in my judgement) some rare invention and
> Methode before not commonly used. And therefore
> (beeing more pleasant than profitable) I have named
> them Floures.
>> The seconde (being indeede morall discourses
> and reformed inventions, and therefore more
> profitable than pleasant) I have named Hearbes.
>> The third (being Weedes) might seeme to
> some judgements neither pleasant nor yet profitable,
> and therefore meete to bee cast away. But as many
> weedes are right medicinable, so may you find in this
> none so vile or stinking, but that it hath in it some
> vertue if it be rightly handled. . . . if you take
> example by the harmes of other who have eaten
> [hemlock] before you, then may you chaunce to
> become so warie, that you will looke advisedly on all
> the Perceley that you gather, least amongst the same
> one braunch of Hemlock might anoy you.

19. *Paradise of Dainty Devices*, ed. Hyder Rollins (Cambridge, Mass.: Harvard Univ. Press, 1927), 11. See his note, 188, for "my" in line 12.

20. *Posies*, 1575, Hv-H3v. The poem is among the "Hearbes."

21. Yvor Winters praises several such poets, including Googe and Turberville, in "The English Lyric in the Sixteenth Century," *Poetry*, (1939), rpt. in *Elizabethan Poetry: Modern Essays in Criticism*, ed. Paul J. Alpers (New York: Oxford Univ. Press, 1967). Many of the poets and poems Winters specifically mentioned are collected in *English Renaissance Poetry*, ed. John D. Williams (Garden City, NY: Doubleday, 1963).

22. Smith, 1:30. Unless otherwise noted, all subsequent references to works relevant to the rhyme controversy will be taken from this work and cited in the text by volume and page number. For clarity, I will continue to use "rime" to refer to the feature of like-sounding syllables at the ends of lines, and will use "rhyme" to refer to the whole metrical system over which the controversialists were arguing.

23. George Duckworth describes heavily spondaic lines as "slow, stately, and calm," as in the thirteen-syllable *Aeneas* VIII, 452:

illi inter sese multa vi bracchia tollunt

On the other hand, "dactylic verses are light, graceful and rapid," as *Aeneas* II, 790-91, where the first line has sixteen and the second has seventeen syllables:

haec ubi dicta dedit, lacrimantem et multa volentem
dicere deseruit, tenuisque recessit in auras.

Vergil and Classical Hexameter Poetry (Ann Arbor: Univ. of Michigan Press, 1969), 3-7. The point here is that both sorts of verses have exactly the same meter.

24. Harvey may be reflecting this confused view of rhyme when he refers to it as "Balductum." The *OED* defines "balductum" as a "posset," a drink combining milk and ale, suggesting a confused mixture. The term may have been a common one for denigrating rhyme; Richard Stanyhurst, in the preface to his tortuous translation of Virgil's *Aeneid*, also dismisses "rude rythming and balducktoom ballads" *(Thee First Foure Bookes of Virgil His Aeneis*, 1582, A4v).

25. As early as 1902 Bastiaan A. P. Van Dam attacked "The Dogma of the 'Extra' Syllables in the Heroic and Blank Verse Line (XVI. and XVII. Century)," in *Chapters on English Printing, Prosody, and Pronunciation (1550-1700)*, ed. Bastiaan A. P. Van Dam and Cornelis Stoffel

133

(Anglistische Forschungen, vol. 9, Heidelberg: C. W. Winter, 1902). He argues against Guest, Mayor, and Saintsbury, each of whom had seen (in different ways) the presence of extra syllables in English non-lyric pentameter verse of the period. Saintsbury specifically refers to his perceived trisyllabic feet as English "equivalence," making him appear to believe that English verse is quantitative, which clearly he does not. Van Dam argues for English elision, on the authority of Edward Bysshe *(Art of English Poetry,* 1702) among others. His argument is marred by an exaggeration of what may be attributed to printers' errors in the period and by an inability to distinguish between elision and synalepha (and hence to grant Mayor and Saintsbury a legitimate portion of their assumptions). Nonetheless the historical evidence supports his conclusion in favor of a verse perceived in the Renaissance as primarily syllabic. See note 26.

26. The presence in English of synalepha, and its conventional association with elision, helps explain the continuing controversy over syllabification and syllabic equivalency in English verse. Italian and French of course have longstanding and linguistically valid practices of elision, of literally combining two syllables into one, as in the transformation of "de Orleans" into "d'Orleans" or "che il" into "che'l." English has very little elision, and that is so closely tied to English grammar that it is no longer recognizable as elision *(e.g.,* from "John his book" to "John's book"). But synalepha, treated as if it were elision, is quite common. Few would dispute Halle and Keyser's inclusion of a "sonorant sequence" in their "correspondence rule (i)": "A position (S, W, or X) corresponds to a single syllable OR to a sonorant sequence incorporating at most two vowels (immediately adjoining or separated by a sonorant consonant)," Morris Halle and S. Jay Keyser, *English Stress: Its Form, Its Growth, and Its Role in Verse* (New York: Harper and Row, 1971), 169. The search for seventeenth-century trisyllabic substitutions has in the vast majority of cases produced instances of what the disyllabic advocates have called elision (as "heav'n" and "pow'r"), but which are in fact technically synalepha and in at least some cases sufficiently distinct from true elision to allow the trisyllabicists to press their case.

27. Harvey elsewhere uses the term in both the general sense of language sounds and sound patterns and the more specific sense of sounds and sound patterns appropriate to versification. In a letter to Spenser (1:102) he says he "would gladly be acquainted with M. DRANTS prosodye," referring to rules for English quantitative verse, and then makes the distinction between specific and general when he warns there can be no succesful "English Artificiall Prosodye" unless there is a

standard orthography, "in all points conformable and proportionate to our COMMON NATURAL PROSODYE."

28. Richard Stanyhurst in his preface "Too Thee Learned Reader" quotes Harvey admiringly and then sets and follows rules for English prosody and spelling that render his translation of Virgil almost unreadable (*Thee First Foure Bookes of Virgil His Aeneis*, B-B2v). This is a typical pedantry of the period.

29. Derek Attridge, *Well-Weighed Syllables: Elizabethan Verse in Classical Metres* (Cambridge: Cambridge Univ. Press, 1974), 111-12, 133, 138-39, and 154-58.

30. Attridge, 182-83.

Catholique: wherto fyre haue dayly prooues sufficient, but one moste famous
of all, practifed of late yeares in Fraunce by Charles the nynth.
Fayne) gladde or defyrous.
Our fir Iohn) a Popishe priest, A faying fit for the grofeneffe of a fheyheade, but fpoken to tawnt vnlearned Priestes.
Difmcount) defcende or fit.   Nye) draweth nere.
                          Embleme.
Both thefe Emblemes make one whole Hexameter. The firft fpoken of Palinodie, as in
reproche of them, that be diftruftful, is a peece of Theognis verfe, intending,
that who doth moft miftruft is moft falfe. For fuch experience in falfhood bree-
deth miftruft in the mynd, thinking no lefle guile to lurke in others, then in hym-
felfe. But Piers thereto ftrongly replyeth with another peece of the fame verfe,
faying, as in his former fable, what fayth then is there in the faythleffe. For if
fayth be the groound of religion, which fayth they dayly falfe, what hold then is
there of thayr religion. And thys is all that they faye.

Iune.

Ægloga fexta.

ARGVMENT.

This Æglogue is wholly vowed to the complayning of Colins ill fuccesse
in his loue. For being (as is aforesaid) enamoured of a Country lasse Ro-
falind, and hauing (as feemeth) fownde place in her heart, he lamenteth to
his deare frend Hobbinoll, that he is nowe forfaken vnfaithfully, and in
his feede Menalcas, another fhepheard receiued difloyally. And this is the
whole Argument of this Æglogue.

Hobbinoll

HOBBINOLL.   COLIN Cloute.

O Collin, here the place, whofe pleafaunt fyte
From other fhades hath weand my wandring mynde,
Tell me, what wants me here, to worke delyte?
The fimple ayre, the gentle warbling wynde,
So calme, fo coole, as no where elfe I fynde:
The graffie ground with daintye Dayfies dight,
The Bramble bufh, where Byrds of euery kynde
To the waters fall their tunes attemper right.

COLLIN.

O happy Hobbinoll, I bleffe thy ftate,
That Paradife haft found, whych Adam loft.
Here wander may thy flock early or late,
Withouten dreade of Wolues to bene ytoft:
Thy louely layes here mayft thou freely bofte.
But I vnhappy man, whom cruell fate,
And angry Gods purfue from cofte to cofte,
Can nowhere fynd, to fhroude my luckleffe pate.

HOBBINOLL.

Then if by me thou lift aduifed be,
Forfake the foyle, that fo doth the bewitch:
Leaue me thofe hilles, where harbrough nis to fee,
Nor holybufh, nor bryere, nor winding witche:
And to the dales refort, where fhepheards ritch,
And fruictfull flocks bene euery where to fee.
Here no night Rauens lodge more black then pitche,
Nor eluifh ghofts, nor gaftly owles doe flee.

But frendly Faeries, met with many Graces,
And lightfote Nymphes can chace the lingring night,
With Heydeguyes, and trimly trodden traces,
Whilft fyfters nyne, which dwell on Parnaffe hight,
Doe make them mufick, for their more delight:
And Pan himfelfe to kiffe their chriftall faces,
Will pype and daunce, when Phœbe fhineth bright:
Such pierleffe pleafures haue we in thefe places.

COLLIN.

And I, whylft youth, and courfe of carelefse yeeres

F.3   Did

Chapter Five

Spenser, Sidney, and the Countess of Pembroke

*Why, a God's name, may not we, as else the Greekes,
have the Kingdome of our owne Language, and measure
our Accentes by the sounde, reserving the Quantitie
to the Verse?*

Spenser, in a letter to Gabriel Harvey

The principal developers of the aesthetic and mimetic possibilities suggested by Gascoigne were Edmund Spenser (1552-1599) and Sir Philip Sidney (1554-86). The professional poet and the popular young nobleman, acquaintances who admired each other's work, were the acknowledged masters of English poetry in their generation.[1] For the most part subsequent generations have concurred, although Yvor Winters' rehabilitation of Gascoigne and the mid-century plain style poets has tended to challenge the traditional estimate of Spenser and Sidney as unquestionably pre-eminent among Elizabethan non-dramatic poets.[2] The contribution of these two to the development of English versification has also been recently challenged. While John Thompson admires Sidney as the first poet fully to exploit the various possibilities of "the metrical system of modern English," he considers Spenser's metrical experimentation in *The Shepheardes Calendar* "not the beginning of a new way in metre, but a turning round and round at a dead end."[3] Sherod M. Cooper, on the other hand, contends that Sidney "does not use metrical variety to create and hold interest."[4] These comments are insufficiently perceptive of Spenser and Sidney's central position in the development of English versification, which should be reaffirmed. In addition, the formal inventiveness and historical importance of Mary Sidney Herbert, Countess of Pembroke (1561-1621), has not been sufficiently emphasized.

Spenser's strophic inventiveness illustrates how variously the new iambic pentameter could be handled, while his elegant aesthetic rhythms achieved a new fluidity for English verse. Sidney, who contributed the most successful of the quantitative experiments and some fine pastoral lyrics, more importantly developed the idea of an English sonnet sequence and showed how various and flexible the English sonnet could be.[5] He was also the first complete master of mimetic rhythms over an iambic pentameter base in non-dramatic English verse. Like Shakespeare, Sidney was able to produce with apparent ease rhythms that were mimetic of statement but appeared the natural voice of a real personality in a variety of moods. Sidney's formal experimentation is perhaps most evident in the psalm translations completed by his sister, the Countess of Pembroke, whose formal ingenuity is at least as impressive as her brother's. What have been called the Sidneian psalms were to provide a rich and various model for subsequent religious lyricists, including George Herbert.

The pastoral lyric was in many ways a characteristic Christian Humanist genre. Its origins in Theocritus and Virgil gave it both Greek and Augustan credentials. In the fifteenth century Baptista Spagnuoli, known as "Mantuan," revived the genre in a Christian neo-Latin much admired by the sixteenth-century pedagogues. The eclogue (or "eglogue") offered both pleasure and instruction, simplicity and sophistication, in a country format appropriate to young and developing poets and readers. Imitations of Virgil and Mantuan appear in England as early as Alexander Barclay's *Certain Eglogues* (1514). Interest in the pastoral lyric apparently strengthened in the 1560s with English versions by such respected poets as George Turberville and Barnabe Googe. None of these early pastorals approached the brilliance with which Spenser's lyrics announced his poetic ambition in his 1579 pastoral *tour de force*, *The Shepheardes Calendar*.

The Shepheardes Calendar is an unusually unified and coherent set of pastoral lyrics written in many different verse forms by a poet who was admired by his peers.[6] At least four of its features were to have profound and longstanding effects on English poetry: its conscientiously unified structure, effective and various use of abundant genres and sources, deliberate audacity, and skillful compendium of verse forms and types. All of these have been amply documented though by no means exhaustively discussed,[7] but it is the fourth that commands our attention. Although Spenser invents no new meters and even his most innovative stanzas have obvious sources and analogues, his skill with so wide a variety of meters and verse forms proclaims for the first time the sheer abundance of possibilities for English versification.

One important effect of the *Calendar* was to help displace poulters measure and fourteeners as the dominant meters in English. Although Spenser uses ballad verses in "July" and ballad-like stanzas in "March," he has no explicit poulters measure and his most common line is the decasyllabic pentameter. With this line he is able to produce such a wide range of stanzaic constructions and rhythmic effects that he becomes one of the first poets to exploit and establish the full possibilities for this relatively new line.

The "January" eclogue shows the line's suppleness for accommodating both rhetorical schemes and mimetic rhythms. A major theme of the eclogue (and, in varying ways, of the *Calendar* as a whole) is Colin's perception of nature as mirror to his mood. In a fine and properly reverse interpretation of the art/nature relationship, the bleak landscape and "feeble flock" both reflect and project the lovelorn shepherd's interior winter:

> Thou barrein ground, whome winters wrath hath wasted,
> Art made a myrrhour, to behold my plight:
>
> (ll. 19-20)

Natural Emphasis

So, too, devices of balance and antithesis underscore and imitate the mutual mirroring that unifies the internal and external worlds of Spenser's pastoral:

> Ye Gods of love, that pitie lovers payne,
> (If any gods the paine of lovers pitie:)

> (ll. 13-14)

> Thou weake, I wanne: thou leane, I quite forlorne:
> With mourning pyne I, you with pyning mourne.

> (ll. 47-48)

> I love thilke lasse, (alas why doe I love?)
> And am forlorne, (alas why am I lorne?)

> (ll. 61-62)

The reflecting coherence of language and syntax was undoubtedly striking to an audience educated according to the new learning of Humanism. Their strong rhetorical training allowed them to appreciate "a prety Epanorthosis," as E. K., the unknown glosser of the *Shepheardes Calendar*, describes lines 61-62. The verse form itself, decasyllabic short ballade stanzas (ababcc), is unremarkable except insofar as Spenser makes it subtly appropriate to the speaker and the genre. The ballade was originally a courtly song form, imported to England from France in the fourteenth century. Since it suggests the sophistication of Chaucer and the professional poets (such as Barclay and Hawes) who later followed him, it is proper for Colin Clout, the sweet singer among the shepherds. But as a simpler version of the Chaucerian rime royal ballade stanza, it is decorous for an English shepherd.[8]

The rhythms with which the figure of the poet sings his complaint are beautifully managed to reflect his plight and display his skill. They are simple rhythms, but not rough, relying

140

on the most obvious kinds of balance and antithesis and depending for their movement on the Surreyan pause after the fourth syllable. There is just enough variety in the cesural position to avoid monotony, but not nearly enough to suggest serious innovation or uncontrolled passion. The fifth stanza is typical of the extent of variety in line movement that Spenser allows in this eclogue. Here, as throughout, the couplet returns to the clearest possible formal balance, in this case fully reinforced by syntactic parallelism and semantic antithesis:

> Such rage as winters,‖ reigneth in my heart,
> My life bloud friesing ‖ with unkindly cold:
> Such stormy stoures ‖ do breed my balefull smart,
> As if my yeare were wast, ‖ and woxen old.
> And yet alas,‖ but now my spring begonne,
> And yet alas,‖ yt is already donne.
>
> (ll. 25-30)

Twentieth-century readers may tend to read such lines as if they were post-Miltonic or even post-Romantic wholes. In fact the rhythm of most of Spenser's decasyllabic poetry is best considered in terms of the hemistich.[9] The tendency to associate Spenser with innovation and with classical and continental models has perhaps obscured his familiarity with his own literature, his devotion to Chaucer, and his deliberate archaizing, sometimes playful (as here) but always part of Spenser's patriotic determination to advance his own language and culture. While he is innovative and inventive, he is also the heir of the ancient English hemistich tradition, and more immediately of Surrey and Gascoigne, who regularized the cesura in decasyllabic verse and at least indirectly underscored its inherence. Spenser remains essentially conservative in this matter throughout his poetic career.[10]

The importance of the hemistich is evident in another of Spenser's rhythmic variations on the decasyllabic line, the rollicking four-stress nine and ten-syllable verse of "February."

141

Natural Emphasis

These rough couplets apparently seek to imitate what Gascoigne and others understood to be Chaucer's "ryding rhyme."[11] Most of these lines are unmanageable if one is looking for whole iambic lines, or even whole pentameter lines. Although the presence and persistence of "dipodic" verse in English poetry has been most familiar in jingles and nursery rimes since the Middle Ages, "February" provides a clear instance of it in another context.[12] As with certain early medieval English verse, the meter of this poem consists of four accented syllables, two on either side of a floating pause within the line. The pause will always be more-or-less in the middle of the line, but its varying position determines the varying rhythms of the lines. They ordinarily have at least nine syllables, despite the tetrameter accentuation, which avoids too regular a mid-line pause. Without the extra one or two syllables which would make the verse decasyllabic, the line would tend toward the dreadful monotony of the *Ormulum*.[13] Lines 9-14 of "February" illustrate something of the variety Spenser achieves by means of cesural placement and accent distribution in this heavily rhythmic versification:

> /　　　　　/　　　　　/　　/
> Lewdly complainest ‖ thou laesie ladde,

> /　　　/　　　　/　　　　　/
> Of Winters wracke, ‖ for making thee sadde.

> /　　　/　　　　/　　　/
> Must not the world wend ‖ in his commun course

> /　　　/　　　　/　　　/
> From good to badd, ‖ and from badde to worse,

> /　　　/　　　/　　/
> From worse unto that ‖ is worst of all,

> /　　　/　　　　/　　/
> And then returne ‖ to his former fall?

More conventional scansions would produce either a highly variable iambic-anapestic tetrameter (which does not convincingly

appear in English verse until the eighteenth century) or a
strained iambic pentameter, usually headless and seldom metrical. In "February" these rough couplets are of course appropriate to the roughness of the season, the rudeness of the unsophisticated young shepherds who speak them, and the comic
disruption that love has caused. Here, as in "January" and
throughout the *Shepheardes Calendar*, Spenser's versification is
perfectly integrated with the seasons, speakers, subjects, and
overall purposes of the poem.

In addition to the simple elegance of Colin's love complaints, which we find in June and December as well as January,
Spenser's decasyllabic verse can carry the rough, usually four-
stress, couplets of "May," the discourse and debate of "October"
(where the hemistich rhythms are suppressed to produce more
prosaic whole-line rhythms proper to intellectual discussion), and
much of the power of the complex strophic constructions in
"April" and "November." In fact Spenser achieves with the
decasyllabic line a variety of effects unanticipated by most earlier
decasyllabic poetry and impossible with the hitherto dominant
fourteeners and poulters measure. Additionally, his use of the
rhythms common to the latter verses, specifically in "March" and
"July," helps to define anew the generic limits of those meters.

Not only are Spenser's meters and rhythms inventive in
both their variety and their cohering appropriateness, so too are
his strophic innovations and variations, which are also the most
original elements of *Shepheardes Calendar* versification.[14] One
example is the way the work's complex coherence is brilliantly
underscored by the strophic relation of Colin's three complaints,
"January," "June," and "December." The reflexive interconnec-
tion of all the forms in *The Shepheardes Calendar* serves to reinforce
the mirror conceit of "January," but the other two complaints
illustrate particularly the poem's formal relationships. Like
Janus, "January's" form (ababcc) looks both backward and forward to its reflection in "December." The stanza form of "June,"
centering the poem and Colin's year, similarly underscores the
Janus and mirror concepts: abababab. It begins like the ballade
of "January" then reverses itself after the first quatrain to become
instead a double ballade stanza, or ballad-like quatrain and its

mirror image. "December" is again composed of short English ballade stanzas.

No one in the history of English verse, including Chaucer and Gascoigne, had produced a poetic structure so thoroughly integrated on so many levels as Spenser's *Shepheardes Calendar*. The simple catalog may have already given way to progression and coherence in English verse,[15] but not to anything so sophisticated as this. It was a new era for English poetry, audaciously presented and amusingly glossed. Like Sir Thomas More's *Utopia*, it assumes a coterie of initiates who can appreciate the accomplishment and catch all the jokes.

Sidney's pastoral lyrics similarly reflect the exuberant experimentation of the late 1570s and early 1580s among both academic and courtier poets. Like Spenser, Sidney apparently perceives the pastoral genre as a rich environment for poetic and thematic exploration. He transforms his own comic prose *Arcadia*, originally in five "bookes or actes," into a heightened and serious, and formally more various, prose "heroic poem." The interchapter lyrics which were a part of the original (now commonly known as the *Old Arcadia)* are important as emblems of the recreative, youthful, and essentially benign pastoral world in the midst of the often threatening environment of Arcadian adventures. The formal richness of those lyrics has been amply documented by William Ringler.[16] A few examples will show something of Sidney's range and achievement with the pastoral lyric.

Sidney's quantitative experiments have been admirably discussed by Ringler and Derek Attridge. A number of these poems are sprinkled through the *Old Arcadia*, with three coming at the end of the first group of eclogues *(OA* 11-13), four at end of the second *(OA* 31-34) and one in the fourth group *(OA* 74). Sidney's ability to balance the phonetic realities of English stress with the abstract and orthographic character of a quantitative system, documented by Attridge, is evident in all of them.[17] Sidney is also able to use the artificial quantitative system to relieve accentual-syllabic monotony without violating too strongly the natural patterns of language. Thus the verse of *OA*

34 follows the asclepiadic pattern if we allow conventional definitions of "long" and "short":

Ō swēet wōods thĕ dēlīght ōf sŏlĭtārĭnēs!

O how much I do like your solitarines!

The vowels of "of," "much," and "your" become long by position, that is, by preceding at least two consonants. In the case of "of" and "your" the double consonants are separated by word boundaries, obviating any natural tendency to equate conventions of length with English stress-emphasis. The poem will also scan as accentual hexameter, albeit not entirely iambic:


```
 /   x    /    x x / x  /x/ x  /
O  sweet woods the delight of solitarines!
```

```
 /  x    /  x x  /   x   /x/x/
O how much I do like your solitarines!
```

```
   x    /   /  x  x   /  x  / x /x/
Where man's mind hath a freed consideration
```

```
x   /  x  x x /  /   x  x/  x /
Of goodnes to receive lovely direction.
```

```
   x   / x  / x  /   /  x x   /   x   /
Where senses do behold th'order of heav'nly hoste,
```

```
x    /   /    x x /   /   x  x /x  /
And wise thoughts do behold what the creator is.
```

(ll. 1-6)

The total rhythmic movement is neither quantitative nor accentual-syllabic, however. Sidney's work with the quantitative conventions has the net effect of placing the strongest accentual emphasis at about the middle of most lines, producing a rise and fall over the entire line. In the first four lines, for example, the strongest stresses are on the second syllable of "delight," on "like," on either "mind" or "freed," and on the second syllable of "receive" or the first of "lovely." This central emphasis reduces the usual tendency of iambics either to build or decline in strength over the course of a line, as in the first line of the Arcadian oracle *(OA* 1), which mostly builds:

Thy elder care shall from thy carefull face
2   1

or in the first lines of the dance of the Arcadian shepherds *(OA* 6), which mostly decline:

We love, and have our loves rewarded.
We love, and are no whit regarded.

Sidney's ability to effect peak emphasis within a line is not limited to his experimentation with artificial quantitative patterning. In the Reason-Passion round of the Arcadian shepherds (OA 27), two dancing groups form geometric figures, initially in opposition, but finally resolved in a circular dance and stand which cast the apparent conflict between Reason and Passion up to the harmonizing will of heaven. Here Sidney relies on midline pauses to effect a dramatic or oratorical phrasing across the individual lines of highly formal couplets, with jerky or emphatic rhythms often emblematic of the stated conflict. Individual lines appear to be disrupted, even as the couplet progression of the whole poem works toward formal harmony:

Reason. Thou Rebell vile, come, to thy master yelde.
Passion. No, Tyrant; no: mine, mine shall be the fielde.

R. Can *Reason* then a Tyraunt counted be?
P. If *Reason* will, that *Passions* be not free.
R. But *Reason* will, that *Reason* governe most.
P. And *Passion* will, that *Passion* rule the rost.

(ll. 1-6)

And so on, in a progressive interchange of asymmetry and balance until the final couplet, spoken by both groups, follows a steady iambic line with a balanced concluding one, which has its cesura after the fourth syllable:

R. P. Then let us both to heavenly rules give place,
Wich *Passions* kill, and *Reason* do deface.

Sidney's skills with lineation and with testing both artificial and natural speaking rhythms against the rhythmic possibilities of accentual-syllabic meters are evident in his pastoral lyrics. So, too, is his interest in a variety of strophic forms, though few of them achieve the cohesion of Spenser's strophic inventions. What is most impressive throughout the *Old Arcadia* lyrics is Sidney's interplay of stress-level variety with binary systems of syllabification, whether long-short or accented-unaccented. His practice (like his theoretical statements in the *Apology for Poetry*) denies entirely the then-common notion that rime was the main feature of metrical harmony in English verse. Sidney was able to show, not only in his quantitative experiments but also in his couplet verse, rimed strophic verse, and the famous double sestina, "Yee Gote-heard Gods" (*OA* 71), that rime could easily be the least important feature of linear or strophic harmony and inventiveness. In this he worked toward an essentially aesthetic formalism, although his characteristic poetic voice, most fully developed in *Astrophil and Stella*, is dramatically mimetic of speaker and sometimes of subject.

Both Spenser and Sidney followed their early experimentations in the pastoral lyric and quantitative verse with efforts to

147

develop and transform continental models to suit the English language and its developing high art of versification. Spenser's most impressive post-*Calendar* efforts were his invention and use of the nine-line Spenserian stanza and his transformation of the Italian *canzone* in the *Epithalamion* and *Prothalamion*. His manipulation of linear rhythms becomes freer and more various while his strophic constructions find a perfect balance between flexibility and formalizing control. Sidney's sonnets and the Sidney-Pembroke psalms tend to reverse the emphasis. Strophic forms tend to be free and various, at least in relation to the traditions of sonnet and psalm the Sidneys inherited, while lineation becomes increasingly controlled.

The question of where Spenser got his stanza for *The Faerie Queene* resists certain identification, though he probably borrowed the idea of an epic stanza from the Italian *ottava rima* epic romances (abababcc) and he may have had in mind Chaucer's *Monk's Tale* stanza (ababbcbc), a less symmetrical version of Spenser's "June" stanza. He certainly borrowed the alexandrine from French verse, but the idea of concluding an otherwise eight-line stanza with it is his own invention. A number of other influences on the Spenserian stanza have also been suggested, including Italian *terza rima* and native rime royal.[18] Whatever his sources, it is an invented stanza of great coherence and flexibility, consisting of nine lines, eight of iambic pentameter and the ninth an alexandrine, riming ababbcbcc. It has been spoken of rhapsodically by George Saintsbury, Enid Hamer, and Frank Warnke, among others.[19]

The medial couplet sometimes serves a function analogous to the allegory itself. One overall technique of *The Faerie Queene* is to set a contrast between appearance and reality, whose relationship is one of the work's central themes.[20] The various heroes encounter events that illustrate how difficult it is, in the wood of this world, to perceive the truth. Spenser's allegory continually suggests that his readers must learn to rely on grace, divine and secular, and must practice care and discernment; readers must be both fully involved in the tasks set before them, yet willing to step sufficiently back from personal involvement to see events in their true proportion. The technique of allegory and this important theme are constantly underscored by the stanzaic turn effected by the medial couplet. In I.ii.26, for example, the perspective shifts from the misleading words of Duessa to Red Cross Knight's inattendance – from the appearance she is creating to the reality of its effect on the knight:

> In this sad plight, friendlesse, unfortunate,
>> Now miserable I *Fidessa* dwell,
>> Craving of you in pitty of my state,
>> To do none ill, if please ye not do well.
>> He in great passion all this while did dwell,
>> More busying his quicke eyes, her face to view,
>> Than his dull eares, to heare what she did tell;
>> And said, Faire Lady hart of flint would rew
> The undeserved woes and sorrowes, which ye shew.

The shift is even more pronounced in the next stanza, where Duessa's feigned reaction follows Red Cross Knight's sincere if distracted banalities:

> Henceforth in safe assurance may yee rest,
>> Having both found a new friend you to aid,
>> And lost an old foe, that did you molest:
>> Better new friend than old foe is said.
>> With chaunge of cheare the seeming simple maid
>> Let fall her eyen, as shamfast to the earth;
>> And yeelding soft, in that she nought gain-said.
>> So forth they rode, he feining seemely merth,
> And she coy lookes: so dainty they say maketh derth.

(I.ii.27)

The medial couplet is also suitable for a variety of other formal and rhetorical effects. Most commonly, it will either summarize or conclude what has preceded or provide a center or pivot for the stanza as a whole. In one example, the medial couplet concludes the first of two elaborations on an opening aphorism:

> A harder lesson, to learn Continence
>   In joyous pleasure, then in grievous paine:
>   For, sweetnes doth allure the weaker sence
>   So strongly, that uneathes it can refraine
>   From that, which feeble nature covets faine:
>   But griefe and wrath, that be her enemies,
>   And foes of life, she better can restraine;
>   Yet vertue vauntes in both their victories,
> And Guyon in them all shewes goodly maisteries.
>
> (II.vi.1)

Epigrammatic techniques in fact pervade this moralizing stanza, all the way to the final couplet where the rest is summarized and summed up in Guyon. In a second example, the pivot or transition effect is apparent in the stanza that concludes Malbecco's transformation from jealous man to Jealousy itself:

> Yet can he never dye, but dying lives,
>   And doth himselfe with sorrow new sustaine,
>   That death and life attonce unto him gives,
>   And painefull pleasure turnes to pleasing paine.
>   There dwels he ever, miserable swaine,
>   Hatefull both to him selfe, and every wight;
>   Where he through privy griefe, and honour vaine,
>   Is woxen so deform'd, that he has quight
> Forgot he was a man, and *Gelosie* is hight.
>
> (III.x.60)

The medial couplet allows the stanza to move from concluding the narrative description of Malbecco to distancing and emblematizing the entire Paridell-Hellenore-Malbecco story. The result is economical and effective closure.

Spenser's alexandrine is a brilliant touch. It can extend the statement of the stanza, summarize it, act as a narrative lead into the following stanza, or (with or without the pentameter line that precedes and rimes with it) provide an element of epigrammatic surprise or closure. There was summary and extension in II.vi.1, for example: "And Guyon in them all shewes goodly maisteries," and ironic summary in I.ii.27: "So forth they rode, he faining seemly mirth, / And she coy looks: so, Dainty they say maketh dearth." The proverb in the second part of this alexandrine breaks up the potentially relentless progress of the couplet and illustrates Spenser's use of the alexandrine's tendency to break in half. Instead of allowing the effect of two trimeter lines, Spenser controls placement of a mid-line pause, and provides here, as elsewhere, various rhythms and effects. Another common use of the pause in the alexandrine is to provide a lead into the next stanza, as in this transition from IV.iv.27-8 and 28-9, where Cambell takes up the arms of his wounded friend Triamond, in order to "purchase honour in his friends behalve" by fighting the previous day's winner, Satyrane:

> The shield and armes well knowne to be the same
> Which *Triamond* had worne, unwares to wight,
> And to his friend unwist, for doubt of blame,
> If he misdid, he on himselfe did dight,
> That none could him discerne, and so went forth to fight.

> There Satyrane Lord of the field he found,
>   . . .

> Who seeing him come on so furiously,
> Met him mid-way with equal hardiment;
> That forcibly to ground they both together went.

> They up again them selves can lightly reare,
> And to their tryed swords them selves betake;

151

Natural Emphasis

Spenser uses the alexandrine most commonly for narrative extension and summary, but also for epigrammatic turn and conclusion. In VI.ix.29 Meliboee asserts the value of decorous behavior, whether of court or country, over the gold and high office that are the usual aspirations of men:

> But fittest is, that all contented rest
> With what they hold: each hath his fortune in his brest.

The Spenserian stanza, so flexible and effective in Spenser's hands, was to achieve less in the hands of its subsequent borrowers. With the exception of a few Romantic works, most notably John Keats's *Eve of St. Agnes*, nothing after *The Faerie Queene* shows any very effective use of the stanza.[21] It may well be that the Spenserian stanza represents its creator's unique formal genius: his ability to construct strophic patterns that are so perfectly coordinated to his overall purposes that they resist transfer to a different context. Like the musical air carefully attenuated to a single set of words, the Spenserian stanza loses much of its force away from *The Faerie Queene*. Precisely why it so happily accommodates the complex mind of its inventor and resists the imposition of other poetic talents, however skilled they may be, remains unclear.

Spenser used received verse forms as well as devising his own, as we have seen from the variety of *The Shepheardes Calendar*. "The Ruines of Time" and *Fowre Hymnes* are in rime royal (ababbcc); "The Teares of the Muses" and "Astrophel" are in ballade stanzas (ababcc); "Ruines of Rome" are in Surrey's English sonnets; "Prosopopoia" is in iambic pentameter couplets; and "Virgil's Gnat" and "Muiopotmos" are in *ottava rima*. In addition Spenser transforms received material, as in the Spenserian stanza. Other examples include the interlocking sonnet form, found in "Visions of the World's Vanitie" (from Du Bellay) as well as in the *Amoretti*; this sonnet form interconnects Surrey's three quatrains and keeps the English couplet: ababbcbccdcdee. "Daphnaida" uses a variation on rime royal, ababcbc, and *Colin Clouts Come Home Again*, composed of iambic pentameter quatrains arranged in verse paragraphs, begins with an unusual seven-line interconnecting introduction: ababcbc.

Spenser's transformation of conventional materials in his two marriage poems, the *Epithalamion* and the *Prothalamion*, is perhaps most impressive of all. Here he takes the complex high lyric tradition of the Italian *canzone* and fuses it with the classical marriage song. The results are slightly differing forms, used for their different purposes, offering persuasive statements of richly conventional attitudes.

The Italian *canzone* developed from the Provençal *canso* and apparently established its main outlines during the first half of the thirteenth century.[22] The *canso* was "a love song of five, six, or seven strophes, plus *envoi* or half-strophe, with lines of equal and unequal length and interlaced masculine or feminine rimes."[23] The medieval French *chanson*, which developed parallel to the Italian version during the fourteenth and fifteenth centuries, helped establish the overall tri-partite structure that was to inform the stanzaic construction of the Petrarchan *canzone*. Specifically, the *chanson* nearly always had five, six, or seven stanzas, with continuing rime from one stanza to another describing structural units of two-two-one, two-two-two, or two-two-three.[24] The *canzone petrarchesca* further codifies the developing practice of tri-partite stanzas. In its strict form, each stanza consists of "two like parts, *piedi*, and one unlike part, *sirima* or *cauda*. There is usually a single *commiato* at the close of the poem in the form of a valediction to the *canzone*. Stanzaic length is indeterminate, varying from a maximum of twenty to a minimum of seven verses. The lines are normally hendecasyllabic with some admixture of heptameters and pentameters."[25]

The similarity of this formal pattern to the Pindaric ode has led to some confusion about the lyric genre of Spenser's epithalamia. Once one has conceded Spenser's reflection of the important classical conventions and noted specific echoes from various models, most notably Catullus 61, one still must account

for the unique power of the lyric forms Spenser constructs.[26]
The breathtaking achievement of the *Epithalamion*, in particular,
has led certain commentators, beginning with Saintsbury, to
maintain that the wedding poems are indeed formal odes.[27]
Saintsbury's attempt to give Spenser the first English importa-
tion of Pindar is, however, anachronistic. Ben Jonson was the
first English poet explicitly to follow Pindar, as in the Cary-
Morison ode, but not until Abraham Cowley's 1651 *Odes Pinda-
rique* was there a substantial adaptation of the tripartite Pindaric
form which Ronsard had followed in his 1550 *Odes*. This is well
after Spenser, whose formal model is the *canzone* heightened with
epithalamic conventions.[28]

The *Epithalamion* has long been recognized as a remarkably
cohesive and carefully structured lyric, despite its fluid narrative
and the individual flexibility of its twenty-four stanzas. In 1926
Cortlandt Van Winkle analyzed the combination of sameness and
variety in the poem's stanzaic structures, and in 1960 A. Kent
Hieatt published his provocative analysis of the breathtaking
time symbolism in the structure of the poem.[29] The stanzas,
including refrain, vary only from seventeen to eighteen lines,
with the concluding stanza a seven-line *envoi*. Three rime
schemes dominate. The lines are mostly iambic pentameter with
the exceptions of concluding alexandrines, trimeter verses interspersed through the stanza (typically at the sixth, eleventh, and
seventeenth lines), and a few tetrameter lines throughout the
poem. The first nine lines of each stanza are the same:
5ababc3c5dcd. Van Winkle suggests French influence on the
rime scheme, with one of Ronsard's stanzas, ababccdeed, particularly close to these uniform openings.[30] This underlying sameness sustains the poem's formal unity and foregrounds the variety. It also reinforces the alternations from formal to personal
occasion, from controlled public praise to outbursts of private
feeling, that characterize the remarkably balanced tone of the
poem. Thus, for example, the poet's formal invocation of the
sun turns into an emphatic personal plea, concluded by the
trimeter line and summarized and turned into the reordering
power of the refrain at the end of the stanza:

O fayrest Phoebus, father of the Muse,
If ever I did honour thee aright,
Or sing the thing, that mote my mind delight,
Doe not thy servants simple boone refuse,
But let this day let this one day be myne,
Let all the rest be thine.
Then I thy soverayne prayses loud wil sing,
That all the woods shal answer and theyr eccho ring.

(ll. 121-28)

    The trimeter lines serve metrical variety and provide emphasis. In addition, like the couplets and alexandrines of the Spenserian stanza, they establish various ordering structures within the stanza, both in conjunction with and in contrast to the rime scheme. In the first four stanzas, for example, the inevitable trimeter sixth line works as: a summary of the first section of the stanza; a personal comment within the flow of the stanza, from which the stanza's first part pivots into a more public tone; an introduction to the stanza's second section; and a conclusion to the stanza's first section. Similarly, the trimeter line that regularly occurs before each stanza's concluding couplet provides variously for a separation of the couplet:

Ne dare lift up her countenance too bold,
But blush to heare her prayses sung so loud,
So farre from being proud.
Nathlesse doe ye still loud her prayses sing,
That all the woods may answer and your eccho ring,

(ll. 162-66)

a lead-in to the couplet:

And let the Graces daunce unto the rest;
For they can doo it best:

155

> The whiles the maydens doe theyr carroll sing,
> To which the woods shal answer & theyr eccho ring,

(ll. 257-60)

or a formal alteration of an otherwise continuous narrative flow, and so an anticipation of the stanza's conclusion:

> Ring ye the bels, to make it weare away,
> And bonefiers make all day,
> And daunce about them, and about them sing:
> That all the woods may answer, and your eccho ring.

(ll. 274-77)

Overall, the *Epithalamion* conveys a graceful lyricism through its skilled and elegant manipulation of strophic structure. But it is also one of Spenser's most euphonious poems. Few poets before Campion could produce lines of complex consonance to match the speaker's description of his bride's flowing hair:

> Her long loose yellow locks lyke golden wyre
> Sprinckled with perle, and perling flowres a tweene,
> Doe lyke a golden mantle her attyre.

(ll. 154-56)

Or produce the slow, end-stopped lines that give way to the increased pace of the run-on line that confirms the bridegroom's impatience:

> Ah when will this long weary day have end,
> And lende me leave to come unto my love?
> How slowly do the houres theyr numbers spend?

156

How slowly does sad Time his feathers move?
Hast thee O fayrest Planet to thy home
Within the Westerne fome.

(ll. 278-83)

Rhythms such as these are only marginally mimetic, if at all, of the poem's theme of time and of the bridegroom's subjective impression of the day's timing and its eternal significance. For the most part Spenser's rhythms are aesthetic (as "Her long loose yellow locks, like golden wyre"), with euphonious phonological patternings usually distant from conversational language registers.

The Prothalamion is an equally euphonious poem, though its ten stanzas are more consistently constructed, perhaps reflecting the more strictly public function of the poet for this "Spousall Verse." Each of the ten stanzas has eighteen lines, with lines 5, 10, 15, and 16 trimeter throughout, and only slight variations in the rime scheme. Insofar as the verse of the *Epithalamion* may be felt as irregular or idiosyncratic, it may be understood as the decorous reflection of a tension between the formal detachment of the public poet and the impatience of the bridegroom. The *Prothalamion*, on the other hand, is all public. Unlike the *Epithalamion*, the *Prothalamion* is presented from a distance, both physical and temporal. The former poem draws us in with progressive vignettes from the point of view of the groom, while the latter paints a past tense portrait of country and city panoramas along the banks of the Thames. Even Spenser's conventional intrusion of himself into the poem is done in terms of his association with London and his disappointments in the public arena. As in the *Epithalamion*, however, Spenser in the *Prothalamion* uses varying line lengths for a variety of structural divisions and rhythmic effects. In the first stanza, for example, the first trimeter line marks a move into the second section of that stanza:

157

Natural Emphasis

> Calme was the day, and through the trembling ayre,
> Sweete breathing *Zephyrus* did softly play
> A gentle spirit, that lightly did delay
> Hot *Titans* beames, which then did glyster fayre:
> When I whome sullein care,

(ll. 1-5)

In the second stanza the first trimeter line is part of a continuous descriptive flow that lasts until the other trimeter line:

> There, in a Meadow by the Rivers side,
> A Flocke of *Nymphes* I chaunced to espy,
> All lovely Daughters of the Flood thereby,
> With goodly greenish locks all loose untyde,
> As each had bene a Bryde,
> And each one had a little wicker basket,
> Made of fine twigs entrayled curiously,
> In which they gathered flowers to fill their flasket:
> And with fine Fingers cropt full featously
> The tender stalkes on hye.

(ll. 19-28)

In the third stanza the first trimeter line is the second line of a four-line descriptive digression:

> With that I saw two Swannes of goodly hewe,
> Come softly swimming downe along the Lee;
> Two fairer birds I yet did never see:
> The snow which doth the top of *Pindus* strew,
> Did never whiter shew,
> Nor *Jove* himself when he a Swan would be
> For love of *Leda*, whiter did appeare:

(ll. 37-43)

And in the fourth stanza the first trimeter line concludes the stanza's first section:

Eftsoones the *Nymphes*, which now had Flowers their fill,
Ran all in haste, to see that silver brood,
As they came floating on the Christal Flood,
Whom when they sawe, they stood amazed still,
Their wondring eyes to fill,

(ll. 55-59)

By the time he came to write these two marriage poems, Spenser was a master of line rhythms and stanzaic construction, arts he had announced in the *Shepheardes Calendar*, developed through his invention and use of the Spenserian stanza for narrative and continued allegory, and shaded with his increasingly varied lineation and internal line rhythms. While Spenser's rhythms and sound patternings are seldom mimetic, either of voice or of subject, their effects are nonetheless powerful. In sonnet 54 of the *Amoretti*, for example, the speaker's impassioned conclusion is belied by the evidence. Far from being the "sencelesse stone" of which he accuses her, the lady has indeed responded to the lover, but she has recognized his posturing for what it is and reacts with amusement:

Of this worlds Theatre in which we stay,
My love lyke the Spectator ydly sits
beholding me that all the pageants play,
disguysing diversly my troubled wits.
Sometimes I joy when glad occasion fits,
and mask in myrth lyke to a Comedy:
soone after when my joy to sorrow flits,
I waile and make my woes a Tragedy.
Yet she beholding me with constant eye,
delights not in my merth nor rues my smart:
but when I laugh she mocks, and when I cry
she laughes, and hardens evermore her hart.
What then can move her? if nor merth nor mone,
she is no woman, but a sencelesse stone.

The simplicity and matter-of-factness of the couplet's rhythms, without the excessive accentuation common to statements of pas-

159

sion or frustration that seek to imitate a distraught state of mind, lead us to the detached perspective of the lady rather than the unseeing involvement of the lover. Or, again, in the remarkable transformation of sonnet 67, patterns of sound serve the wonder of the speaker's amazement, but (with the possible exception of the panting hounds) without the mimetic effects of even something as mild as Gascoigne's "Wherein my dazled eyes onely behold":

> Lyke as a huntsman after weary chace,
>   Seeing the game from him escapt away,
>   Sits downe to rest him in some shady place,
>   with panting hounds beguiled of their pray:
> So after long pursuit and vaine assay,
>   when I all weary had the chace forsooke,
>   the gentle deare returnd the selfe-same way,
>   thinking to quench her thirst at the next brooke,
> There she beholding me with mylder looke,
>   sought not to fly, but fearelesse still did bide:
>   till I in hand her yet halfe trembling tooke,
>   and with her own goodwill hir fyrmely tyde.
> Strange thing me seemd to see a beast so wyld,
>   so goodly wonne with her owne will beguyld.

There are sometimes unusual and attention-getting rhythms, as in line 8:

<pre>
 / x   x /   x /   /   x x   /
thinking to quench her thirst II at the next brooke
                        3   4 2   1
</pre>

But mimetic effects are largely confined to syntax, where unusual patterns reflect some of the wonder of the speaker's voice, as in line 11:

till I in hand her yet half trembling tooke

Spenser began his poetic career influenced by French poetics, like his favorite English model, Chaucer. Not only did Spenser translate Du Bellay, the quantitative experiments of the "Areopagus" were in imitation of the *Pléiade* and the school of Baïf, and *The Shepheardes Calendar* goes back through the 1503 *Kalendar and Compost of Shepheardes* to a popular French source and contains explicit reflections of Clement Marot.[31] Also like Chaucer, Spenser's most enduring contribution to English poetics lies in his Englishing of both French and Italian materials and giving them a new native vitality. Unlike Chaucer, however, Spenser was the heir of Renaissance Humanism, and his experiments on behalf of English poetry were also done in avowed imitation of the great classical masters, especially Virgil. To a great extent Spenser succeeded in the Renaissance ideal of asserting a new and localized classicism through an eloquent and flexible vernacular literature. More importantly, he showed that English verse could support a beautiful and various poetic. Spenser, the master of pleasing aesthetic rhythms, was the English poet who fully and finally overcame the Lydgatian model for English artifice.

Spenser's *Amoretti*, most unusually concluded by the successful wedding portrayed in the *Epithalamion*, was one of many responses to the popularity of Sidney's *Astrophil and Stella*. The latter's publication in 1591 provoked a deluge of sonnet sequences, which were the lyric phenomena of the 1590s.[32] In Sidney's work the sonnet tradition arrived fully in England, and through his mastery it was established as a major lyric form for English verse. In addition, *Astrophil and Stella* at last reveals the full potential for rhythmic tensions and metrical variations in the iambic pentameter line, in this case primarily in service to Sidney's formal imitation of voice and statement.

The sonnet already had a 300-year history by the time Wyatt imported it in the 1520s.[33] In the fourteenth century, when Petrarch turned to the sonnet as his principal lyric form for the *Canzoniere*, he had a firm tradition from which to work. Like the earliest sonnets, Petrarch's lyrics are usually fourteen-

161

line hendecasyllabic verses with invariable octave rime (abbaabba) and a variable sestet, usually riming cdecde or cdcdcd.[34] Wyatt allowed for the octave/sestet structure even as he changed the sestet to conclude with a couplet. At least some sense of the eight/six structure remained in Surrey's sonnets although his English sonnet more easily suggested the fourfold rhetorical structure implied by the three quatrains and couplet (see chapter 3).

Sidney's sonnet forms reflect both the English tradition and fresh borrowing from Petrarch, from whom he took not only standard metaphors but the remarkable idea of the sequence, including the short lyric *canzoniere* that are a feature of Petrarch's work. *Astrophil and Stella* consists of 108 sonnets and eleven songs distributed through the second half of the sequence (one each after sonnets 63, 72, 83, 85, 92, 104, and five after sonnet 86). Both sonnets and songs are in various forms.

Critics have noted how thoroughly Sidney both borrows and adapts his Petrarchan materials; on the one hand he claims to disdain received forms and conventions, and on the other hand he exploits their full potential as vocabulary for the problems of love, as shorthand for complex emotions and ideas, and as cultural expectations against which to test the reality of his own experience.[35] The first sonnet announces the complexity of the intent, both rejecting previous authors and calling on tradition at the same time. The first quatrain (of a formal and conventional octave riming abababab) describes the speaker's desire to win the lady's pity, and so her grace, through the revelation of his true love in verse. The second quatrain traces his study of previous writers in his search for inspiration. The familiar sestet affirms this poet's independence from tradition and dependence on the lady for his poetry:[36]

> But words came halting forth, wanting Invention's stay,
> Invention, Nature's child, fled step-dame Studie's blowes,
> And others' feete still seem'd but strangers in my way.
> Thus great with child to speake, and helplesse in my throwes,
> Biting my trewand pen, beating my selfe for spite,
> 'Foole,' saide my Muse to me, 'looke in thy heart and write.'

Despite the amusing and individualized portrait of the distracted poet-lover, this sonnet's premise is conventional. The picture of the lady resides in the poet's heart, and, like Dante and Petrarch before him, Sidney's verse will receive its virtue from a focus on the lady. The sestet is the by-now standard English cdcdee, with the *c* and *d* rimes assonant with the *a* and *b* rimes. Yet even as this poem acknowledges the speaker's predecessors, most specifically conjuring up Petrarch, it deliberately rejects them. However much this lover will in fact follow Petrarch and the others, he will feign not to, and this becomes an important attitude for the sequence as a whole. What is true of the poem's statement is also true for Sidney's characteristically mimetic versification: "others' feete," usually pentameter and decasyllabic, are specifically rejected in this hexameter sonnet with its twelve-syllable lines.[37]

If Sidney is testing the limits and validity of Petrarchan conventions throughout the sequence, he is also exploring the range of the sonnet form itself. The entire sequence is as formally and prosodically complex as the revealed and purported emotions of the courtly speaker. Among the first eight sonnets there are no two forms exactly alike.[38] In addition, he appears to be exploring sound relationships other than rime. Not only are the *c* and *d* rimes assonant with the *a* and *b* rimes in the first sonnet, there are assonances or concluding consonances in the rime words of Sonnets 2 through 8 as well.

Sonnet 5 is a particularly rich example of Sidney's development of sound patterns:

It is most true, that eyes are form'd to serve
The inward light: and that the heavenly part
Ought to be king, from whose rules who do swerve,
Rebels to Nature, strive for their owne smart.
    It is most true, what we call *Cupid's* dart,
An image is, which for ourselves we carve;
And, fooles, adore in temple of our hart,
Till that good God make Church and Churchman starve.
    True, that true Beautie Vertue is indeed,
Whereof this Beautie can be but a shade,

> Which elements with mortall mixture breed:
> True, that on earth we are but pilgrims made,
> And should in soule up to our countrey move:
> True, and yet true that I must *Stella* love.

The poem's structure is dominated by figures of repetition and parallelism and by the development of a logic ultimately transcended (though not rejected) by the lover's obsession. This is a common strategy throughout *Astrophil and Stella*. Here both the logic and its apparent contradiction are set out not only in parallel words and syntax but in dense sound parallels and reflections as well. Since there was some collapsing of the distinction between Middle English "er" and "ar" in the sixteenth century, "carve" and "starve" may even be considered exact rimes with "serve" and "swerve."[39] The result, in any case, is a sound pattern that hovers between rime and assonance. The major resonances in this poem, however, are in the consonance of the *c* and *d* rimes and the *a* and *e* rimes, so that the turn of the conclusion nonetheless echoes the initial affirmation of the poem. There is a fair amount of mid-line consonance and alliteration as well.

Sidney's skills as a mimetic artist are subtle here but impressive. Just as the sounds of the poem echo each other and remind the reader of what they are on the surface distinguished from, so love of Stella echoes love of virtue; just as the various rimes are transformations of each other, so love of Stella is a form of the love of virtue. A standard submerged equation, which the poem refuses to make explicit, is that Stella is true beauty and true beauty is virtue. Sidney implies the similarity but insists upon the distinction. To say that all virtue is beautiful is not the same as to say that all beauty is virtuous; logically, we are left with an undistributed middle term. The poem's conclusion may therefore provoke three succeeding reactions from the reader. At first one assumes a contrast between service of virtue and service of Stella. Next, one recognizes the Neoplatonic equation of beauty with virtue, and that therefore what is stated as contrast should be congruent. Finally, one sees that in fact two different kinds of truth are being enunciated here:

divine (hence the starving "Church" and "Churchman") and human (subject to that pagan "good God," Cupid). From the Christian perspective the speaker is in danger of idolatry; from the perspective of the love tradition the speaker must adore Stella. The poem therefore allows for the Neoplatonic understanding of the beauty-virtue equation, but leaves the reader reminded that such virtue is secular at best and dangerous to the Christian soul at worst.

As the poem's rhetorical structure and the echoing sound patterns imitate the distinctions and equations the statement makes and suggests, so the rhythms reinforce the affectation of detached logic. The first two lines are enjambed, both effecting emphasis on the first phrase of their following lines:

>   . . . to serve
> *The inward light:* and that the heavenly part
> *Ought to be king* . . .

The repetition of "true" in parallel phrases at the beginning of the first two quatrains and more variously at the beginning, middle, and end of the sestet also influences the rhythm, carrying with it the emphasis of rhetorical conviction. That conviction is both confirmed and altered by the final "True, and yet true that I must *Stella* love." The last line also contains what I call rhythmic ambiguity, defined more fully in relation to Jonson, in chapter 7: a rhythmic tension resulting from a metrical foot that can legitimately be read as either an iamb or a trochee. Ordinary phrasal patterns, and the expectation we have of sonnet rhythms generally, would render the first two feet a conventional initial trochee and iamb:

>   /   x   x   /
> True, and yet true that I must *Stella* love

165

Natural Emphasis

But the entire context of the poem, including its rhetorical structure and stance, points to an emphatic stress on "yet," and hence the unusual double trochee at the beginning of the line:

> /   x   /   x   x / x   / x   /
> True, and yet true that I must *Stella"* *love*

The result is rhythm mimetic of the speaker's voice making the distinctions appropriate to logical argument.

The dramatic effects Sidney achieves with his rhythms are apparent throughout *Astrophil and Stella*. The reader is often encouraged to join in a performance by choosing rhetorical over metrical stress, although the meter remains the basic guide to emphasis and the legitimate expectation of an experienced reader of metrical poetry. In addition, scene, audience, and the speaker's dangers and conflicts are dramatically conveyed in impassioned heavy accentuation, as in the first line of sonnet 20:

> Flie, fly, my friends, I have my death wound; fly

or the last line of sonnet 71:

> 'But ah,' Desire still cries, 'give me some food.'

Sonnet 71 is also a subtle modification of the ideas presented in sonnet 5. The later poem states the Neoplatonic equation between Stella and virtue, with the speaker's problem not love of Stella, but the insufficiency of the intellectual and spiritual aspects, the rational virtue, of that love.

Sidney was also a master of rhythms that imitate statement. In line 3 of sonnet 5, for example, a trochaic third foot culminates a trisyllabic rise in emphasis, a climb "up" in pitch and other elements of stress:

166

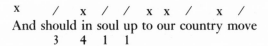

```
x      /   x  /  /  x x  /   x  /
And should in soul up to our country move
      3   4  1  1
```

The climbing effect achieved by an overall ascending accentuation is even more pronounced in the first line of sonnet 31 where it is accomplished over a consistent iambic meter:

```
        x   /   x  /   x   /   x   /   x   /
With how sad steps, ô Moone, thou climb'st the skies
      4   3   2   1   3   1   3   1   4   1
```

Like Gascoigne in "Lullabie," Sidney is also able to exploit the mimetic possibilities of meter itself. With only the slightest evident control of metrical emphasis, Sidney transforms standard iambic pentameter lines with initial trochees into galloping rhythm:

```
        /  x   x  /   x  /   x  /   x  /
Having this day my horse, my hand, my launce
```

```
        /  x   x  /   x  / x  /   x   /
Guided so well, that I obtain'd the prize
```

(Sonnet 41, ll. 1-2)

One need only alter the first line to its exact semantic and metrical equivalent to see how effective is Sidney's control:

Natural Emphasis

Having this day my horse and hand and launce

Sidney was unquestionably an exceptional formalist who heard language in relation to its content. In *Astrophil and Stella* he took the traditions of the sonnet and of Petrarchism and gave them new life even as he more closely imitated Petrarch than anyone except the translators had done in England up to that point. Sidney also took iambic pentameter and hexameter lines and gave the former new flexibility and the latter at least a limited currency for English verse. His use of hexameters may have helped in the decline of poulters measure and fourteeners for serious verse. Five of the *Astrophil and Stella* sonnets and two of the songs (the third and fifth) are in hexameters. The only lyric in fourteeners, the seventh song, is a virtual study of how to break up long lines in unconventional ways. The rollicking music of the common meter is completely undercut, with the long-lined verse carrying the tinge of humor that it has sustained (outside of hymnody and other song contexts) to the present day. Sidney further tolls its death knell in the *Arcadia*, where the unspeakable Mopsa is elegized in a poulters measure sonnet (OA 3) beginning:

What length of verse can serve brave *Mopsa's* good to show,
Whose vertues strange, and beuties such, as no man may them know?
Thus shrewdly burdned then, how can my Muse escape?
The gods must help, and pretious things must serve to shew her shape.
Like great god *Saturn* faire, and like faire *Venus* chaste:
As smooth as *Pan*, as *Juno* milde, like goddess *Isis* faste.

So much for the original English heroic line.

Astrophil and Stella is the fruition of Sidney's experiments with both quantitative and native measures, experiments largely preserved in the lyrics from the *Arcadia*. Whatever interest his specifically quantitative experiments may hold, for the most part Sidney's versification follows what he described in his *Apology for*

Poetry as the "Moderne" kind: syllabic verse with "some regard of accent."[40] He is deceptively casual about accentuation. His attitude is liberating, but his meters are in clearly derivable iambic or trochaic accentual feet, with no evidence in his "Moderne" verse of strophic constructions that allow for trisyllabic feet, much less trisyllabic substitutions for disyllabic feet in his consistently iambic verse. Nonetheless, he is a master of rhythmic variety within the iambic metrical context, and he sometimes seems to anticipate the more daring accentuation we associate with Donne.

If the forms of *Astrophil and Stella* are essentially conservative despite the dramatic stance and sometimes complex accentuation within lines, the strophic constructions of the Sidneian psalms show Sir Philip and especially his sister Mary engaged in a contest with God's own abundant variety, an exercise in Davidian stance whose influence can be traced well into the seventeenth century.[41] Sidney completed his translation/imitations of the first forty-three psalms without precisely repeating a verse form, much as he had managed to do with the first eight sonnets of *Astrophil and Stella*, though without the restraints of the sonnet form and consequently with even greater variousness. Twelve of the forty-three poems rely on feminine endings to lend variety to the strophic constructions, and seven of the poems make use of what has been called "counterpoint," or the riming of lines of unequal length.[42]

The Countess of Pembroke is even more inventive and complex in the remaining psalms, with her contribution to English verse among the least acknowledged major achievements in the history of English poetry. Although it was and continued to be well known that she was the author of the vast majority of the Sidneian psalms, until recently she has received very little explicit credit for her accomplishment. The Psalms were not published in their most influential period, the early seventeenth century, but circulated widely in manuscript. Of three such early manuscripts in the Huntington Library, two attribute the entire collection to Sir Philip Sidney, and the third, which lacks a title page, has his name following Psalm 43 but no mention of

169

the Countess of Pembroke. Despite this official anonymity, Ben Jonson knew and admired her work, while Donne and Herbert found inspiration for their own various religious versifying in what Hallett Smith, in this century, has called "a school of English versification."[43] As her modern editor has noted, Pembroke, like her brother, is far more than a translator. "By recreating the Psalms as Elizabethan poems, the Countess compels us to read them afresh," even more than does Sidney, whose "share in translating the psalms, most critics have agreed, is decidedly inferior to that of his sister."[44]

The magnitude of Pembroke's lyric accomplishment is astonishing. She not only provides different forms for the 107 poems which translate Psalms 44-150, but also manages different forms for the twenty-two sections of Psalm 119, for a total of 128 separate lyric forms, which in turn do not precisely copy any of Sidney's forty-three verse constructions. Such variety inevitably leads to awkward syntax on occasion, and her meters and rhythms are not usually very subtle, but her forms are often highly complex and even daring. A review of some of the basic components of her variety and some of the ways in which she very probably had substantial impact on the direction of lyric versification will conclude this chapter.

Like Sidney, Pembroke frequently varies her stanza constructions by the use of feminine endings, counterpoint, internal rime, and inventive strophic constructions. She also makes consistent use of headless iambics, sometimes in conjunction with feminine endings. The result is a fair number of trochaic lines, apparently generated from that combination (in 44, 69, 71, 81, 86, 90, 99, 119P, and 136). Psalm 90 has a particularly interesting interweaving of iambic and trochaic movements, though the poem as a whole is not among her most successful. She is not afraid to experiment with extended strophes and complex rime schemes, with the number and variety of examples too numerous to catalogue here. The lyrics of 119 offer particularly rich examples. 119D is composed of four stanzas constructed 3Ab4b1a3cDe4e1d4c (where lower case represents masculine and upper case feminine rime). 3A and 3D are consistently headless in all four stanzas. In this, as throughout, Pembroke is careful and precise in meeting the contract she has set for herself. She also works with anagrammatic patterns, as in 117, whose first letters spell out "Praise the Lord," and 111, whose twenty lines of pentameter couplets run alphabetically from A-U (a feature not made obvious in the modern edition, but set off in bold face in two of the three manuscripts I have reviewed, HM 100 and HM 117). These formal anticipations of Herbert (among others) are supported by other suggestions of Herbert's debt to Pembroke. The first four lines of Pembroke Psalm 108, for example, are evocative of the first half of Herbert's "Easter" in content, and of the last half in form:

> To sing and play my heart is bent,
>   Is bent God's name to solemnize
> Thy service O my tongue, present:
>   Arise my lute, my harp arise.

The first stanza of Pembroke's 92 may also anticipate Herbert's "Easter," while the accentual elegiac couplets of 111 may be formally reflected in Herbert's "Thanksgiving." In 130 a song-like lyric stanza combines with an impassioned, heavily-accented series on the speaker's discomfort, to suggest Donne perhaps more than Herbert. It illustrates again the extent of Pembroke's probable influence on the seventeenth-century religious lyric:

> From depth of grief
>   Where droun'd I ly,
> Lord for relief
>   To thee I cry:
> My earnest, vehement, crying, prayeng,
> Graunt quick, attentive, hearing, waighing.

(first of six stanzas)

171

Natural Emphasis

Psalms 120-127 present Pembroke's quantitative experiments, interesting as part of the general classical experimentation of the Sidney circle, but also as evidence of her own ear for the interjection of anapestic rhythms into essentially iambic accentual patterns across the artificial rules for quantitative verse. In this, Pembroke offers one of the earliest examples of trisyllabic substitution for disyllabic feet, a practice that does not fully come into its own until the Romantic period, but for which there are some models in Jonson (see chapter 7) and the late Elizabethan and Jacobean lyricists. Like her contemporaries, Pembroke will remain consistent in her syllabic patterning throughout a poem. Unlike many Romantic poems, there are not different syllable-counts in analogous lines from stanza to stanza, but like Romantic poems, Pembroke's quantitative Psalms will have variety of movement within individual lines, so that iambic and anapestic or dactylic rhythms interweave differently from stanza to stanza. In the first poem of the quantitative sequence, Psalm 120, each unrimed quatrain contains lines of eleven, eleven, nine, and ten syllables, as in the first stanza:

> As to th'Eternall often in anguishes
> Erst have I called, never unanswered
> Againe I call, againe I calling
> Doubt not againe to receive an answer.

(The -ed ending is pronounced throughout the Pembroke Psalms.) An accentual-syllabic scansion of the last line would put an anapest in the third foot:

> x / x / x x / x / x
> Doubt not againe to receive an answer

The ten-syllable rule is kept in the fourth line of each of the poem's six stanzas, but with substantial varying of the anapestic movement. In stanza two it falls on the fourth foot, following a trochaic substitution, and so produces almost the effect of a four-syllable (five, because of the feminine ending) prose run (for a discussion of rhythmic prose clausulas, see chapter 8):

> / x   x / / x x   x / x
> Poison'd abuse, ruine of beleevers

And there is similar variety in the fourth lines of each stanza. The rule for this patterning, and for similar patterning in 121, appears to be that trisyllabic feet may occur in any position in the line, but there must be an equal number of syllables in strophically analogous lines.

Psalms 122 and 123 are not strophically constructed, but are in dactylic hexameters with variable syllabic number. Lines 1-2 in 122, for example, are the longest and shortest of the poem's seventeen lines with thirteen and sixteen syllables respectively:

> O fame | most joy|full! O | joy most | lovely de|lightfull
>
> Loe, I do | heare Godds | temple, as | erst, soe a|gaine be fre|quented

Psalm 125 offers an example of sapphics. As with most sapphics of this period, Pembroke's stanzas of three eleven-syllable lines followed by one five-syllable line respond neatly to the accentual iambic pentameter tradition. The result is an unrimed accentual iambic poem with feminine endings, similar in its sophisticated movement to Sidney's and Campion's efforts:

> As Sion standeth very firmly steadfast,
> Never once shaking: soe, on high, Jehova
> Who his hope buildeth, very firmly stedfast,
>   Ever abideth.
>
> (stanza 1)

Natural Emphasis

Throughout, strophic complexity combines with experiments in intralinear rhythmic variety to produce one of the most impressive records of versifying in the Renaissance, one that clearly had substantial influence on subsequent poets. The Countess of Pembroke was more than a mechanic of verse, however. A good many of her poems bear frequent rereading, and show an ear sensitive to the best features of the various prose translations of the Psalms she probably encountered. Psalm 47, verse 7b, is rendered by the 1560 Geneva Bible:

Sing praises *everie one* that hathe understanding

by the 1568 Bishop's Bible:

syng psalmes (all you that hath) skyll

and by the Book of Common Prayer:

sing ye praises with understandyng.

Pembroke expands this into an exuberant anthem that captures very well the tone of praise inherent in the prose translation:

> . . . praise, praise our king,
> Kings of the world your judgments sound,
> With Skillful song his praises sing.

Her conclusion to this Psalm extends the tonal interpretation into a textual one. Here the Geneva Bible has "The shields of the world belong to God," and the Book of Common Prayer, "God .

174

. . doth defend the earth as it were with a shield." Pembroke concludes in good Protestant fashion:

> Hee, greatest prince, great princes gaines;
> Princes, the shields that earth defend.

The full range of Pembroke's artistry is beyond the scope of this book, but it is a subject that will reward far more attention than it has yet received.

Together Spenser and Sidney represent a new inventiveness and coherence for English verse, especially in their use of the newly ubiquitous iambic pentameter line. While their artistry appears highly self-conscious, their verse gives an impression of ease, of the art used to hide art which Sidney had found and praised in "divers smally learned Courtiers."[45] Spenser's verse flows with the authority and the graceful unobtrusiveness of the rivers he so much admired, while Sidney's fictive voice carries the tone and conviction of a living speaker. These aesthetic and mimetic achievements of the foremost non-dramatic poets of their time provide the solid base from which subsequent verse experiments may range. In addition, the Countess of Pembroke not only continued but expanded the Sidney influence, offering an independent ingenuity and formal inventiveness that makes her the first known woman to have a solid and wide-ranging, though largely uncredited, impact on the development of English poetics. Accentual-syllabic English verse has not only arrived in the work of these three, it has shown its potential for flexible and individual artistry.

NOTES

1. Sidney praised *The Shepheardes Calendar* in his *Apology for Poetry*, one of only four English works and the only truly contemporary one to receive such attention (the others were Chaucer's *Troilus and Creseyde*, *The Mirror for Magistrates*, and Surrey's lyrics; *Elizabethan Critical Essays*, ed. G. Gregory Smith, 2 vols. [Oxford: Oxford Univ. Press, 1904], 1:196). Spenser's admiration for Sidney is found in his letters and in his elegy, *Astrophel*. Among the testimonies to their pre-eminence among

175

Natural Emphasis

their colleagues are statements by Puttenham and Meres, the 1593 memorial lyric collection dedicated to Sidney, *The Phoenix Nest*, the description of Spenser's 1599 funeral and his burial next to Chaucer in Westminster Abbey, and the large portion of verse by these two in the elegant 1601 pastoral collection, *England's Helicon*.

2. Yvor Winters, "The English Lyric in the Sixteenth Century," *Poetry* (1939); rpt. in *Elizabethan Poetry: Modern Essays in Criticism*, ed. Paul J. Alpers (New York: Oxford Univ. Press, 1967), 93-125. Douglas Peterson, in *The English Lyric from Wyatt to Donne* (Princeton: Princeton Univ. Press, 1967) admires Sidney but offers Wintersian hesitations about Spenser.

3. John Thompson, *The Founding of English Metre* (New York: Columbia Univ. Press, 1961), 139, 127.

4. Sherod M. Cooper, *The Sonnets of Astrophil and Stella: A Stylistic Study* (The Hague: Mouton, 1968), 47. For general comments on Sidney's rhythms, see Robert Montgomery, Jr., *Symmetry and Sense: The Poetry of Sir Philip Sidney* (Austin: Univ. of Texas Press, 1961), 77-99; David Kalstone, *Sidney's Poetry: Contexts and Interpretations* (Cambridge, Mass.: Harvard Univ. Press, 1965), 32-36, 71-83, 133-78; A. C. Hamilton, *Sir Philip Sidney: A Study of His Life and Works* (Cambridge: Cambridge Univ. Press, 1977), 86-106. J. G. Nichols, in *The Poetry of Sir Philip Sidney: An Interpretation in the Context of His Life and Times* (New York: Barnes and Noble, 1974), 137-39, apparently disagrees with Cooper, as I do, but much depends on how one defines metrical variety. Nichols' contrast of Sidney with Gascoigne is limited but basically accurate.

5. Derek Attridge, *Well-Weighed Syllables: Elizabethan Verse in Classical Metres* (Cambridge: Cambridge Univ. Press, 1974), describes the experiments and makes the case for Sidney's achievement, 173-87.

6. First published in 1579, it went through seven editions by 1617.

7. For a background summary of the discussion and documentation, see *The Works of Edmund Spenser, A Variorum Edition*, ed. Edwin Greenlaw et al., vol. 7, The Minor Poems: Volume One, ed. C. G. Osgood and H. G. Lotspeich (Baltimore: The Johns Hopkins Univ. Press, 1943), 571-655. For more recent discussion see Hallett Smith, *Elizabethan Poetry* (Cambridge, Mass.: Harvard Univ. Press, 1952), 34 ff.; William Nelson, *The Poetry of Edmund Spenser* (New York: Columbia Univ. Press, 1963), 57 ff.; S. K. Heninger, Jr., "The Implications of Form for *The Shepheardes Calendar*," *Studies in Renaissance*, 9(1962)309-21; and Susanne Woods, "Variety and Coherence in the Verse of Spenser's *Shepheardes Calendar*," in *Spenser at Kalamazoo*, ed. David A. Richardson

(Cleveland: Cleveland State Univ. Press, 1979), 148-67. Thompson (88-127) notes the abundance of strophic forms in the *Calendar* but concludes that Spenser's use of meter was uninventive. I would stress that although Spenser did nothing precisely new with his meters, the versatility and coherence of his formal construction belies Thompson's sense of the *Shepheardes Calendar* as a "turning round and round at a dead end" (127).

8. This is Gascoigne's "ballade" stanza, and I shall use the term "ballade" to apply to the iambic pentameter ababcc sizain throughout the rest of this book. For its more complex forms and history, see Helen Louise Cohen, *The Ballade* (New York: Columbia Univ. Press, 1915).

9. I am grateful to Sears Jayne for this observation.

10. See the discussion of the Spenserian stanza. Paul J. Alpers judges the unit of Spenserian versification to be the line, rather than the foot, half-line, or stanza: "Spenser's treatment of the line as an independent unit can be seen in every stanza of *The Faerie Queene.*" *Poetry of* The Faerie Queene (Princeton: Princeton Univ. Press, 1967), 46. He also believes that cantos are independent narrative units in the work. As will be seen, I have some basic disagreements with him and with William Empson, whose discussion of the rhythms of *The Faerie Queene* Alpers cites and admires.

11. Although there are more recent examples, as Ferrars' verse in *The Mirror for Magistrates*. Spenser, unlike Ferrars, recognizes the particular usefulness of this verse for comedy.

12. Paul Fussell, Jr. defines dipodic verse as "constructed rhythmically so that, in scansion, pairs of feet must be considered together," *Encyclopedia of Poetry and Poetics*, ed. Alex Preminger (Princeton: Princeton Univ. Press, 1965); it may be more generally defined as an accentual verse dependent for its rhythm on a medial pause.

13. This work proved that English poets could, very early, write precise syllabic verse, but apparently and fortunately Orm's work was not imitated. The "Introduction" begins:

> All mannkinn, fra thatt Adam wass
> Thurrh Drihten wrohht off eorthe
> Anan till thatt itt cumenn wass
> Till Cristess doeth o rode,
> All for till helle forr thatt gilt
> That Adam haffde gilltedd.

177

The Ormulum, ed. Robert Holt, 2 vols. (Oxford: Clarendon Press, 1878).

14. See, *e.g.*, W. L. Renwick, *Edmund Spenser: An Essay on Renaissance Poetry* (London: Arnold, 1925), 189, and Hallett Smith, 33-51.

15. Leonard Nathan, "Gascoigne's 'Lullabie' and Structures in the Tudor Lyric," contrasts early Elizabethan practice with the typical medieval "enumeration" or catalog poem. *The Rhetoric of Renaissance Poetry from Wyatt to Milton*, ed. Thomas O. Sloan and Raymond B. Waddington (Berkeley and Los Angeles: Univ. of Calif. Press, 1974), 58-72.

16. In *The Poems of Sir Philip Sidney*, ed. William Ringler (Oxford: Clarendon Press, 1962), 569-72. All texts of Sidney poems are from this edition.

17. Attridge, 173-87.

18. In the seventeenth century Thomas Rymer assumed Spenser's stanza was a transformation of *ottava rima* ("Preface to the *Translation of Rapin's Reflections on Aristotle's Treatise of Poesie*," 1674, in *Critical Essays of the Seventeenth Century*, ed. J. E. Spingarn, 3 vols. [Oxford: Oxford Univ. Press, 1908], 2:168). This view went unchallenged until George Saintsbury argued that no other English poet had thought of adding an alexandrine to *ottava rima*, and that Spenser's stanzas are too organic to be considered as eight lines plus one (George Saintsbury, *A History of English Prosody*, 3 vols. [London: Macmillan, 1906-10], 1:363-65). Other critics then looked for additional sources for the stanza. In 1926 E. F. Pope remarked that "when Spenser sought a medium for his epic, he had as authoritative precedents the classic hexameter, the alexandrine of the French, the *terza rima* of Dante, the *ottava rima* of Boiardo, Ariosto, and Tasso and the decasyllabic heroic line of his own country" ("The Critical Background of the Spenserian Stanza," *Modern Philology*, 24(1926):31-53, 37. Pope is wrong about the ready accessibility of a "decasyllabic heroic line"; it scarcely existed until Marlowe and Spenser himself, despite Surrey's Virgilian model. She makes an interesting case for the *Monk's Tale* stanza, and then finally and rather curiously rejects it in favor of an eight-line Italian madrigal form derived from the *terza rima*. In 1928 Leicester Bradner suggested "that the three notable features of the rime scheme invented by Spenser are the medial couplet, the concluding couplet, and the *c* rime in the sixth line connecting the latter to the rest of the stanza." He noted English models for at least two of these features: two nine-line stanza forms by anonymous authors in Tottel's *Miscellany*, and the *Monk's Tale* stanza ("Forerunners of the Spenserian Stanza," *Review of English Studies*,

4(1928):207-08). Enid Hamer pursues the native origins of the stanza by linking it to rime royal (*The Metres of English Poetry* [London: Methuen, 1930], 159).

19. Saintsbury and Hamer, *loc cit.*; Warnke, in *The Encyclopedia of Poetry and Poetics:* "This form was invented by Edmund Spenser for his *The Faerie Queene*, and, despite some similarity to *ottava rima* and to the linked octave used by Chaucer in *The Monk's Tale*, it stands out as one of the most remarkably original metrical innovations in the history of English verse."

20. Recognition of this theme underlies discussions of *The Faerie Queene* by Kathleen Williams, *Spenser's World of Glass* (Berkeley and Los Angeles: Univ. of Calif. Press, 1966), and A. Bartlett Giamatti, *The Play of Double Senses* (Englewood Cliffs, N.J.: Prentice-Hall, 1974), among other important works on Spenser. It is an assumption behind Nelson's discussion of the thematic centering of various books of *The Faerie Queene*, as well as Alpers' very different approach, in *The Poetry of The Faerie Queene*.

21. A review of poems written in the stanza is mostly a survey of inconsequential verses and ambitious failures. See Philip G. Davis, "A Check List of Poems 1595 to 1833, Entirely or Partly Written in the Spenserian Stanza," *Bulletin of the New York Public Library*, 77(1974):314-28.

22. E. H. Wilkins traces its Italian development back to the court of Frederick II (1194-1250). The thirty or so poets he calls the "Fredericans" merged Provençal and Northern French lyric with the German *minnesong* to produce the basic structures that were in turn imitated in the French *chanson* and firmly established by Petrarch in the fourteenth century. *A History of Italian Literature*, revised by Thomas G. Bergin (Cambridge, Mass.: Harvard Univ. Press, 1974), 18. See also Wilkins, "The Canzone and the Minnesong," in *The Invention of the Sonnet and Other Studies in Italian Literature* (Rome: Edizioni di Storia e letteratura, 1959), 41-50.

23. Warner Forrest Patterson, *Three Centuries of French Poetic Theory (1328-1630)*, 2 vols. (Ann Arbor: Univ. of Michigan Press, 1935), 1:41-42.

24. Gaston Paris, *La Littérature Française au Moyen Age* (Paris: Hachette, 1913), 199.

25. Joseph G. Fucilla, "Canzone," in *The Encyclopedia of Poetry and Poetics.*

26. See Cortlandt Van Winkle, *Epithalamion* (New York: F. S. Crofts, 1926), 6-26, for parallels and analogues for that poem.

27. Saintsbury, *A History of English Prosody*, 1:362. See also B. E. C. Davis, *Edmund Spenser: A Critical Study* (Cambridge: Cambridge Univ. Press, 1933), 200.

28. Carol Maddison, *Apollo and The Nine* (Baltimore: Johns Hopkins Univ. Press, 1960), 289: "The *Epithalamium's* [sic] claim to being an ode is that it is an occasional lyric poem, written in an elevated style, celebrating an event generalized to appear of vast importance. Thus is resembles an ode. But the epithalamium like the sonnet, the usual elegy, whether amorous or funeral, and the ancient type of epigram, has so long been discriminated from the large lyric genre that there seems little point in removing it from its historical sub-genre and throwing it back into the undifferentiated mass, especially when this reclassification will offer no new key to the interpretation of the poem, nor will the *Epithalamium's* [sic] inclusion among English odes contribute to the clarification of that already confused genre." Maddison is very careful of formal analogues to the ode and sees none here. See also her discussion of Cowley, 369-401, as the father of more modern conceptions of an English Pindaric ode.

29. Van Winkle, 37-39; A. Kent Hieatt, *Short Time's Endless Monument* (New York: Columbia Univ. Press, 1960). See also Enid Welsford's discussion and critique of Hieatt's suggestions, in *Spenser, Fowre Hymnes, Epithalamion: A Study of Edmund Spenser's Doctrine of Love* (New York: Barnes and Noble, 1967), 191-206.

30. Van Winkle, 38. The similar form is from Ronsard's *Amours*. His Pindaric *Odes* are quite different, with a strophe beginning aabccbcdcdee . . . and an antistrophe beginning aabccbdedeff . . . . *Le Premier Livre Des Odes*, 1550, in *Oeuvres Complètes de Ronsard*, ed. Gustave Cohen, 2 vols. (Paris: Librairie Gallimard, 1950), 1:358 ff.

31. The 1503 *Kalendrier des Bergiers* combined practical advice, homespun moralizing, and recreative verses in a manner reminiscent of an almanac. Spenser has obviously borrowed some of these almanac features in order to make a "Calendar for every yeare." For further discussion of French influence on Spenser and other English poets, see Anne Lake Prescott, *French Poets and the English Renaissance* (New Haven: Yale Univ. Press, 1978).

32. For discussions of the sonnet in England, see J. W. Lever, *The Elizabethan Love Sonnet* (London: Methuen, 1956), and L. C. John, *The Elizabethan Sonnet Sequence* (New York: Columbia Univ. Press, 1938).

John, 18-26, describes the outburst of sonnet sequences in English after 1591.

33. Wilkins traces its first appearance to poets in the Sicilian court of Holy Roman Emperor Frederick II (1194-1250) and credits the senior member of the group, Giacomo da Lentino, with its invention. He also argues that the form derives from the Sicilian folk *canzuna*, an eight-line song, with the sestet a purely artistic invention and addition. *The Invention of the Sonnet and Other Studies in Italian Literature*, 11-39.

34. See E. H. Wilkins, *The Making of the Canzoniere and Other Petrarchan Studies* (Roma: Edizioni di Storia e letteratura, 1951).

35. See, for example, Kenneth Myrick, *Sir Philip Sidney as a Literary Craftsman*, 2d ed. (Lincoln: Univ. of Nebraska Press, 1965), 300-01, 309-13; Montgomery, 100-19; Kalstone, 107, 179-81; Neil Rudenstine, *Sidney's Poetic Development* (Cambridge, Mass.: Harvard Univ. Press, 1967), 149-269 *passim*, and 272-73; Hamilton, 84-86; and Nichol, 153.

36. Ringler summarizes this and all of Sidney's verse forms with characteristic thoroughness and accuracy in *The Poems*, 569-72.

37. Even Sidney's use of hexameters is a disingenuous borrowing, this time from the French Petrarchists. Hexamater sonnets are common in Ronsard. See, for example, xx-xxii of *Le Second Livre des Amours* (xxii: "Que ne suis-je insensible? où que n'est mon visage") and "À La Rivière du Loir" ("Respon moy, meschant Loir: me rens-tu ce loyer"), in *Oeuvres Complète*, ed. Cohen, 1:129, 321.

38. 1. 6abababcdcdee; 2. 5abbaabbacdcdee; 3. 5abababccdeed; 4. 5ababababccdccd; 5. 5ababbbabacdcdee; 6. 6ababbabaccdeed; 7. 5ababababcdcdee; 8. 6abbaabbacdcdee. Sonnet 9 returns to the form of the second sonnet, abbaabbacdcdee, the most common single form throughout the sequence.

39. E. J. Dobson, *English Pronunciation 1500-1700*, 2d ed., 2 vols. (Oxford: Clarendon Press, 1968), 2:558-60, especially 559 and 560, n. 2. For evidence that Sidney may have heard this usually Northern pronounciation, see the "preserved/swarved" rime in his Psalm 37, ll. 70-71. Edition cited in note 42.

40. Smith, 1:204. See discussion of the "ryme" controversy in chapter 6 for further reference to Sidney's metrical comments.

41. For the importance of the Sidneian Psalms to seventeenth-century English religious poetry, see Barbara K. Lewalski, *Protestant Poetics and the Seventeenth-Century English Lyric* (Princeton: Princeton Univ. Press, 1979), 241-44, 275-76, and 301.

42. Feminine endings: 3, 6, 11, 13, 14, 19, 21, 22, 24, 32, 37, 42, and 43; counterpoint: 6, 20, 23, 33, 38, 39, and 41. Counterpoint is a term most often used in discussions of Herbert's verse. See chapter 8. Texts of the Sidneian Psalms are taken from *The Psalms of Sir Philip Sidney and the Countess of Pembroke*, ed. J. C. A. Rathmell (New York: NYU Press, 1963), with reference to the three seventeenth-century manuscript versions at the Huntington Library, HM 100, HM 117, and EL 11637.

43. For the Pembroke influence on Herbert and Donne, see Lewalski, 244, 275. Jonson's reference to the psalms is in his *Conversations with William Drummond of Hawthornden* in 1619. Hallet Smith, "English Metrical Psalms in the Sixteenth Century," *Huntington Library Quarterly*, 9(1946):323-55.

44. Rathmell, xx and xxvi.

45. *Apology for Poetry*, in Smith, 1:203.

Chapter Six

Late Elizabethan Verse and Verse Theory

*Every language hath her proper number
or measure fitted to use and delight.*

Daniel, "Defence of Rhyme"

In the late Elizabethan period a number of factors contributed to a literary climate in which both Sidney's "smally learned courtiers" and professional writers and theoreticians could find abundant inspiration and audience for their verses. These factors included the models of Sidney and Spenser, the popularity of miscellanies and song books, and a court centered around a queen who embodied courtly love's ruling lady and who encouraged (if she did not lavishly remunerate) poetry and song. Among the many courtier-poets of this period Sir Walter Ralegh (1552?-1618) stands out as both representative and particularly talented. His lyrics reflect the variety and vitality with which English poets were exploring the range of the new versification, evident also in the sonnet craze of the 1590s and in the production of poetry collections, most notably *The Phoenix Nest* (1593) and *England's Helicon* (1600). Alongside this abundance of poetic riches, the rhyme controversy wound its way to a belated close in the theory and practice of two fine lyricists, Thomas Campion (1567-1620) and Samuel Daniel (1563?-1619).

Ralegh was in many ways the quintessential courtier/lover/ poet of the later Elizabethan period. His relationship with the

Queen was more special than most, but it was not unique.[1] His extant poetry not only documents certain aspects of that association and of the conflation of the Lord/Vassal, Lady/Lover relationship that was such an integral part of Elizabeth's rule, it also provides a useful summary of the development of verse from Gascoigne through the beginning of the seventeenth century. Although the Ralegh canon remains uncertain, there is a core of poems that are clearly his and others that are very probably by him. Even doubtful cases provide examples of courtly poetry of the later Elizabethan period, and, insofar as they are in Ralegh's stylistic manner, will serve to illustrate principles of verse development whether or not their author is surely known.[2]

Although precise dating, as well as authorship, is often a problem with Ralegh poems, certain key lyrics are easily dated and others suggest probable occasions or can at least be given a *terminus ante quem*. We therefore know rather more about Ralegh's poetic development than we do about any other non-professional poet of this period, with the possible exception of Sidney. It is a rich and observable development, reflecting both changing tastes in verse and Ralegh's own developing poetic voice.

Among the poems which can be certainly dated are three commendations which provide interesting touchstones for middle and late Elizabethan and early Jacobean verse styles. Ralegh's earliest known and first published poem, "in commendation of the Steele Glasse," appeared as three ballade stanzas prefaced to Gascoigne's blank verse satire in 1576. In 1590 Ralegh provided two commendatory poems for Spenser's *Faerie Queene*, the first and better known of which is a sonnet titled "A Vision upon this conceipt of the Faery Queen." In 1614 Ralegh published another sonnet commending his cousin, Arthur Gorges, on his translation of Lucan's *Pharsalia*. The styles of these three poems are strongly reminiscent of Gascoigne, Spenser, and Ben Jonson, arguably the most influential poets of their times and all of them Ralegh's acquaintances. The same year Gorges published his translation of Lucan, Ralegh published his own prose masterpiece, *The History of the World*, whose frontespiece is faced by

Jonson's "The Mind of the Front," an extended sonnet consisting of four quatrains and a couplet.

"In commendation of the Steele Glasse" is in conservative, end-stopped iambic pentameter with an unvarying pause after the fourth syllable. Ornamental alliteration also serves to define phrasal units and to underscore the initial four-syllable group:[3]

> Swete were the sauce would please ech kind of tast;
> The life likewise were pure that never swerved;
>
> (ll. 1-2)

A variation in the alliterative pattern is the primary source of prosodic variation in the poem, as in the second stanza:

> Though sundry mindes in sundry sorte do deeme,
> Yet worthiest wights yelde prayse for every payne;
> But envious braynes do nought (or light) esteme,
> Such stately steppes as they cannot attaine.
> For whoso reapes renowne above the rest,
> With heapes of hate shal surely be opprest.
>
> (ll. 7-12)

In the best tradition of Gascoigne's own verse, and in specific imitation of the insistent regularity of "The Steele Glas" line structure, Ralegh offers a straightforward aphoristic verse in which the occasional polysyllabic word provides some rhythmic variety, with devices of balance and parallelism, the rhetorical schemes favored by orators, dominating the structure of the poem.

The first of Ralegh's two commendations of *The Faerie Queene* provides an interesting contrast.[4] Here he makes limited but excellent use of enjambment (lines 2-3 and 9-10), uses the norm of the pause after the fourth syllable but varies from it,

185

and includes a fair number of polysyllabic words. The poem depends for its aesthetic power on a trope (the central conceit of the Faerie Queene banishing Petrarch's Laura from fame) rather then on the schematic structures that carried the "Steele Glas" commendation:

> Methought I saw the grave, where *Laura* lay,
> Within that Temple, where the vestall flame
> Was wont to burne, and passing by that way,
> To see that buried dust of living fame,
> Whose tumbe faire love, and fairer vertue kept,
> All suddeinly I saw the Faery Queene:
> At whose approch the soule of *Petrarke* wept,
> And from thenceforth those graces were not seene.
> For they this Queene attended, in whose steed
> Oblivion laid him down on *Lauras* herse:
> Hereat the hardest stones were seene to bleed,
> And grones of buried ghostes the hevens did perse.
>   Where *Homers* spright did tremble all for griefe,
>   And curst th'accesse of that celestiall theife.

The alliterative patterns of the earlier poem have been replaced by more subtle echoes of assonance ("grave . . . lay," l. 1; "Temple . . . vestall," l. 2; "burne . . . / . . . buried dust," ll. 3-4; "seene . . . bleed," l. 11; "grones . . . ghostes," l. 12). Line 10, "Oblivion laid him downe on Lauras herse," is an impressive transformation of convention as well as an exceptionally elegant line rhythmically.

If Ralegh's "Steele Glas" commendation is very like Gascoigne's work, and his sonnet in praise of *The Faerie Queene* is reminiscent of Spenserian coherence, metaphor, and euphony, "To the Translator of Lucan" is strongly reminiscent of Ben Jonson's poems, especially in his own commendations and his epigrams (see chapter 7). Although it is a sonnet, it does not develop a central metaphor but rather offers a logical argument for the virtue of Arthur Gorges and therefore for the appropriateness of his translation. It uses the octave/sestet division to help structure the argument, but otherwise the poem is an epideictic epigram. Its versification also suggests Jonson's influence. Mid-line pauses are more varied than in earlier verses, enjambment is more severe and more important to the total movement of the poem, and the apparently straightforward language is belied by the wrenched accent and ambiguity of the concluding couplet:

> Had *Lucan* hid the truth to please the time,
> He had beene too unworthy of thy Penne:
> Who never sought, nor ever car'd to clime
> By flattery, or seeking worthlesse men.
> For this thou hast been bruis'd: but yet those scarres
> Do beautifie no lesse then those wounds do
> Receiv'd in just, and in religious warres;
> Though thou hast bled by both, and bearst them too.
> Change not, to change thy fortune is too late.
> Who with a manly faith resolves to dye,
> May promise to himselfe a lasting state,
> Though not so great, yet free from infamy.
>   Such was thy *Lucan*, whom so to translate
>   Nature thy Muse (like LUCANS) did create.

The rhythm of the thirteenth line reflects the new daring that both Jonson and Donne, in ways only slightly different, had already explored and were to explore further:

```
         / x    x /   x   /    / x   x /
Such was I thy Luc I an, whom I so to I translate
```

The trochaic fourth foot and the prosaic accentuation were unusual even for Jonson, though not for Donne. Although it will fit accentual-syllabic foot meter, the line's mid-line pause after the fifth syllable hearkens back to Wyatt and earlier, tempting a four-accent reading based on the hemistich:

187

<pre>
      /   /   /   /
Such was thy Lucan || whom so to translate
</pre>

Rather than reflecting a normative awkwardness, such a line in a well-wrought sonnet -adds an emphatic tone appropriate to Ralegh's epigrammatic conclusion.

Ralegh seems to have been interested in pacing and line movement from early in his poetic career, despite the rigidity of the "Steele Glas" verses. Most of the Ralegh poems published in the 1593 *Phoenix Nest* date from the 1580s and show definite though conservative exploration of varying techniques.[5] "Calling to minde mine eie long went about," for example, uses initial trochees in the first, third, and fifth lines of the first of three ballade stanzas, and in the fourth and fifth lines of the second stanza. The third stanza, however, which moves toward the concluding testament of unwavering faithfulness, is relentlessly iambic with either no pauses or the usual one after the fourth syllable:

> But when I found my selfe to you was true,
> I lov'd my selfe, bicause my selfe lov'd you.

The variant published in 1589 by Puttenham as an example of "Ploche, or the Doubler" is equally regular:

> Yet when I saw my selfe to you was true,
> I loved my selfe, bycause my selfe loved you.

Two of Ralegh's most elegant lyrics, both probably written somewhat later than "Calling to minde," are "The Nimphs reply" to Christopher Marlowe's "passionate Sheepheard" and the poem beginning "Nature that washt her hands in milke." Both illustrate how sound patterns affect the flow of an otherwise regularly iambic line, and both show the interest in intralinear phrasing that characterizes Ralegh's later verse. From "The Nimphs reply" we have this sophistication of the alliterative impulse:

> Time drives the flocks from field to fold,
> When Rivers rage, and Rocks grow cold,
> And Philomell becommeth dombe,
> The rest complaines of cares to come.
>
> The flowers doe fade, and wanton fieldes
> To wayward winter reckoning yeeldes.

(ll. 5-10)

There is more being done with sound than just alliteration. The concluding consonance of "field to fold," for example, affects the pace of the line more than the alliteration does, and line 10 is a mouthful of accountability less because of the "w" alliteration than because of the obscured word boundary that comes from the "r" linking in "winter reckoning." The poem is throughout more prosodically ponderous than the lighter Marlowe lyric. The relative lengthening of lines and slower rhythms is in part a function of the somewhat more numerous double consonant groups: world, field, fold, complaines, fieldes, yeeldes, gownes, belt, straw, and clasps. The Marlowe poem has only fieldes, yieldes, and gowne, straw, and clasps. This may be a lesson from quantitative poetics or it may simply be the exercise of English sounds to affect the pacing of a poem.

"Nature that washt her hands in milke" adds a tetrameter couplet to conventional quatrains (4a3B4a3B4cc in stanza one; 4aBaBcc in the rest) producing lyric stanzas that Ralegh manipulates superbly to serve the changing purposes of the poem. The first half describes a standard "cruel fair," with the courtly song tradition emphasized in the feminine endings of lines 2 and 4 in each stanza:

Nature that washt her hands in milke
  And had forgott to dry them,
In stead of earth tooke snow and silke
  At Loves request to trye them,
If she a mistresse could compose
To please Loves fancy out of those.

Her eyes he would should be of light,
  A Violett breath, and Lipps of Jelly,
Her haire not blacke, nor over bright,
  And of the softest downe her Belly,
As for her inside hee'ld have it
Only of wantonnesse and witt.

At Loves entreaty, such a one
  Nature made, but with her beauty
She hath framed a heart of stone,
  So as Love by ill destinie
Must dye for her whom nature gave him
Because her darling would not save him.

The first two stanzas establish a pattern of end-stopped lines with a slight enjambment between the fifth and sixth lines, linking the couplet as a unit. The third stanza varies that movement slightly but significantly. The fourth line provides an inadequate rime and wrenched accent if the word is to be pronounced "destínie"; if the last syllable is to receive some form of stress, then we have an instance of a stressed syllable riming with the unstressed second syllable of "beauty," common enough in the fifteenth century but most unusual in the late sixteenth century. Something is clearly out of line, a conviction reinforced by the slight enjambment between lines 4 and 5 and the feminine endings of 5 and 6.

    The unease that the versification provokes at the end of the third stanza is confirmed by the second half of the poem. The cruel fair becomes merely an occasion for meditating on devouring time, which is the true subject of the poem:

But Time which nature doth despise,
  And rudely gives her love the lye,
Makes hope a foole, and sorrow wise,
  His hands doth neither wash, nor dry,
But being made of steele and rust,
Turnes snow, and silke, and milke to dust.

The Light, the Belly, lipps and breath,
  He dimms, discolours, and destroyes,
With those he feedes, but fills not death,
  Which sometimes were the foode of Joyes;
Yet Time doth dull each lively witt,
And dryes all wantonnes with it.

Oh cruell Time which takes in trust
  Our youth, our Joyes and all we have,
And payes us but with age and dust,
  Who in the darke and silent grave
When we have wandred all our wayes
Shutts up the story of our dayes.

The schematic balance and parallelism that characterized the verse in the "Steele Glas" commendation is here, emphasizing the relentless inevitability of time and the grave, but the schemes are sufficiently varied to keep the movement interesting. Notice, for example the pause patterns in the first of these three last stanzas:

> But Time I which nature doth despise,II
>   And rudely gives her love the lye,II
> Makes hope a foole, I and sorrow wise,II
>   His hands doth neither wash, I nor dry,II
> But being made of steele and rust,II
> Turnes snow, II and silke, II and milke I to dust.

This is an excellent poem, whose initial conceit has the Petrarchan sophistication of Sidney or Spenser, and whose turn to moral aphorism anticipates the Jonson-like poetry Ralegh would write in his later years.[6]

Natural Emphasis

Ralegh is not simply a transition poet with derivative verse styles that span rich Elizabethan and Jacobean periods in England. His own voice is evident from first to last: a grim wit and sense of irony, concern with time, mutability, reputation, and honor, inventive handling of metaphors usually taken from nature and seldom extended, plain language with an occasional elegant phrase or image, and a strong sense of the line as a poetic unit (as opposed to Spenser, for example, for whom the rhythmic unit is often the half-line or a series of lines). Even with these observable characteristics, he also may be seen to reflect the poetry of his time, from Gascoigne to Jonson, and with his excellent ear it is not surprising that he learns to vary the Surreyan lines much as his professional contemporaries were doing. He is also willing to experiment with lineation, as in his holograph "Ocean to Scinthia," a long poem to Queen Elizabeth, indirectly petitionary, which does not represent a final draft but is more than a first. He breaks off lines, worries less about completing quatrains than about achieving the effect of strong emotion, and can be seen in his punctuation to be somewhat concerned with linear rhythms. In one of the most moving and sophisticated poems of the early seventeenth century, "The Passionate Man's Pilgrimage," he uses unequal lines in the *canzone* tradition to assist in achieving a remarkable compromise between simplicity and sophistication.[7]

> Blood must be my bodies balmer,
> No other balme will there be given
> Whilst my soule like a white Palmer
> Travels to the land of heaven,
> Over the silver mountaines,
> Where spring the Nectar fountaines:
> And there Ile kisse
> The Bowle of blisse,
> And drink my eternal fill
> On every milken hill.
> My soule will be a drie before,
> But after it will nere thirst more.

(ll. 7-18)

More commonly Ralegh uses standard pentameter and tetrameter lines with counterpoint and parallelism effected by an overlay of rhetorical schemes. His poetry displays a variety of sound and rhythmic patterns available to the newly attuned Elizabethan ear.[8]

Some of the use Elizabethan poets made of that variety is evident in the two pre-eminent Elizabethan poetry collections in which Ralegh's verse appeared. *The Phoenix Nest* is a memorial to Sir Philip Sidney, and consists of poems by fellow Oxonians and poets of some gentility, including Edward de Vere, Earl of Oxford ("E. O."), and Fulke Greville, later Lord Brooke, along with professional writers such as Nicholas Breton and Thomas Lodge.[9] *England's Helicon* (1600), is a wide-ranging collection of high quality lyrics, either pastoral in their original mode or made so for the sake of the volume's theme.[10] It contains poems by many of the same poets who appear in *The Phoenix Nest*, including Ralegh, Breton, and Lodge, along with a substantial number of Sidney's lyrics, three by Spenser, one by Shakespeare, and works by at least twenty-three other poets. As we might expect in such sophisticated late Elizabethan verse collections, there is a fair amount of formal variety and metrical ease.

The Phoenix Nest contains eighty-one poems plus a prose defense of the late Earl of Leicester and a prose "Dialogue betweene Constancie and Inconstancie." The lyrics are strophically conservative for the most part, with pentameter and tetrameter ballade stanzas or rime royal dominating the collection. Lodge's lyrics are the most various and inventive. They include one of the earliest published examples of a trochaic tetrameter poem ("Muses helpe me, sorrow swarmeth"), a complex trochaic/iambic lyric ("Strive no more": 2a3bba5cc), several in ballade stanzas, and one English sonnet ("Midst lasting griefes, to have but short repose"). Several forms anticipate the inventive counterpoint lyricism of the seventeenth-century poets. One lyric in eight stanzas formed 5a5B5a2B may have helped suggest a form for Herbert's "Sacrifice." Lodge's poem, on quite a different topic, begins:

> The fatall starre that at my birthday shined,
> Were it of Jove, or Venus in hir brightnes,
> All sad effects, sowre fruits of love divined,
>   In my Loves lightnes.

Another example of complex counterpoint construction is in the five stanzas beginning:

> My bonie Lasse thine eie,
>   So slie,
> Hath made me sorrowe so:
> Thy crimsen cheekes my deere,
>   So cleere,
> Have so much wrought my woe.

(3a1a3bc1c3b.) Lodge's contributions are atypical of *The Phoenix Nest* poems in their strophic variety.[11] More typical is his ease of lineation, though he injects perhaps more aesthetic variety into metrically regular lines than do most of the poets in the volume.

One *Phoenix Nest* poem worth special note is the epitaph on Sidney ("Another of the same") usually attributed to Sidney's close friend, Fulke Greville. It is a late poulters measure lyric, arguably the most successful extant. Its effectiveness makes it the exception that proves the rule that poulters measure is limited for serious verse. The form itself is so rollicking that rhythmic pacing must depend on syntactic pauses running counter to the cesural pause, which is hard to sustain without the lines breaking down altogether. Greville's deliberately plain and emphatic epitaph begins:

> Silence augmenteth grief, writing increaseth rage,
> Staled are my thoughts, which loved and lost the wonder of our age;
> Yet quickened now with fire, though dead with frost ere now,
> Enraged I write I know not what; dead, quick, I know not how.

The rhythmic power of this stanza depends on a fine balance between the metrically directed movement created in part by the precise mid-line cesura of the first and third lines and in part by the less predictable pause patterns of the second and fourth lines. The first stanza establishes the heavy rhythms usual to poulters measure, but also suggests the speaker's turmoil. This sets the base rhythm and model for changes that run throughout the poem. Finally, in a triumph of phrasing over the regular insistence of a metrical base at its most unyielding, the poem concludes:

> Now rhyme, the son of rage, which art no kin to skill,
> And endless grief, which deads my life, yet knows not how to kill,
> Go, seek that hapless tomb, which if ye hap to find
> Salute the stones that keep the limbs that held so good a mind.

Greville has deliberately chosen this meter as an appropriate container for the unsubtle passions of rage and grief. He acknowledges the quantitative theorists (such as Sidney himself) in his insistence that "rhyme" is "no kin to skill," but he achieves tremendous poignancy in the pose of artlessness underscored by "rhyme's" most discredited form, poulters measure.

As a whole, *The Phoenix Nest* is a collection of mostly competent and sometimes impressive verse. Perhaps the most interesting formal variation in the volume is in the different manifestations of ballade stanzas (ababcc). They range from pentameter, as in Breton's "Com yonglings com, that seem to make such mone," to tetrameter, as in Matthew Roydon's long elegy on Sidney beginning "As then, no winde at all there blew," to the Earl of Oxford's trimeter lyric beginning "What cunning can express."

England's Helicon is much more strophically various, suggesting that the model of Spenser's *Shepheardes Calendar* produced a tendency to use pastoral lyrics for formal experimentation. The first edition contained 150 poems (to which nine were added in the second, 1614 edition). Of these only a few are in some form of ballade stanza, while the majority are in long or complex stanzas. The largest single contribution to the volume comes from Bartholomew Yong, whose twenty-five lyrics from his translation of Montemayor's Spanish pastoral romance, *Diana*, represent the formal range of the volume as a whole.

Yong's poems include the standard lyric forms. "Neere to the River banks, with greene" begins a poem in tetrameter ballade stanzas. Even more simply, "When that I poore soul was borne" is in headless tetrameter quatrains riming abab, and "I see thee jolly Sheepheard merrie" is in iambic tetrameter quatrains with feminine endings. More complex are the stanzas of the shepherd songs by "Faustus" ("Eclipsed was our Sunne": 3a5b3a5bb3c5d3c5dd) and by "Firmius" ("If that the gentle wind": 3a4b3aa4b3c5d3cc5dd). Even more interesting is the pastoral epithalamion which sustains feminine rimes across seven stanzas that interweave pentameter and trimeter lines, possibly on the model of the *canzone*. The poem is not entirely successful, but its first stanza is a fairly typical example of the late Elizabethan attempt at euphonious variety in both strophic construction and linear rhythms. Note especially the variation in rhythmic pacing from the third to the fourth line:

Let now each Meade with flowers be depainted,
    Of sundry colours sweetest odours glowing:
Roses yeeld foorth your smells so finely tainted,
    Calme winds the greene leaves moove with gentle blowing,
      The Christall Rivers flowing
      With waters be encreased:
    And since each one from sorrow now hath ceased,
      From mournfull plaints and sadnes.
    Ring foorth faire Nimphs your joyfull Songs for gladnes.

In the light of this rich lyricism, it is perhaps surprising that the controversy over rhyme should have continued. It had its last real gasp around the time of *England's Helicon*, and from one of the finest rhyme-writing lyricists in the history of English verse, Thomas Campion. If Sidney was the most successful English quantitative poet, Campion was the most interesting theoretician of quantitative verse. His musical training and his excellent ear for verbal sound combined to make his 1602 *Observations in the Art of English Poetry* a more compelling case for quantity than most, and his poetic practice (which at first glance bears little relation to his theory), a fine example of the new elegancies of which English verse was capable.

Campion's attack against rhyme is the standard one: the feature of rime encourages a lack of attention to the internal movement of the line, and syllabic number is an insufficient meter for developing the rhythms and euphonies available to the language:

> As in Musick we do not say a straine of so many
> notes, but so many sem'briefes (though sometimes
> there are no more notes than sem'briefes), so in a
> verse the numeration of the sillables is not so much to
> be observed as their waite and due proportion.

> (2:328-29)

As he gets down to cases, however, Campion often reflects conservative accentual-syllabic practice. He notes that English iambic pentameter provides "those numbers which Nature in our English destinates to the Tragick and Heroik Poeme," confirming its comparability to Latin dactylic hexameters. He also discusses the correctness of certain substitutions: "The Iambick verse in like manner being yet made a little more licentiate, that it may thereby the neerer imitate our common talke, will excellently serve for Comedies; and then we may use a *Sponde* in the fifth place, and in the third place any foote except a *Trochy*, which never enters into our Iambick verse but in the first place, and then with this caveat of the other feete which must of necessity follow" (2:338). While he is speaking of quantitative rather than accentual feet, he is nonetheless descriptive of current accentual-syllabic practice.

Natural Emphasis

Campion's practice follows his theory only indirectly. Except for the examples he gives in the *Observations*, all his extant English verse is in the despised rhyme. Yet Campion's rhyme takes such care of its intralinear sounds and rhythms, and there is such clear attention to the devices of sound that appear to affect English syllabic length, that he may well be considered the first truly successful writer of English verse whose rhythms depend primarily on syllabic quantity. The relation between his theorizing about English verse and his most effective practice is perhaps clearest if one compares his most famous example of rimeless "true versifying," the poem beginning "Rose-cheekt Lawra," with almost any of the poems from his several books of airs. "Rose-cheekt Lawra," though not one of Campion's best poems, is arguably the best lyric to come out of the discussions of quantitative meters in English:

> Rose-cheekt *Lawra*, come
> Sing thou smoothly with thy beawtie's
> Silent musick, either other
> > Sweetely gracing.
> Lovely formes do flowe
> From concent devinely framed;
> Heav'n is musick, and thy beawtie's
> > Birth is heavenly.
> These dull notes we sing
> Discords need for helps to grace them;
> Only beawty purely loving
> > Knowes no discord,
> But still mooves delight,
> Like cleare springs renu'd by flowing,
> Ever perfect, ever in them-
> > selves eternall.

In this curious conflation of Plato and Catullus, Campion has produced a rimeless poem of great euphony. I have read this poem aloud to classes of English majors, all with the text before them, and then asked what was unusual about it. Only after concentrating on the printed text did anyone recognize the

absence of rime. Campion's focus on syllabic quantity and relationship has sensitized him to appropriately English aesthetic
patterns of consonance, assonance, and alliteration which are
apparent to the ear, far from prosaic, and generally successful.
Consonance and alliteration are as much a part of the process as
the more obvious assonances available to a poet focusing on an
idea of syllabic quantity. The "s" sounds of lines 2-4, for example, or the "f" sounds in lines 5-6 are sufficiently evident to provide a pattern, but sufficiently varied to prevent the old alliterative monotony. The complex of "s" and "d" sounds in lines 9-10
is nothing short of masterful:

> These dull notes we sing
> Discords need for helps to grace them;

This is superb aesthetic patterning, more literary than vocal in
its remoteness from conversational registers, but euphonious and
graceful. Unlike Lydgate's equally aesthetic verse, the sounds of
Campion's verse are neither discordant nor dull, but rather provide an intricate weaving of consonance in support of lyricism
reminiscent of the musical patterning it explicitly seeks to imitate.

Although "Rose-cheekt Lawra" eschews end rime, it is
syllabic. Its four four-line strophic units are each composed of
lines of five, eight, eight, and four syllables (assuming both
"framed" and "heavenly" to be disyllabic). The only real difference between this poem and Campion's lyrics in his books of airs
is therefore the presence of end rime in the latter. Not surpris-
ingly, end rime is usually the least important prosodic feature in
Campion's verse. His stanzas are variously composed, some
keeping a single measure throughout and some as complex or
almost as complex as "Rose-cheekt Lawra." An example of the
former is the consistent iambic pentameter of "When thou must
home to shades of underground," where the patterning of what
are usually called "long" vowels provides the "chiefe life" of the
verse, as in the first stanza:[12]

Natural Emphasis

> When thou must home to shades of under ground,
> And there ariv'd, a newe admired guest,
> The beauteous spirits do ingirt thee round,
> White Iope, blith Hellen, and the rest,
> To heare the stories of thy finisht love,
> From that smoothe toong whose musicke hell can move.

The movement from back to front vowels makes this a ponderous, ominous mouthful. The result is not strictly mimetic, but it supports the heavy tone the words suggest. Similarly in "Now winter nights enlarge" there is a complex of consonances, particularly "s," "w," and the liquids, "r" and "l," as in the first of the two stanzas:

> Now winter nights enlarge
>   The number of their houres,
> And clouds their stormes discharge
>   Upon the ayrie towres:
>   . . .

> Now yellow waxen lights
>   Shall waite on hunny Love,
> While youthfull Revels, Masks, and Courtly sights,
>   Sleepes leaden spels remove.

The elegant subtlety of phonological patterning comes in part from Campion's willingness to limit the assonance or consonance in stressed syllables, where they clearly establish a pattern, but to echo their limited patterning by including those sounds in a fair portion of unstressed syllables as well. Consider the "r" sounds in the first four lines, for example, or the "l" sounds in the unstressed syllables in the last four lines reinforcing the more obvious "l" consonance in the stressed. The effect is to point up the consonance without allowing it to overpower the other elements, phonological and semantic, that make up the rhythm and sound of the poem. This graceful patterning is equally evident in the initial consonance of "lights," "Love," and "leaden";

although they alliterate, they are not quite close enough together to project a pattern of alliteration.

These examples offer only a brief suggestion of Campion's skill with verbal sounds. Despite his theorizing about quantatititive verse, and his stated dismissal of rhyme, he is a brilliant writer of accentual-syllabic rimed verse. His theory brings to his practice a profound concern for the sounds of his verse and an ability to render end rime virtually irrelevant in the complexity of sound patterning that pervades entire lines and stanzas. This is not, however, some new form of English quantitative verse. Although his sound patterns are evident and interesting, they are not systematic. Campion's skills develop new rhythmic possibilities, a new attention to the way sounds inform an accentual-syllabic line; they do not establish new meters. Sidney, who was able to see the analogy between accent and quantity, used his experimentation to develop a more varied accentuation in his verse, and Campion, who made the analogy between music and verbal quantity, modeled the possibilities for various and flexible overlays of rhythm, including a sense of syllabic length, across the more objectifiable accentual syllabic stress meters.

Samuel Daniel's reponse to Campion's *Observations*, the 1603 *Defence of Ryme*, is in many ways a signal of Jacobean poetic concerns as well as a summary theoretical statement describing and defending English accentual-syllabic verse. For the latter, Daniel at first appears simply to follow Sidney in acknowledging the analogue between classical quantity and English accent, but he takes it a step further:

> For as Greeke and Latine verse consists of the
> number and quantitie of sillables, so doth the English
> verse of measure and accent. And though it doth not
> strictly observe long and short sillables, yet it most
> religiously respects the accent; and as the short and
> long make number, so the acute and grave accent
> yeelde harmonie. And harmonie is likewise number;
> so that the English verse then hath number, measure,
> and harmonie in the best proportion of Musicke.

> (2:360)

Natural Emphasis

He is of course asserting the musicality of English rhyme in response to Campion. In addition, he is noting the importance of accent and levels of accentuation to the movement of English verse. Proper handling of accentuation produces "harmonie," or interesting and appropriate verse rhythms. sysll 52

Daniel's response to Campion has often been praised for its common sense.[13] Less often noticed is the extent to which this treatise, written under Elizabeth but published in the first year of James's reign, anticipates important emphases and attitudes of the Jacobean period.[14] Daniel's initial argument appeals to nature over art, hardly a new topic but one that received a special emphasis between Shakespeare and Milton:

> We could well have allowed [Campion] his numbers,
> had he not disgraced our Ryme, which both Custome
> and Nature doth most powerfully defend: Custome
> that is before all Law, Nature that is above all Arte.
> Every language hath her proper number or measure
> fitted to use and delight, which Custome,
> intertaininge by the allowance of the Eare, doth
> indenize and make naturall.
>
> (2:359)

Daniel finds conventions of quantity artificial not only for English verse, but in general:

> Even the Latines, who professe not to be so licentious
> as the Greekes, shew us many times examples, but of
> strange crueltie in torturing and dismembering of
> words in the middest...that sometimes, unlesse the
> kind reader out of his owne good nature will stay
> them up by their measure, they will fall downe into
> flatte prose, and sometimes are no other indeede in
> their naturall sound.
>
> (2:364)

Art should serve and display nature, and not be treated "as if Art were ordained to afflict Nature, and that we could not goe but in fetters" (2:365).

The appeal to nature is joined by an appeal to reason, specifically as an answer to the authority of classical practice so admired by Ascham and other Humanists:

> Me thinkes we should not so soone yeeld our
> consents captive to the authoritie of Antiquitie,
> unlesse we saw more reason; all our understandings
> are not to be built by the square of *Greece* and *Italie*.
> We are the children of nature as well as they; we are
> not so placed out of the way of judgement but that
> the same Sunne of Discretion shineth uppon us.
>
> (2:366)

Daniel extends the questioning of authority that accompanied both Humanist textual scholarship and the Protestant movement to include the questioning of the great Humanist models themselves. Like Francis Bacon's "Booke of Gods workes" and "Booke of Gods word," Daniel's "great booke of the world" and "the all-overspreading grace of heaven" replace or at least become the test for classical authority. Induction, except in religious matters, is to replace deduction as the primary epistemology.[15]

Another anticipation of Bacon and of Ben Jonson is Daniel's insistence on the primacy of matter over manner. Although Thomas Elyot, Ascham, and the other Humanists had insisted upon the importance of matter, they cited it as inexorably bound up with manner. Thus, for example, Elyot's rhapsody in his 1531 *Boke Named the Governor:*

> Lorde God, what incomparable swetnesse of wordes
> and mater shall a student finde in the saide warkes
> of Plato & Cicero: wherein is joyned gravitie with

dilectation: excellent wysedome with divine
eloquence: absolute vertue with pleasure incredible.

(Bk. I, ch. xi; Fv)

Or Ascham's admonition in *The Scholemaster* (1570):

Ye know not, what hurt ye do to learning, that care
not for wordes, but for matter, and so make a
devorse betwixt the tong and the hart.

(1:6)

Daniel, like Bacon after him, tends to make just such a
"devorse":

When we heare Musicke, we must be in our eares in
the utter-roome of sense, but when we intertaine
judgement, we retire into the cabinet and innermost
withdrawing chamber of the soule. . . . The most
judiciall and worthy spirites of this land are not so
delicate, or will owe so much to their eare, as to rest
uppon the outside of wordes, and be intertained with
sound; seeing that both Number, Measure, and
Ryme is but as the ground or seate, whereupon is
raised the work that commends it.

(2:381)

Similarly, Bacon is largely referring to the sounds of words
when he announces the "first distemper of learning" to be "when
men studie words, and not matter . . . for wordes are but the
Images of matter, and except they have life of reason and invention: to fall in love with them, is all one, as to fall in love with a
picture."[16] Ironically, Jonson may have been referring to Daniel

himself when in his 1619 "Conversations" with William Drummond of Hawthornden he denigrates those poets "that have no composition at all; but a kind of tuneing, and riming fall, in what they write. It runs and slides, and only makes a sound."[17]

Daniel's theory was mostly ahead of his practice. His poetry is conservatively Spenserian in its use of metaphor and its unquestioning acceptance of Petrarchan techniques and conventions, as in the sonnet sequence *Delia* (1592). Nothing, for example, could be more accepting of the virtue inherent in loving a cruel fair than sonnet 6:

> Faire is my Love, and cruell as she's faire;
> Her brow-shades frownes, although her eyes are sunny;
> Her smiles are lightning, though her pride dispaire;
> And her disdaines are Gall: her favours Hunny.
> A modest Maide, deckt with a blush of honor,
> Whose feete doe tread greene paths of youth and love,
> The wonder of all eyes that looke upon her:
> Sacred on earth, design'd a Saint above.
> Chastitie and Beautie, which were deadly foes,
> Live reconciled friends within her brow:
> And had she pitty to conjoyne with those,
> Then who had heard the plaints I utter now.
> O had she not beene faire, and thus unkinde,
> My Muse had slept, and none had knowne my minde.

The premise is completely artificial; the professional poet delights to have an occasion to write poetry. Yet it is a charming poem – ingenuous in its enjoyment of art, smooth, balanced, and pleasant to read. Daniel is equally conservative in his historical poetry and its reliance on the *Mirror* tradition.[18] But a poem like "Musophilus" (1603), with its forward-looking vision of fame in new worlds centuries thereafter, and its praise of a contemplative life, suggests the reasoning of Jonson as well as the calm reflection and Arcadian pleasures of Spenser. Of all his poetry, Daniel's "Musophilus" most nearly corresponds to his *Defense of Ryme*, which not only codified the practice of Elizabethan poets,

205

including Ralegh and even Campion, but anticipates the emphasis on nature, reason, and induction that was to characterize the intellectual atmosphere of Jacobean England. With Daniel's treatise, there is finally a theoretical paradigm for English versification that was to last at least until the twentieth century. Although the terminology is not precisely the same, Daniel in effect establishes a distinction between (in modern terms) meter and rhythm, in which meter is syllabic number with careful accentuation, and rhythm is a function of the various levels and patterns of stress-accent available to the poet.

Campion contributed to the increasing richness of English accentual-syllabic rhyme by his effective attention to intralinear assonances and consonances. Daniel, in theory as well as practice, recognized the importance of patterning various levels of stress into the acentuation of the line. A poet such as Ralegh reflects these developments, and in his own particular attention to mid-line pauses contributes to yet another way in which the secure but apparently rigid new English meters could be made flexible and various. These elements are developed further, within the characteristic voices of the specific poets, by the great versifiers of the earlier seventeenth century, from Jonson to Herbert.

NOTES

1. Ralegh was the middle, and the lowest born, of Elizabeth's three principal favorites (Sidney's uncle, Robert Dudley, whom Elizabeth made Earl of Leicester, was the first, and Robert Devereux, Earl of Essex in his own right, was the last). There were others (such as Christopher Hatton) who also felt free to address the Queen in a somewhat more personal vein than the conventional adulation of such professional poets as Spenser and Jonson (as in *The Faerie Queene* or *Cynthia's Revels*). Ralegh borrowed his original motto, *Tam Marti Quam Mercurio*, from Gascoigne after the latter's death, but not long thereafter was permitted the special acknowledgment of the queen's affection in his use of *amore et virtute* as his motto. See Walter Oakeshott, *The Queen and The Poet* (London: Faber and Faber, 1960), Philip Edwards, *Sir Walter Ralegh* (London: Longmans, 1953), and Pierre Lefranc, *Sir Walter Ralegh, Écrivain* (Quebec: Laval, 1968).

2. Agnes M. C. Latham analyzes the evidence and many of the problems in notes to her edition of *Poems of Sir Walter Ralegh* (London:

Routledge and Kegan Paul, 1951), 95-162. For a slightly different view of some of the same issues, see Lefranc, 75-98.

3. Texts: *Poems of Sir Walter Ralegh*, ed. Latham. I have checked the commendatory poems against their first printings, and the others against various manuscript versions in the Huntington Library and the British Library.

4. The second commendation, fourteen lines of poulters measure couplets, appears a deliberate attempt to acknowledge the ascendency of Spenser's complex pentameters over the older popular verse, but is otherwise of little formal interest.

5. This is Latham's assumption, supported by manuscript evidence and further argued by Michael Rudnick, *The Poems of Sir Walter Ralegh: An Edition* (unpublished Ph.D. diss., Univ. of Chicago, 1970), 29.

6. A strong tradition says that Ralegh added a final couplet to the last stanza of this poem shortly before his death:

> From which earth, and grave, and dust,
> The Lord shall raise me up, I trust.

For the evidence that this tradition may well be true, see Rudnick, 49-52.

7. In part because the strong tradition that ascribes this poem to Ralegh begins after his death, and in part because some critics find it alien to their understanding of either his personal or poetic styles, the authenticity of this poem has recently been challenged. For a summary and response see Susanne Woods, "'The Passionate Mans Pilgrimage': Ralegh is Still in the Running," *Modern Language Studies*, 8(1978):12-29. Whether or not Ralegh wrote this poem (it would probably have been after his 1603 condemnation for treason), it is a good example of subtle variation of line lengths and rhythms in the earlier seventeenth century. I have deliberately deleted the comma Latham places in 1.18.

8. John Hollander argues for a late-developing verbal lyricism in "The Poem in the Ear," *Vision and Resonance* (New York: Oxford Univ. Press, 1975).

9. *The Phoenix Nest, 1593*, ed. Hyder Rollins (Cambridge, Mass.: Harvard Univ. Press, 1931), xvi-xvii. Texts are from this edition.

10. *England's Helicon*, ed. Hugh MacDonald (Cambridge, Mass.: Harvard Univ. Press, 1950), xx. Texts are from this edition.

11. They are not exclusive in complexity, however. Among the more adventuresome is a poem, also printed in *England's Helicon*, beginning "Sweete Violets (Loves paradice) that spred." It consists of two stanzas formed 5ab3C6d3e6ed3C5ba5fgfg, plus a concluding pentameter couplet.

12. Texts are from *The Works of Thomas Campion*, ed. Walter R. Davis (New York: Norton, 1967).

13. See *Elizabethan Critical Essays*, ed. G. Gregory Smith, 2 vols. (Oxford: Oxford Univ. Press, 1904), 1:xlix; E. W. Tayler, *Literary Criticism of Seventeenth Century England* (New York: Knopf, 1967), 47; Derek Attridge, *Well-Weighed Syllables: Elizabethan Verse in Classical Metres* (Cambridge: Cambridge Univ. Press), 234.

14. It was first published in the fall of 1603 along with Daniel's "Panegyrick" to King James; the treatise was an equally important offering, since the King had intellectual interests and had himself written a solid treatise on versification.

15. *The Twoo Bookes of Sir Francis Bacon, of the proficiencie and advancement of Learning, divine and humane* (London, 1605), was a principle influence in that shift.

16. *Advancement of Learning*, Bk. I, 18v-19 (E3v-E4).

17. *Ben Jonson*, ed. C. H. Herford and Percy and Evelyn Simpson, 11 vols. (Oxford: Oxford Univ. Press, 1925-52), 8:585.

18. *The Civil Wars* (first published 1595) is in a mostly end-stopped ottava rima.

Chapter Seven

The Aesthetic Achievement of Jonson and Herrick

The study of [poesy] . . . offers to mankinde a certaine rule, and Patterne of living well, and happily; disposing to us all Civill offices of Society.

Jonson, *Timber: or Discoveries*

Ben Jonson (1572-1637) was the most prominent and immediately influential of the Jacobean poets. His career as a poet and playwright is well documented not only by such usual sources as the Stationers' Register but also by Jonson's own effort to participate in the classical fame he endeavored to impart to his patrons and friends. No poet had previously dared publish his own *Workes*, as Jonson did in an impressive 1616 folio edition, or so conspicuously planted himself in a public epideictic poem, as in the Pindaric ode "To the immortall memorie and friendship of that noble paire, Sir Lucius Cary, and Sir H. Morison." In a dramatic move from "counter-turne" to "stand," Jonson describes the late Henry Morison as having "leap'd the present age," to live[1]

with memorie; and *Ben*

The Stand

Jonson, who sung this of him, e're he went Himselfe to rest.

209

Natural Emphasis

Jonson's life and personality are also reflected in the works of his contemporaries and especially his "sons," poets who learned from him, socialized with him, and were willing both to praise and admonish an aging laureate.[2] Among the poets claiming kinship were Thomas Carew, Sir John Suckling, Richard Lovelace, and Robert Herrick (1591-1674). Herrick's life touched less directly on the cavalier experience than did some of the others' (though Herrick's royalist sympathies lost him his country living between 1647 and 1660), but in topic and approach he may be taken as reasonably typical of the Sons of Ben. He may also be the best, at least in terms of his ability to integrate Jonson's poetics of naturalness and restraint into his own elegant and deceptively simple verse. Although Herrick's pastoral lyricism (with an occasional Rabelaisian touch) may well have been out of favor by the time his collected poetry appeared in 1648 (*Hesperides* combined with his *Noble Numbers*), his versification remains a forward-looking product of Jonson's important influence. Together Jonson and Herrick show both the impetus behind a plain style best expressed in couplets and its projection toward the couplet essays, epistles, and satires that were to characterize the ages of Dryden and Pope.

Jonson was both a product and transformer of his literary age. His association with Sir Walter Ralegh is but one example of active involvement in the literary and intellectual worlds of his time, which included the rhyme controversy and the new science popularized by Sir Francis Bacon.[3] Jonson's theory of versemaking unsurprisingly reflects the Jacobean context in which he flourished. As a classicist in the Senecan and neo-Stoic traditions of the seventeenth century (rather than the Ciceronian and neo-Platonic traditions of the sixteenth century) Jonson was an advocate for clarity and restraint, and for language and form which serve meaning and lucidly convey the author's voice. His statements about versification reflect that advocacy and suggest a theoretical basis for Jonson's own practice, itself a trim and masterful version of late Elizabethan rhythmic variety.

The "Conversations" with William Drummond of Hawthornden (1619) begin with a record of Jonson's reaction to both

Campion and Daniel and his praise of the couplet (which Daniel had condemned):

> Jonson said that he had ane intention to perfect ane
> Epick Poeme intitled Heroologia, of the worthies of
> his Country, rowsed by fame, and was to dedicate it
> to his Country, it is all in Couplets, for he detesteth
> all other Rimes, said he had written a Discourse of
> Poesie both against Campion and Daniel especially
> this last, where he proves couplets to be the bravest
> sort of verses, especially when they are broken, like
> hexameters and that crosse Rimes and Stanzaes
> (becaus the purpose would lead him beyond 8 lines to
> conclude) were all forced.
>
> (Herford and Simpson, 1:132)

Despite the intemperate tone, which the humorless Drummond slavishly conveys, Jonson's standards for versification are clear: verse should serve meaning, and line movement is most elegant when it allows for internal pauses. Daniel had objected to couplets because they were used in "long and continued Poemes" where they become "verie tyresome and unpleasing, by reason that still, me thinks, they run on with a sound of one nature, and a kind of certaintie which stuffs the delight rather than intertaines it" (Smith, 2:382). He preferred stanzas of "alternate or crosse Ryme" which he believed contributed to a more subtle and complex musicality than is available in couplets or blank verse; Daniel was of course arguing for the charm of the feature of rime, as well as for a whole native system of versification. Jonson, however, would not have his "purpose" confined by stanzaic units, presumably such as the *ottava rima* stanza common to both narrative and epigrammatic poetry. He implies that strophic constructions take on a life of their own, forcing the poet to depart from his meaning in order to serve the demands of the verse form. Verse should instead be used to formulate and

211

clarify subject matter. Despite his generally forward-looking approach described in the last chapter, Daniel's focus on the sounds of verse might be taken as itself an example of Bacon's first "distemper of learning," when men "studie words, and not matter."[4] Jonson's own emphasis on "matter" is everywhere evident, as in Drummond's report that Jonson always wrote his poetry "first in prose, for so his master Cambden had learned him" (Herford and Simpson, 1:143). Jonson considered Daniel himself "no poet."

Though Jonson rejects surface and display for their own sakes, he is not altogether rejecting the new euphonies of which English verse was capable. He found deliberately rough verse a potential impediment to the clarity he advocated. Although he considered John Donne "the first poet in the World in some things," he also claimed that Donne "for not keeping of accent deserved hanging," and added "that Done himself for not being understood would perish" (Herford and Simpson, 1:135, 133, and 138).

The equation of artistic elegance with clarity is apparent not only in his comments to Drummond about Donne, but also throughout *Timber, or Discoveries*, a collection of notes and meditations on his reading. In a paraphrase of the sixteenth-century Spanish Humanist, Juan Luis Vives, for example, Jonson follows the Horatian principle that delight is an aid to knowledge, smoothness to clarity:

> A man should so deliver himself to the nature of the
> subject, whereof he speakes, that his hearer may take
> knowledge of his discipline with some delight: and so
> apparell faire, and good matter, that the studious of
> elegancy be not defrauded; redeeme Arts from their
> rough, and braky seates, where they lay hid, and
> overgrowne with thornes, to a pure, open, and flowry
> light: where they may take the eye, and be taken by
> the hand.

> (Herford and Simpson, 8:566-67)

He nonetheless reserves the bulk of his concern for excesses of ostentation rather than excesses of elegance. In paraphrasing Quintillian's catalogue of the faults of "wits," for example, Jonson adds a few of his own. There are "wits" who are to be chided because they "labour onely to ostentation; and are ever more busie about the colours, and surface of a worke, then in the matter, and foundation: For that is hid, the other is seene" (Herford and Simpson, 8:585). Like Bacon, who insisted that all learning be applied "to use, and not to ostentation," Jonson continually objects to mere show. His insistence on matter over manner explains the terms of Jonson's feud with his onetime friend and colleague of the masque, Inigo Jones:

> O Showes! Showes! Mighty Showes!
> The Eloquence of Masques! What need of prose,
> Or verse, or sense, t'expresse Immortall you?
>
> ("An Expostulation against Inigo Jones,"
> (ll. 39-41).

With Jonson's emphasis on substance, it at first appears difficult to account for his strong and continuing interest in versification, apparently the most superficial of the arts of manner. The "Conversations" are full of reference to metrical topics, and many of the comments in *Timber* are concerned with poetic form. The resolution of this apparent contradiction is suggested by Bacon, whose ideas Jonson so often admired and shared.

For Bacon as for Sidney, poetry is one of the three branches of human learning (the other two are history and philosophy), but it is the one of which he seems most suspicious. While history relates to man's memory and philosophy to his reason, "poesie" relates to the third part of human understanding, the imagination. Bacon defines poesie as

> a part of learning in measure of words for the most
> part restrained: but in all other points extreamely

213

> licensed: and doth truly refer to the Imagination:
> which beeing not tyed to the Laws of Matter; may at
> pleasure joyne that which Nature hath severed: &
> sever that which Nature hath joyned, and so make
> unlawfull Matches & divorses of things.[5]

Poetry may therefore be taken to refer either to verse or to fiction generally, to either an external manner of communication or to an essential mode of dealing with nature. Bacon goes on to make that double reference explicit. Poesie, he says

> is taken in two senses in respect of Wordes or Matter:
> in the first sense it is but a *Character* of stile, and
> belongeth to Arts of speeche. . . . In the later, it is
> (as hath beene saide) one of the principall Portions of
> learning: and is nothing else but FAINED
> HISTORY, which may be stiled as well in Prose as
> in Verse (Bk. II, 17v).

Sidney had insisted that verse was "but an ornament and no cause to Poetry: sith there have beene many most excellent Poets, that never versified, and nowe swarme many versifiers that neede never aunswere to the name of Poets" (Smith, 1:159-60). Jonson makes the same distinction in the "Conversations," telling Drummond that he "thought not Bartas a Poet but a Verser, because he wrote not Fiction" (Herford and Simpson, 1:133). He is even more explicit in *Timber*, noting that "hee is call'd a Poet, not hee which writeth in measure only; but that fayneth and formeth a fable, and writes things like the Truth." (Herford and Simpson, 8:635).

After a brief Humanist attempt to make matter and manner inseparable (as in the comments by Elyot and Ascham cited in chapter 6) we return to the familiar medieval distinction between the arts of first and second rhetoric, or what Bacon calls the "Arts of speeche" as opposed to the disposition of knowledge. But insofar as poesie is one of the "principall Portions of learning" it allows for the rejection and transformation of nature, something of which Bacon did not wholly approve. There is an important paradox here. Insofar as poetry refers to verse it is a mere *"Character* of stile," inhabiter of the world of manner, surface, and "ostentation" rather than "use." Yet when Bacon describes poetry as "a part of Learning in measure of words for the most part restrained," he is surely referring to poetry as verse, and order and restraint are undoubted values throughout *The Advancement.* When he adds that poetry is "in all other points extremely licensed" he is surely referring to its imaginative and fictional qualities. Although verse "belongeth to the Arts of Speeche," then, it provides formal regulation of the licenses of fantasy, and so deserves an attention and respect not conceded to other merely stylistic features of rhetoric.

Ben Jonson's theory and practice fit precisely into this Baconian context. Jonson sees versification as a restraining influence on the excesses of fantasy, and he is the first major advocate of verse forms that best accommodate the natural shapes of rational discourse over verse forms that merely convey sensuous musicality. Like Bacon, he emphasizes the natural and substantive over the fantastical and ostentatious. Meters and rhythms should derive from and convey natural speech, unlike the wrenched accents of Donne or the artificial classicism of Abraham Fraunce, who "in his English Hexameters was a foole" ("Conversations," Herford and Simpson, 1:133). Subject matter should dictate stylistics in all things, including versification. This doctrine of decorum explains Drummond's apparent confusion over Jonson's comment "that Verses stood by sense without either Colours or accent, which yett other tymes he denied" (Herford and Simpson, 1:143). It also accounts for Jonson's preference for couplets, which allow the shape of the idea to control the length of the poem.

Jonson preferred his couplets to be "broken," however, and his rich use of pauses to produce various and powerful line rhythms provides his major legacy for English verse practice. Gascoigne and Spenser both worked well with intralinear pauses, but both tended primarily to follow the Surreyan pattern of the

215

pause after the fourth syllable. Spenser's use of the half-line and the stanza allowed him to think in terms other than the line, yet he used enjambment fairly seldom.[6] Sidney used the pause well and mastered the handling of various stress levels across the line. The dramatists, including Jonson and Shakespeare, paid particular attention to a variety of phrasal patterns across an iambic base, while certain more rhetorical courtier poets, including Ralegh, showed a talent for intralinear phrasing. But Jonson is arguably the first complete master of various patterns of pause and enjambment in a wide variety of non-dramatic poetic genres.

Something of Jonson's attitude toward rigid cesural patterns may be gathered from his one poem specifically about versification, the delightful "Fit of Rime against Rime." For the sake of his "fit," Jonson assumes the usual Humanist position against rhyme as a barbaric invention whose end rime and simple-minded syllabic measure ignored the true weight and harmony of syllabic relationship:

> Wresting words, from their true calling;
> Propping Verse, for feare of falling
>   To the ground.
> Joynting Syllabes, drowning Letters,
> Fastning Vowells, as with fetters
>   They were bound!
>
>   (ll. 7-12)

Not only does this illustrate the probable confusion between simple syllabics and rough accentuation that Ascham and Harvey's comments suggested, it also offers an example of Jonson's own interpretation of what makes "Rime" into doggerel. An obvious feature of this section is the relentless pause after the third syllable of each octosyllabic line. In addition the poem's lines are tiresomely end-stopped; "Rime," here, is a strict syllabic system with jog-trot pauses underscored by the end rime. In the best Ascham tradition, Jonson wishes rhyme's inventer "joynts tormented," "Cramp'd for ever," and he concludes:

Still may Syllabes jarre with time
Stil may reason warre with rime,
>>>Resting never.

>>>(ll. 52-54)

Jonson suggests that rime or rhyme is too artificially confining for the natural movement of language. Not only must one accommodate strict syllabic measure and the sure return of like-sounding syllables, one is also apparently confined to phrasal patterns that either coincide with the line itself or follow regular and insistent patterns of cesural convention.

Though this is Jonson's only poem specifically about versification, concepts of "weight," "measure," and "proportion" abound in his poems, often with direct implications for verse.[7] His concern with verse technique is evident in his own skill at weighing syllabic effect, measuring the rhythm of his verse, and proportioning his phrasal rhythms within and across his metrical structures. Like Campion, Jonson often appears to think in terms of the musical analogy, but he avoids elaborate euphonies. He is the great poet of subtle aesthetic effects, keenly tied to vocal tone. Two of his most notable skills are his lineation (including mid-line pauses and run-on lines) and his success with rhythmic ambiguity and other rhythmic tensions.

Jonson had great respect for the formal possibilities of the poetic line. Inessential as verse may be to the fictional writing that is the essence of "poesie," when Jonson thinks of poetry he often thinks specifically in terms of verse. So in *Timber* he notes that "*A Poeme* is not alone any worke, or composition of the Poets in many, or few verses; but even one alone verse sometimes makes a perfect *Poeme*." (Herford and Simpson, 8:635). He goes on to give examples from Virgil, Martial and Lucretius. These examples have the precision of insight and epigrammatic force we might expect, but they are also effective rhythmic units, as this from Martial:

217

Natural Emphasis

Omnia, Castor, emis: sit fiet, ut omnia vendas.

(Liber 8, epig. 19)

Jonson also assumes a respect for the formal attributes of verse in his advocacy of the couplet, which could adapt itself to content without verses as such becoming superfluous. Both his appreciation of single-lined "poems" and his preference for couplets are also part of his emphasis on density and thought, which in turn makes him a superb epigrammaticist. Of the 133 poems in Jonson's *Epigrammes* all but seventeen are written exclusively in couplets, and, of the remaining, three are short poems that consist of a single riming tercet. Jonson's appreciation for Virgil and Martial and his preference for the couplet are also parts of a larger concern with the formalizing powers of lineation. He does not limit himself to the couplet; both *Forrest* and *Under-wood* contain considerable variety in stanzaic form and line length. His skill with a variety of formal structures is apparent in his song lyrics as well, many of which are as euphonious, rhythmical, and strophically interesting as Campion's.[8] In the songs, lineation is used for aural effect and to complement musical settings. In many of Jonson's classical imitations he shows equal attention to the importance of lineation. His "Epode" properly alternates pentameter and trimeter lines, as the classical model directs. His Cary-Morison ode follows Pindar not only in the tri-partite strophic structure of "turne," "counter-turne," and "stand" but in the heavy enjambment associated with Pindar as well.[9]

For the most part, however, Jonson's verse is in relatively simple couplet or strophic patterns, usually pentameter or tetrameter. His masterful lineation is not so much a function of stanzaic creativity, as it was for Spenser and Campion, as of his ability to vary rhythms within and across iambic lines. Jonson achieved a remarkable control of a line movement which conveys both tone and content with grace and force.

His translation of the popular Martial epigram (Book X, Epigram XLVII), which Surrey had also translated, shows Jonson's characteristic departure from the less sophisticated model of

218

Surreyan iambics. Surrey's version is in tetrameter quatrains, a simple and longstanding English verse form which Surrey informs with clear iambics and regular cesural patterning.[10] Jonson's poem is in his preferred iambic pentameter couplets, but a more important difference is in the position and length of the mid-line pause. Surrey's version starts with a fine balance of pauses: in the first line the pause occurs after the second syllable and in the second line it is placed before the penultimate syllable. For the rest of the poem, however, there is no variation in the placement of the cesura; it is either in the standard mid-line position or there is no break in a line at all. Jonson's version is obviously more complex:[11]

> The things that make the happier life, are these,
> Most pleasant Martial; Substance got with ease,
> Not labour'd for, but left thee by thy Sire;
> A Soyle, not barren; a continewall fire;
> Never at Law; seldome in office gown'd;
> A quiet mind; free powers; and body sound;
> A wise simplicity; freindes alike-stated;
> Thy table without art, and easy-rated;
> Thy might not dronken, but from cares layd wast;
> No sowre, or sollen bed-mate, yet a Chast;
> Sleepe, that will make the darkest howres swift-pac'd;
> Will to bee, what thou art; and nothing more:
> Nor feare thy latest day, nor wish therfore.

In some ways Jonson's version is a more accurate translation than Surrey's. Martial's poem, for example, begins:[12]

> Vitam quae faciunt beatiorem
> iucundissime Martialis, haec sunt.

Formally Jonson is even closer to Martial. Like the original, Jonson's poem has thirteen lines (Surrey's has sixteen), and Jonson imitates Martial's pacing, an attempt Surrey apparently did not make. Compare Jonson's lines 5-6 with Martial's:

219

> lis numquam, toga rara, mens quieta;
> vires ingenuae, salubre corpus.

Although he reverses Martial's pattern of pauses across these two lines, Jonson achieves the intralinear listing effect that Surrey does not have. Surrey's less strict imitation remains a very close translation, however, with a tone perhaps closer to the original than Jonson's. Surrey's simplicity seems better to accommodate the serene geniality of Martial than Jonson's slightly tortuous varying pause patterns.

In his original verses, however, Jonson's variable lineation works well. "On My First Daughter" derives a good deal of its impact from the use of phrasing within the lines, all of which are end-stopped except for line 5, where there is a slight enjambment:

> Here lyes to each her parents ruth,
> *Mary*, the daughtere of their youth:
> Yet, all heavens gifts, being heavens due,
> It makes the father, lesse, to rue.
> At sixe moneths end, shee parted hence
> With safetie of her innocence;
> Whose soule heavens Queene, (whose name she beares)
> In comfort of her mothers teares,
> Hath plac'd amongst her virgin-traine:
> Where, while that sever'd doth remaine,
> This grave partakes the fleshly birth.
> Which cover lightly, gentle earth.

The last three lines are particularly powerful, with the pauses after "where" in the tenth line and "lightly" in the last line framing the steady iambics of line 11.

The first of these last three lines also provides a good example of Jonson's rhythmic ambiguity. This I define as the potential for more than one metrical scansion, either of which may be considered acceptable. In most cases there will be an obvious reading which, whether or not it is preferred, allows for a reasonable alternative within the metrical foot at least, and sometimes, as in this case, across the whole line. While line 10 scans easily as iambic tetrameter,

```
     x    /  x  / x  /  x  /
Where, while that sever'd doth remaine
```

one can also read the first foot as an initial trochee, a scansion encouraged both by the pause after "where" and the contrastive stress on "that." The effect is to emphasize the contrast, putting severe strain on the iambic rhythms of the rest of the line. In modern terms, the line becomes "sprung," with an excess of accent to syllables. Again in modern terms, one could read this as a trimeter line consisting of two amphimachs and an iamb:

```
     /   x  /   / x  /   x   /
Where, while that I sever'd doth I remaine
```

The ambiguity resides not merely in the performer's choice, but in fundamental decisions about the meter itself. Whatever scansion one gives the line, the tension between "that" and the first syllable of "sever'd" supports the tone: as we are pulled from an accented "that" to the more lightly stressed "sev-" we feel the speaker's own tension on giving up his daughter, to the earth and to heaven, and the tension between the earthly and the heavenly in Christian grief.

Rhythmic ambiguity is a device Jonson uses commonly. The last line of his epigram "On Chev'rill," for example, seems to demand a contrastive stress on the third syllable that would produce a rare trochee at the second foot:

No cause, nor client fat, will Chev'rill leese,
   But as they come, on both sides he takes fees,

221

And pleaseth both. For while he melts his greace,

<pre>
 x   /   /   x   x   /   x   /   x   /
</pre>
For this: that winnes, for whom he holds his peace.

One could also read the second foot of the last line more conventionally as an iamb. The effect of this metrical question is to produce a rhythmic ambiguity that raises the emphasis on both words, "that" and "winnes," thereby heightening the epigram's deliberate irony. Similarly, in the epigram "On Death" the second foot of the first line may either be read as an iamb or as a trochee, with contrastive stress on "feares" to effect a parallel with "mournes":

<pre>
   / x /   x x   /   x / x /
</pre>
He that feares death, or mournes it, in the just,
Shewes of the resurrection little trust.

Rhythmic ambiguity is a form of rhythmic tension but it is different in kind from more usual sorts. There is no question about the *meter* in, say, line 12 of "To My Booke," although a phrasal break and an ascending accentuation at the end of the line is typical of Jonson's skill with rhythmic tension:

<pre>
                           x   / x   /
To catch the world's loose laughter, or vaine gaze
                           4   3   2   1
</pre>

There are particularly impressive examples of phrasing and various rhythmic tensions in "On My First Son":

Farewell, thou child of my right hand, and joy;
My sinne was too much hope of thee, lov'd boy,

Seven yeeres tho'wert lent to me, and I thee pay,
   Exacted by thy fate, on the just day.
O, could I loose all father, now. For why
   Will man lament the state he should envie?
To have so soone scap'd worlds, and fleshes rage,
   And, if no other miserie, yet age?
Rest in soft peace, and, ask'd, say here doth lye
   BEN. JONSON his best piece of *poetrie*.
For whose sake, hence-forth, all his vowes be such,
   As what he loves may never like too much.

This is Jonson at his characteristic best. The lines are slowed by an abundance of intralinear pauses, balanced (as in line 1) and varied (as in lines 2-6) within and across a line. His use of enjambment (lines 5-6 and 9-10) typically serves both his meaning and his rhetorical emphases. The line break at "For why / Will man lament the state he should envie?" focuses strikingly on the question and demonstrates the overwhelming effects of grief even as it preserves the coherence of an implied answer in a traditional Christian consolation. The extended line becomes, then, both a rhetorical yet a very real inquiry. Lines 9 and 10 provide a clearer example of phrasal ambiguity, in this case in service to a summarizing epitaph that opens up the implications of the poem. The younger Benjamin, literally "son of my right hand," becomes his father's best "piece of poetrie," like the work of the elder's right hand. The poem itself, therefore, takes on the identity of the one it seeks to commemorate as it becomes identified also with Jonson, the author of both. The conflation of father, son, and poem inform the meaning of the last line, where the word "like" refers simultaneously to the acts of feeling for ("liking"), fashioning according to ("likening"), and seeing one's self reflected in. As the poet warns himself to maintain the appropriate aesthetic distance from his creations, which he may fruitfully love only while avoiding indecorous pride, the tension between his affection and renunciation underscores metrically the portrayal of profound loss. Line 10 can be read as iambic with a climbing accentuation in the second and third feet:

```
  x    /      x  /  x   /   x  / x  /
BEN. JON I SON his I best piece I of po | etrie
     4     3      2      1
```

```
  x    /      x  /   /  x    x  / x  /
BEN. JON I SON his I best piece I of po | etrie
```

Or as an unmetrical four-stress line :

```
      /           /        /  /
BEN. JONSON his best piece of poetrie.
```

However it is read, this line holds a rhythmic as well as a semantic focus for the poem. Jonson would probably have considered line 10 a properly decasyllabic line with a deliberate improper wrenching of accent. This is a Jonsonian kind of mimetic rhythm, with the wrench toward the unmetrical mirroring the speaker's sorrow and painful recognition.

Jonson's appreciation for rhythmic phrasing leads him to write polymetrical verse, an important phase in the development of a clearly accentual-syllabic English lyric. Although neither Jonson nor his contemporaries apparently thought anapestic or other trisyllabic feet could freely substitute for iambs in "rhyme," it is clear that by Jonson's time certain lyric constructions could take meters that combined trisyllabic and disyllabic feet, as long as the lineation was consistently parallel in succeeding stanzas. In "Her Triumph," the fourth poem of *A Celebration of Charis in ten Lyrick Peeces*, Jonson mixes feet but (like Sidney and Pembroke before him) keeps the formula the same in all verses. The first stanza illustrates the complex pattern which is followed exactly by the other two stanzas:

```
x  x   /  x  x  /    x  x  /
```
See the cha | riot at hand | here of Love,

```
x  /  x  /  x  / x
```
Wherein | my La | dy rideth!

```
x    x   /   x x  /   x x  /
```
Each that drawes | is a Swan, | or a Dove,

```
x   /   x  /    x  /  x
```
And well | the Carre | Love guideth.

```
x  x  /   x  /    x  / x
```
As she goes, | all hearts | doe duty

```
x  /  x  /  x
```
Unto | her beauty;

```
x  x /   x   x  /    x  x  /
```
And enam | our'd, doe wish, | so they might

```
x x  /   x  x /
```
But enjoy | such a sight,

```
x   x   /   x   x /   x  x  /
```
That they still | were to run | by her side

```
x  x    /    x  x   /   x x /  x   /
```
Thorough Swords, | thorough Seas, | whether she | would ride.

The analogous concluding phrases of stanzas two and three are

```
x  x  /   x   /
```
of the El | ements strife

```
x  x  /   x /
```
O so sweet | is she.

Natural Emphasis

The poem's meters and its energetic rhythms follow the anapestic title, "Her Triumph" (the accent was on the second syllable of "triumph" in this period). They evoke the trumpeting appropriate to so eager a blazon. Jonson appears aware of the lyrical range of anapestic rhythms and their potential for comedy. Post-Romantic readers familiar with the elegance and often high seriousness of Shelley's anapestic lyrics may not expect Jonson's subtle humor. The musicality of "Her Triumph" has long been recognized, but its underlying ambivalence about the Lady's virtue has tended to elude anthologists, who continue to reprint it separate from the comic context of the whole work. The poem follows the second of the sequence, "What hee suffered." In that poem, while the Lady repents of the Speaker's enamourment, he suffers the pains proper to his situation as a middle-aged lover, prefacing "Her Triumph" with the headless iambic tetrameter lines common to all but two of the sequence's ten lyrics:

> Looser-like, now, all my wreake
> Is, that I have leave to speake,
> And in either Prose, or Song,
> To revenge me with my Tongue,
> Which how Dexterously I doe,
> Heare and make example too.

> (ll. 21-26)

Jonson's anapestic constructions, like his headless tetrameter, provide a vehicle for complex tones which might be labeled serious humor: the speaker both reveals feeling and puts it into perspective at the same time. As in *Charis,* the speaker of "My Picture left in Scotland" is an older man of some "weight" whose "subtile feet" must serve to entice where a fair face is absent:

> I now thinke, Love is rather deafe, then blind,
> For else it could not be,
> That she,

Whom I adore so much, should so slight me,
And cast my love behind:

```
x   /    x /    x   x /    x x    /
```
I'm sure | my lan | guage to her, | was as sweet,
    And every close did meet
In sentence, of as subtile feet,
    As hath the youngest Hee,
That sits in shadow of *Apollo's* tree

Oh, but my conscious feares.
    That file my thoughtes betweene,
Tell me that she hath seene
    My hundred of gray haires
    Told seven and fortie years,
Read so much wast, as she cannot imbrace
    My mountaine belly, and my rockie face,
And all these through her eyes, have stopt her eares.

The partly anapestic line 6 is simply one feature of a strophic complexity that both illustrates and lightens the speaker's complaint.

Another feature of Jonson's verse is his ability to resolve variety of lineation and intralinear complexity with lines so regular that they have the effect of surprise. This shows that English versification had developed two full steps from the inception of a clear accentual-syllabic model. The first step was the development of techniques that would vary the regular rhythms directed by the meter. The second step was to use those devices of variety in such subtle ways that the reader scarcely notices how far the lines have departed from a congruence between meter and language rhythms, so that the reimposition of congruence comes as surprise, reordering, or formal closure. Jonson's epigram "On Lucy, Countess of Bedford" (LXXVI), begins with regular iambic rhythms that correspond with the iambic meter:

```
    x   / x    / x  / x   / x  /
```
This morning, timely rapt with holy fire

227

Natural Emphasis

In the next five lines there are only slight variations in this steady regularity, then in lines 7 and 8 the tension becomes more daring:

```
x   /    x  /  x     /   x  /  x  /
I meant the day-starre should not brighter rise
     1    4      3        2    1
```

```
 x  /   x  /  x     /  x  /x   /
Nor lend like influence from his lucent seat.
 4  3   2  1
```

Onely a learned, and a manly soule
   I purpos'd her; that should, with even powers,
The rock, the spindle, and the sheers controule
   Of destinie, and spin her owne free houres.
Such when I meant to faine, and wish'd to see,
My *Muse* bad, *Bedford* write, and that was she.

A somewhat different example occurs in the fifth section of *Charis*, written in tetrameter. "His discourse with Cupid," begins:

Noblest *Charis*, you that are
Both my fortune, and my Starre!
And do governe more my blood
Than the various Moone the flood!
Heare, what late Discourse of you,
Love, and I have had; and true.

The heavy regularity, the sure return of rime, and even the venerable tradition of tetrameter couplets itself, all contribute to the stiff, old-fashioned, and apparently simple-minded posture of the speaker. As he sets out to praise his Charis, the steadiness of the rhythms dominates the movement of the poem. Again the movement is so subtly varied at first that we hardly notice how thoroughly the original regularity has been abandoned. At line 43 the poem moves toward its close with a series of run-on lines containing substantial rhythmic tension. The concluding lines return to regular tetrameter rhythms, but with the third accent less heavily stressed than the other three. The resulting formal grace reminds the reader that although the speaker and his feelings are in some ways laughable, they are also true. The poem offers insight into the pathos of the human condition as well as its folly:

> But alas, thou seest the least
> Of her good, who is the best
> Of her Sex; but could'st thou *Love*,
> Call to mind the formes, that strove
> For the Apple, and those three
> Make in one, the same were shee.
> For this Beauty yet doth hide,
> Something more than thou hast spi'd.
> Outward Grace weake love beguiles:
> Shee is *Venus*, when she smiles,
> But shee's *Juno*, when she walkes,
> And *Minerva*, when she talkes.

Jonson had great range as a versifier. From his lyric constructions (whether for masque, play, or occasional poems) to various tetrameter poems (compare, for example, the ryhthmic differences between "On my first Daughter" to many of the lines from *Charis*, including the immortal "Far I was from being stupid / For I went and called on Cupid") to his wonderfully varied phrasing and lineation especially in pentameter poetry, Jonson's "plain style" obscures one of the subtlest verse geniuses of English letters. His range and his particularly skillful use of couplets make him not only the legitimate father of the "Sons of Ben" who modeled their versifying on his, but the equally legitimate grandfather of the Augustan versification of Dryden, Pope, and that other Johnson. Jonson had a profound effect on the shape and direction of English verse-making.

Robert Herrick is in some ways atypical of Jonson's "sons." Unlike Suckling, Lovelace, and Waller, whose Cavalier verse had some (and in Waller's case, much) direct influence on late seventeenth-century practice, Herrick wrote lyrics virtually outmoded in subject matter, if not altogether in style, by the time they appeared in 1648. As William Jay Smith has noted, Herrick is the poet of small things, of flowers and children and country occasions.[13] Yet he is a good poet in which to observe the success of the aesthetic impulse in English Renaissance verse. His subjects, however slight they may appear to be, are translucently presented. Herrick offers an elegance of phrasing over relatively simple meters that produces sometimes astonishingly sophisticated rhythms. Further, behind the apparently small topics are important comments about time and art that are fully characteristic of the Cavalier poets generally.[14] The most impressive single element of Herrick's versification is his use of couplets. Not only are the vast majority of his poems written in couplets (mostly pentameter or tetrameter), many of these are sophisticated lyrics with the same subtle euphonies we more commonly expect in what have been called "varied" lyrics, or lyrics of strophic construction.[15] Consider the tetrameter lyric "To Electra":

> More white than whitest Lillies far,
> Or snow, or whitest Swans you are:
> More white then are the whitest Creames,
> Or Moone-light tinselling the streames:
> More white then *Pearls*, or *Juno's* thigh;
> Or *Pelops* Arme of *Yvorie*.
> True, I confesse; such Whites as these
> May me delight, not fully please:
> Till, like *Ixion's* Cloud you be
> White, warme, and soft to lye with me.

This is a rich compendium of Petrarchan catalogue, Ovidian sensuality, and Catullan seduction, with its classicism underscored by restrained, end-stopped couplets. The severity of that classicism is tempered by a skilled Jonsonian use of mid-line pauses, culminating in the perfect balance of lines 7 and 8 followed in line 9 by a pause after the first syllable, then an enjambed run into the final line's series of sensuous attributes:

> True, I confesse; ǁ such Whites as these ǀ
> May me delight, ǀ not fully please: ǁ
> Till, ǀ like *Ixion's* cloud you be
> White, ǀ warme, ǀ and soft ǀ to lye with me.

The lyric richness is also a function of Herrick's euphonies, as in the Campionesque "Or Moone-light tinselling the streames," and of the visual imagery that so often accompanies it. Often Herrick's short couplet lyrics conflate lyric and epigram. Like the more usual epigram (which Herrick also wrote), such lyric poems are short, succinct, and make a point by a witty twist, usually at the end. Unlike the epigram, however, these lyrics are personal or descriptive in stance, as in "Cherry-pit":

> Julia and I did lately sit
> Playing for sport, at Cherry-pit;
> She threw; I cast; and having thrown,
> I got the Pit, and she the Stone.

Or "Zeal required in Love":

> I'le doe my best to win, when'ere I wooe:
> *That man loves not, who is not zealous too.*

Also epigrammatic insofar as it epitomizes its subject is "Upon Julia's Voice," about as mimetic a poem as Herrick wrote:

231

So smooth, so sweet, so silv'ry is thy voice,
As could they hear, the Damn'd would make no noise,
But listen to thee, (walking in thy chamber)
Melting melodious words, to Lutes of Amber.

The euphonies of consonance and assonance are immediately apparent. Less obvious is the characteristic subtlety of line rhythms. After three lines in which there is the conventional pause after the fourth syllable (with an extra pause after the second syllable in the first line), the four/six phrasing is reversed to produce a six/four phrasing in the last line. The "melodious" first section of that line is foregrounded while the shorter second section effects an elegant closure.

Herrick's perfect phrasing is crucial to the translucent ease apparent throughout his verse. His phrases are themselves pleasant rhythmic units, smoothly following the metrical direction. Interest and variety come from his handling of the phrase in relation to the line and from the relations between monosyllabic and polysyllabic words. He often alternates end-stopped with run-on lines, though never automatically. He similarly alternates monosyllabic with polysyllabic words. In "Art above Nature, to Julia," he refers to patterned variety of the very type he practices as "wild civility" (l. 14), a phrase that also provides the climax of his brilliant example of it, "Delight in Disorder":

A sweet disorder in the dresse
Kindles in cloathes a wantonnesse:
A Lawne about the shoulders thrown
Into a fine distraction:
An erring Lace, which here and there
Enthralls the Crimson Stomacher:
A Cuffe neglectfull, and thereby
Ribbands to flow confusedly:
A winning wave (deserving Note)
In the tempestuous petticote:
A carelesse shooe-strong, in whose tye
I see a wilde civility:
Doe more bewitch me, then when Art
Is too precise in every part.

The apparently simple and potentially confining tetrameter couplets are rendered "wilde" by the careful placement of run-on lines, varying phrasings, and juxtapositions of monosyllabic with polysyllabic words that are the essence of Herrick's rhythmic art.

Herrick's verse is in many ways the quintessence of aesthetic verse as I have defined it: it produces pleasing patterns that are not mimetic in any obvious sense, but serve meaning, in part by euphony and in part by drawing attention to the poem's tone through careful and various patternings across an evident meter. Unsurprisingly, Herrick's topics are the subjects of aesthetic philosophy: beauty, art, and time. Herrick, like Jonson, had a strong classical sense of fame and the triumph of art over time. Unlike Jonson, who associated his own fame with that of the people he praised, but like Shakespeare in the *Sonnets*, Herrick affirmed the power of poetry itself to overcome time.[16] The pursuit of a natural beauty in life and art is perhaps best summarized in "Corinna's going a Maying," where the last stanza provides a model for and challenge to *carpe diem* poetry from Marvell to Keats. One of his longer poems, it is composed of stanzas in which pentameter couplets frame tetrameter couplet quatrains. The art of the poem frames the natural Maytime world, giving the temporality of experience the timeless perspective of art. The conclusion makes these relationships explicit:

> Come, let us goe, while we are in our prime;
> And take the harmlesse follie of the time.
>> We shall grow old apace, and die
>> Before we know our liberty.
>> Our life is short; and our dayes run
>> As fast away as do's the Sunne:
> And as a vapour, or a drop of raine
> Once lost, can ne'er be found againe:
>> So when you or I are made
>> A fable, song, or fleeting shade;
>> All love, all liking, all delight
>> Lies drown'd with us in endlesse night.
> Then while time serves, and we are but decaying;
> Come, my *Corinna*, come, let's goe a Maying.

Natural Emphasis

Appropriate to the low style of a pastoral invitation, there are fewer polysyllabic words in this poem than is usual in Herrick, but the patterning of end-stopped to run-on lines is very precise. The artistry comes primarily from the phrasing and lineation and from the structure of the stanza itself, which is used variously throughout the poem with a skill reminiscent of Spenser. All these combine to produce a charming poem that handles major themes with such grace that we are deceived into thinking it a trifle. This is *sprezzatura* indeed, and a fair example of the English Renaissance high art of versification.

NOTES

1. All citations from Jonson's poems and from his prose commonplace book, *Timber: or, Discoveries*, are taken from *Ben Jonson*, ed. C. H. Herford and Percy and Evelyn Simpson, 11 vols. (Oxford: Clarendon Press, 1925-52). All Jonson references are to this edition and are cited in the text.

2. For an outline of the careers of several of the poetic "sons," see Kathryn McEuen, *Classical Influences on the Tribe of Ben* (Cedar Rapids: Torch Press, 1939); Jonson's followers in the drama are discussed by Joe Lee Davis, *The Sons of Ben* (Detroit: Wayne State Univ. Press, 1967). I will have nothing directly to say about Jonson as a dramatist, since his characteristic and innovative versifying is more readily apparent from the non-dramatic poetry. Jonas Barish has suggested that Jonson's greatest theatrical achievement is in fact his use of prose: *Ben Jonson and the Language of Prose Comedy* (Cambridge, Mass.: Harvard Univ. Press, 1960), 273-99.

3. Jonson not only provided "The Minde of the Front" for Ralegh's 1614 *History of the World*, he claimed to have written parts of the book itself. See his "Conversations with William Drummond of Hawthornden" (1619), in Herford and Simpson, 1:138. For Jonson's literary acquaintances and activities, see especially 1:48-88; Herford and Simpson suggest a mutual affection between Jonson and Bacon, 1:77. See Bacon's *Advancement*, Bk. I, 18v.

4. Even more strongly: "The excesse of Feasts, and apparell, are the notes of a sick State; and the wantonesse of language, of a sick mind" (8:592). Jonson was firm in his belief that language directly reflects the mind: "There cannot be one colour of the mind; an other of the wit" (8:593); "*Language* most shewes a man: speake that I may see thee. It springs out of the most retires, and inmost parts of us, and is the Image

234

of the Parent of it, the mind" (8:625). Wesley Trimpi, *Ben Jonson: A Study of the Plain Style* (Princeton: Princeton Univ. Press, 1961), provides the fullest consideration of Jonson's intellectual background and its application to his stylistic assumptions. I find Jonson much less "plain" than Trimpi does, but agree that Jonson uses formal control most often as an agent for clarity.

5. *Advancement*, Bk. II, 17v. All further references will be to this first edition, and will be given in the text.

6. Of the 495 lines in *Faerie Queene* I.i, for example, I count only thirty-one sufficiently enjambed to detract from the pause at the end of the line. Interestingly, enjambment tends to be mimetic of action and confusion in this canto; the only stanza with three enjambed lines is sixteen, where the dragon Error is disturbed from her den.

7. On "weight," see Jonson's translation of Horace, Bk. 2, ll. 378 and 456, and the Cary-Morison Ode, l. 50; "measure," see "To my chosen Friend . . . Thomas May," l. 7; "number," see "Proludium," l. 7. For other examples, see Steven L. Bates and Sidney D. Orr, *A Concordance to the Poems of Ben Jonson* (Athens, Ohio: Ohio Univ. Press, 1978).

8. Consider, for example, *Forrest* VII, "Follow a shaddow, it still flies you," and the uncollected lyric, "Slow, slow, fresh fount, keepe time with my salt teares" (Herford and Simpson, 8:93, 328).

9. Susanne Woods, "Ben Jonson's Cary-Morison Ode: Some Observations on Structure and Form," *Studies in English Literature*, 18(1978):57-74.

10. See chapter 3.

11. This poem was frequently translated in the early seventeenth century. Another notable version is one by Sir Henry Wotton, collected in *Reliquiae Wottonianae* (1564).

12. *Epigrams*, ed. Walter C. A. Ker (London: Heinemann, 1920) II, 188-90.

13. *Herrick*, ed. William Jay Smith (New York: Dell, 1962), 17.

14. The often high seriousness of Herrick's apparently slight lyrics has become increasingly evident from recent detailed studies of his work. See, for example, Roger B. Rollin, *Robert Herrick* (New York: Twayne, 1966); Robert H. Deming, *Ceremony and Art: Robert Herrick's Poetry* (The Hague: Mouton, 1974); and *Trust to Good Verses: Herrick Tercentenary Essays*, ed. Roger B. Rollin and J. Max Patrick (Pittsburgh: Univ. of Pittsburgh, 1978).

15. A. E. Elmore refers to the balanced couplet poems of Herrick's 1648 volume as "uniform" poems and notes that they comprise "about twelve hundred of the more than fourteen hundred poems" in the volume. "Herrick and the Poetry of Song" in Rollin and Patrick, 65-75. All Herrick texts are from *Herrick's Poetical Works*, ed. L. C. Martin (Oxford: Clarendon Press, 1956).

16. See for example "His Poetrie his Pillar," "Lyrick for Legacies," "To live merrily, and to trust to Good Verses," "Verses," "Poetry perpetuates the Poet," and the last poem in *Hesperides*, "The Pillar of Fame."

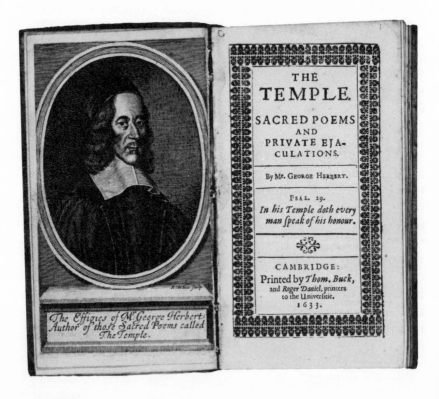

Chapter Eight

The Mimetic Achievement of
Shakespeare, Donne, and Herbert

There is in love a sweetness readie penn'd
Copie out onely that, and save expense.

Herbert, "Jordan[II]"

By the end of the sixteenth century English accentual-syllabic versification had proved itself a reliable and flexible tool for expressing a wide range of poetic genres and voices. Aristotelian imitation and harmony were not only basic to the instincts of the great English Renaissance poets, they became consciously honed skills. William Shakespeare (1564-1616), John Donne (1572-1631), and George Herbert (1593-1633) provide particularly brilliant examples of the variety and sophistication of a primarily mimetic versification traceable from the late Elizabethan to the early Caroline period, through drama and lyric. The formal richness of these three has been often and variously studied.[1] This chapter will confine itself to elements characteristic of their verse styles and pertinent to the development of English versification generally. Shakespeare, following Marlowe, developed for his drama an immensely flexible blank verse iambic pentameter which was to become for at least three hundred years the quintessential English heroic line, and established the rhythms succeeding generations have considered basic to the movement of English verse. Donne brought the speaking voice

237

convincingly into the lyric. Herbert reflected God's own abundance in his rich and varied verse constructions, offering a verse mimetic of the mind's contemplative processes in contrast to the presentational dramatic mimesis of Shakespeare and Donne.

Shakespeare's dramatic blank verse may be traced in a direct line back to Surrey's introduction of iambic pentameter blank verse to English. The first extant play in rimeless iambic pentameter is *Gorboduc*, presented in 1562, first at the Middle Temple and then at Elizabeth's court. The work was the combined effort of Thomas Sackville, whose greater fame lies in his subsequent contributions to *The Mirror for Magistrates*, and Thomas Norton. Norton had published a translation of Calvin's *Institutes* the year before (1561) and had there rendered quotations from Virgil in English pentameter blank verse. This suggests not only a reading of Surrey's *Aeneid*, but an appreciation of this verse as equivalent to the Latin high style. As with serious epic, so with serious drama; Norton and Sackville's choice of blank verse for *Gorboduc* has a clear and progressive logic.[2]

In the mid sixteenth century, however, verse considered appropriate to drama was as varied, one might say as confused, as English verse generally. Fifteenth-century miracle and morality plays, such as the Wakefield and Townley Cycles, relied on both neo-alliterative lines and on various rime constructions tagging more-or-less accentual lines. A tendency toward alliteration in dramatic verse persisted into Shakespeare's time, with his early plays often using alliteration for schematic reinforcement (as in *1 Henry VI*, "The fraud of England, not the force of France"). Tudor interludes relied on a variety of riming patterns, a tradition persisting well into the 1580s. From early in the century until late into Elizabethan times there are numerous plays in fourteeners, quatrains, riming couplets with occasional stanzaic constructions, and combinations of these.[3] The verse of plays that precede such Senecan experiments as *Gorboduc* was equally conservative. John Bale's *King Johan* (1538), for example, was written in the familiar Lydgatian pentameter, mostly in couplets but with occasional extended rime and interpolated rime royal stanzas.[4] The heritage of *Gorboduc* was nonetheless to take hold, first through Gascoigne's *Jocasta* (1566), which increased the range and flexibility of the blank verse line in drama, and most especially and powerfully through Christopher Marlowe's *Tamburlaine*. Probably written in late 1587, Marlowe's play begins by rejecting the confused and various versifying that had preceded it:

> From jygging vaines of ryming mother wits,
> And such conceites as clownage keepes in paye:
> We'l lead you to the stately tent of Warre,
> Where you shall heare the Scythian *Tamburlaine*,
> Threatning the world with high astounding termes,
> And scourging kingdomes with his conquering sword,
> View but his Picture in this tragicke glass,
> And then applaud his fortunes as you please.

"Marlowe's Mighty line," with its "perfect ease and authoritative sonority," was to have a profound impact on English drama.[5] Robert Greene and Thomas Kyd produced serious plays in the newly flexible meters almost immediately, and Shakespeare may have been inspired to write for the theatre shortly afterward.[6]

From Surrey to Norton and Sackville, from Norton and Sackville to Marlowe, the transmission of iambic pentameter blank verse as the most appropriate line for serious "overreaching," particularly in drama, became firmly established. Both the increasing skill of the line's early developers and its genuine appropriateness for serious verse in English helped to establish it above the contenders, particularly the ubiquitous fourteener. Marlowe's work suggested a greater freedom and heightened lyricism for this unrimed verse than either his predecessors or riming contemporaries had been able to provide.

For Shakespeare, as for Marlowe, blank verse originally suggested a heightened oratory for which the pentameter line was the principal unit. Shakespeare's earliest plays are dominated by relentlessly end-stopped verse. Gloucester's speech in

Natural Emphasis

I.i *1 Henry VI* offers an example of about as much enjambment
as one finds in the entire play:

> His sparkling eyes, replete with wrathful fire,
> More dazzled and drove back his enemies
> Than midday sun fierce bent against their faces.

(ll. 12-14)

Not only are the play's lines usually end-stopped, but intralinear
pauses are rare and usually confined to or at least accompanied
by the standard cesural pause after the first syllable. Thus
Gloucester to Winchester, I.iii.53-56:

> Winchester goose, I cry, "A rope! a rope!"
> Now beat them hence, why do you let them stay?
> Thee I'll chase hence, thou wolf in sheep's array.
> Out, tawny coats! Out, scarlet hypocrite!

The rigidity loosens up somewhat over the course of *2 Henry VI*
and *3 Henry VI*, but it is often a loosening in service to Shakespeare's expanded and expansive metaphors. In V.iv of *3 Henry
VI*, for example, Queen Margaret expatiates on the Lancastrian
situation at great length, developing a ship conceit to and perhaps beyond its logical extension. The rhythms are in service to
the delineation of metaphor, and, while not particularly mimetic
(except perhaps of Margaret's elaborate self-dramatizing), they
are more varied than is common in Shakespeare's very earliest
plays:

> Why, is not Oxford here another anchor?
> And Somerset another goodly mast?
> The friends of France our shrouds and tacklings?

240

And though unskillful, why not Ned and I
For once allow'd the skillful pilot's charge?

(ll. 16-20)

Richard III, while remaining highly schematic, shows substantial development in versification. The play begins with enjambment, of which there was some in *3 Henry VI*, but instead of the extended metaphor of that play we have the compressed "son/sun/king" metaphor which Richard uses as a point of departure for a "descant" on his own deformity:

Now is the winter of our discontent
Made glorious summer by this son of York.

(1.i.1-2)

The play's first encounter, between Richard and his brother, The Duke of Clarence, fully illustrates the transformation. The lines allow internal pauses, break naturally from one character to another, and the language manages to be characterizing and idiomatic over sustained pentameter. Shakespeare has learned how to direct his versification instead of being directed by it.

It is difficult to summarize Shakespeare's "characteristic" versification; it is in many ways as varied as his characters. One can summarize some obvious elements, foregrounded early in such verse *tours des forces* as *Romeo and Juliet* or *A Midsummer Night's Dream*. Noble characters speak in blank verse; low born characters speak in prose. When the nobility is lowered to prose or the low born raised to verse a moral or spiritual fall or rise is often assumed. Rimed verse, when sustained, is usually the language of love or fantasy; couplets are otherwise used for a variety of purposes, from speech and scene closure to postures of restraint or incantation.[8] In II.i of *All's Well That Ends Well* Helena persuades the King of France to submit to her healing ministrations, a persuasion symbolized by the varying concord of

241

the couplets spoken by the characters. At first the speakers rime only with themselves; then Helena insists on riming with the King; finally his capitulation is signaled by his riming with her:

> King. Make thy demand.
>
> Hel.   But will you make it even?
>
> King. Ay, by my sceptre and my hopes of heaven.
>
> (ll. 191-92)

Helena's concluding persuasion comes in a incantatory paean to the powers of Phoebus, god of healing and of course of the transforming poetry she speaks. It is metaphor and language unusually florid for Shakespeare's middle period and relatively fresh for one of the so-called "problem plays":

> King. Art thou so confident? Within what space
> Hop'st thou my cure?
>
> Hel.   The greatest grace lending grace,
> Ere twice the horses of the sun shall bring
> Their fiery torcher his diurnal ring,
> Ere twice in murk and occidental damp
> Moist Hesperus hath quench'd her sleepy lamp,
> Or four and twenty times the pilot's glass
> Hath told the thievish minutes how they pass,
> What is infirm from your sound parts shall fly,
> Health shall live free, and sickness freely die.
>
> (ll. 159-68)

E. K. Chambers has provided a series of "Metrical Tables" which offer a useful outline of Shakespeare's verse practices over the course of his career, even though Chambers' chronology is necessarily approximate and one might quarrel with individual readings, whether for textual or other reasons.[9] For the most part his analysis supports what most of us would assume instinctively: That rime is more common in early and middle than in later plays; that prose is most common to the comedies, peaking in the middle part of Shakespeare's career with *Merry Wives of Windsor* and *Much Ado About Nothing;* that prose is nonetheless a part of the vast majority of plays (only *Richard II* and *King John* are entirely in verse); and that Shakespeare becomes increasingly freer with his enjambment and intralinear pauses as his career progresses. One may compare the rigidity of the early histories, for example, with this enjambment in *The Tempest*, cited by G. L. Brook:[10]

> This ancient morsell: this Sir Prudence, who
> Should not upbraid our course:

> (II.i.286-87)

Beyond these broad and rather obvious elements of Shakespeare's use of versification are two more subtle in execution and more difficult to analyze: his use of verse as an aid to staging and thematic highlighting, and his use of verse as an aid to characterization. Both of these involve sophisticated mimetic skills, and it is here that Shakespeare's most impressive accomplishments as a versifier reside.

Richard Flatter has studied Shakespeare's plays as guides to their own performance, and although his reliance on the *First Folio* creates some problems, he provides ample evidence that Shakespeare had specific actions in mind when he put together his plays.[11] There are everywhere hints on staging and emphasis. One of the most interesting from a metrical point of view is what Flatter calls "metrical gaps": metrically incomplete lines within a clear metrical framework. Flatter catalogues a number of these, but misses two which are particularly characteristic. The first is the incomplete line that concludes *As You Like It*, I.ii, as Orlando, who has in the space of two scenes moved from

243

prose to verse to a single passionate couplet, concludes with a rhapsody two feet short of the pentameter norm:

> Thus must I from the smoke into the smother,
> From tyrant Duke unto a tyrant brother.
> But heavenly Rosalind!

The line suggests a two-beat pause as the seriously endangered youngest son of the late Sir Roland de Boys has his thoughts gripped by love. Only after an apparently irrelevant moment of distraction can Orlando flee from Duke Frederick's court, and from the stage.

The second example is more complex. In *Hamlet*, III.iii, the Prince of Denmark decides not to kill Claudius, who is apparently in prayer. Any theory which posits that Hamlet delays his revenge must surely accommodate his lack of opportunity up until that point. The king is routinely surrounded by his retainers, and one can argue that the well-educated (if imaginative) Hamlet has not had proof of Claudius's guilt sufficient to force him to what will appear as regicide. But after "the mouse trap" Claudius's guilt is unquestionable, at least to Hamlet who has heard from the Ghost the details of his uncle's murderous act, and he has the rare good fortune of finding Claudius alone. In Hamlet's soliloquy the claims of the pagan revenge code come up against assumptions about Christian grace. Whether Claudius is truly praying and in a state of grace is something known only to Claudius and God; in assuming that grace, Hamlet puts himself in the place of God. The revenge code requires death of the body. It does not insist upon the sure death of the soul. By assuming what only God knows, Hamlet loses his opportunity for revenge, becomes more hasty and arrogant in his behavior, and so murders Polonious and terrifies Gertrude. One difficulty in understanding *Hamlet* is that all this perfectly recognizable tragic material occurs primarily in the way Shakespeare handles pauses and metrical gaps:

244

Now might I do it pat, now 'a is a-praying;
And now I'll do't – and so 'a goes to heaven,
And so I am reveng'd. That would be scann'd:
A villain kills my father, and for that
I, his sole son, do this same villain send
To heaven.
Why, this is hire and salary, not revenge.
'A took my father grossly, full of bread,
With all his crimes broad blown, as flush as May,
And how his audit stands who know save heaven?
But in our circumstance and course of thought
'Tis heavy with him. And am I then revenged,
To take him in the purging of his soul,
When he is fit and season'd for his passage?
No!
Up, sword, and know thou a more horrid hent:
When he is drunk asleep or in a rage,
Or in th'incestious pleasure of his bed,
At game a-swearing, or about some act
That has no relish of salvation in't –
Then trip him, that his heels may kick at heaven,
And that his soul may be as damn'd and black
As hell, whereto it goes. My mother stays,
This physic but prolongs thy sickly days.

(ll. 73-96)

The metrical gaps are used for two different purposes in this passage. The first instance promotes a four-foot pause that suggests deeply interior thought unsuitable even for soliloquy. It directs four beats of silence. The second, the single "No," does not appear to direct a long pause, but does suggest very strong emphasis. This emphatic negation is the turning point of the play. In assuming he knows how Claudius's "audit stands" Hamlet has chosen to put himself in place of heaven. In choosing alliance with hell, itself the ultimate negation, he has committed not only classical hubris but Christian pride. The tragic hero has made his choice, and his mistake. The scene concludes with chilling irony as Claudius announces his absence from grace:

Natural Emphasis

> My words fly up, my thoughts remain below:
> Words without thoughts never to heaven go.

In instances such as these, Shakespeare's versification is mimetic of action. In uncountable instances it is mimetic of character, and of changes in character. Othello's fall into rougher verse and finally into prose is one obvious and touching example. Lear's smooth iambics similarly move to increased enjambment and broken phrasing as he becomes aware of his daughters' perfidy, and finally, as Lear begins to go mad, his verse tumbles into some of the most heavily accented and cacophonous in all of Shakespeare:

> Blow, winds, and crack your cheeks! rage, blow!
> You cataracts and hurricanoes, spout
> Till you have drenched our steeples, drowned the cocks!
> You sulph'rous and thought-executing fires,
> Vaunt-couriers of oak-cleaving thunderbolts,
> Singe my white head! And thou, all-shaking thunder,
> Strike flat the thick rotundity o'th'world,
> Crack Nature's moulds, all germains spill at once,
> That makes ungrateful man!
>
> (III.ii.1-9)

The ultimate madness is spoken in prose. In contrast, Lear's recovery is presented in gentle monosyllabic blank verse:

> Be your tears wet? Yes, faith. I pray weep not.
> If you have poison for me, I will drink it.
> I know you do not love me, for your sisters
> Have (as I do remember) done me wrong:
> You have some cause, they have not.
>
> (IV.vii.71-75)

Finally, when Lear accepts Cordelia's death, it evokes that amazing line of five trochees, emphasizing not only the terrible negation of death but also the complete reversal of Lear's fortunes:

> Why should a dog, a horse, a rat, have life,
> And thou no breath at all? Thou'lt come no more,
> Never, never, never, never, never.

> (V.iii.307-09)

The Tempest, one of Shakespeare's last plays, displays among its many other rhythmic felicities a delightful compendium of differing voices. From the lumpish monosyllabic and heavily accentuated verse of Caliban to the smooth innocence of Miranda and shadings in between, Shakespeare's rhythms reflect character. Thus for example Shakespeare differentiates between the rhythms of Miranda's impassioned concern, tending toward periodic sentences, and her father's authoritative short sentences, both cast over the heavily enjambed iambic pentameter common to Shakespeare's later plays:

> *Mir.* If by your art, my dearest father, you have
> Put the wild waters in this roar, allay them.
> The sky it seems would pour down stinking pitch
> But that the sea, mounting to th'welkin's cheek
> Dashes the fire out. O! I have suffered
> With those I saw suffer! a brave vessel
> (Who had, no doubt, some noble creature in her)
> Dash'd all to pieces! O, the cry did knock
> Against my very heart! Poor souls, they perished.
> Had I been any god of power, I would
> Have sunk the sea within the earth or ere
> It should the good ship so have swallow'd, and
> The fraughting souls within her.

> *Pros.*   Be collected.
> No more amazement. Tell your piteous heart
> There's no harm done.

247

Mir.	O, woe the day!

Pros.	No harm.

(I.ii.1-15)

Or, in a different example, in II.i the balanced good sense of
Gonzalo, the "honest old councillor," appears in the balance of
his lines. Although the pattern of heavy enjambment continues,
most of the intralinear pauses fall at or about the middle of the
line, giving an impression of steadiness and regularity:

> Beseech you, sir, be merry. You have cause
> (So have we all) of joy; for our escape
> Is much beyond our loss. Our hint of woe
> Is common. Every day some sailor's wife,
> The masters of some merchant, and the merchant,
> Have just our theme of woe; but for the miracle,
> (I mean our preservation), few in millions
> Can speak like us. Then wisely, good sir, weigh
> Our sorrow with our comfort.

(II.i.1-9)

In this same scene, the cynical Sebastian and Antonio
respond to Gonzalo's and Adrian's observations of the island's
loveliness with curt prose phrases, as in lines 46-56:

Adrian. The air breathes upon us here most sweetly.

Sebastian. As if it had lungs, and rotten ones.

Antonio. Or, as 'twere perfumed by a fen.

Gonzalo. Here is everything advantageous to life.

Ant. True, save means to live.

Gonz. How lush and lusty the grass looks! How green!

248

Ant. The ground indeed is tawny.

Seb. With an eye of green in't.

Ant. He misses not much.

Seb. No; he doth but mistake the truth totally.

While Gonzalo and Adrian speak in easy iambic movements, enjoying the wonder they perceive in their surroundings, the villainy of Antonio and Sebastian becomes evident not only in their cynicism and their apparent inability to see the beauties the others see, but also in their relentlessly prosaic speech rhythms. There is no heightening either in their language or the rhythms in which they speak, a subtle but definite and effective contrast with the language of the other characters in the scene. Shakespeare's mastery of mimetic rhythms is evident not only in the sharp contrasts between Prospero and Caliban or Stephano and Ferdinand (for example), nor in the perfect contrastive uses of prose and poetry throughout the play, but even in a scene such as this, where prose and poetry mix and appear to merge so that only the most prosaic of speakers, Antonio and Sebastian, stand out. It is no wonder that for all his immeasurable influence, and for all the attention focused on almost every aspect of Shakespeare's work, the power of his deceptively regular versification has remained elusive. Shakespeare was no innovator, but he was a master of the new mimetic versification and all that it implied for dramatic language.

John Donne (1572-1631) was an excellent student of vocal characterization and dramatic tension in verse. In accommodating these techniques to the lyric, Donne created a dramatic lyricism more various than that of his predecessors in the art, Wyatt and Sidney. While Donne was able to create a variety of characters and moods, from the cynical young courtier of "Goe and catch a falling star," through the witty lover of "The Flea," the metaphysical one of "The Extasy," and the loving husband and priest of God of the majority of his *Songs and Sonnets* (1633), virtually all of his verse was characteristically rougher than the verse of his contemporaries. Wyatt's phrasal rhythms and sometimes awkward accentuation were historically based. Donne, however, comes after Sidney, who was able to portray the courtier's voice with conviction over more manageable iambic rhythms.

In the four and a half centuries since his death, Donne's verse has created problems even for his admirers. Not only did Jonson claim he "deserved hanging" for his rough accentuation, Coleridge wrote that "Donne's muse on dromedary trots," and in this century even H. J. C. Grierson and T. S. Eliot, between them largely responsible for elevating Donne into the canon of Major English Poets, had reservations about his versification.[12] Donne's precipitous fall from critical favor in the late seventeenth century and through the eighteenth century was in large part based on the judgment of his meters as confusing and barbarous, with John Dryden's comments leading the way:

> Would not Donne's *Satires*, which abound with so
> much wit, appear more charming, if he had taken
> care of his words, and of his numbers? . . . I may
> safely say it of this present age, that if we are not so
> great wits as Donne, yet certainly we are better
> poets.[13]

In this century there has been general agreement on two counts: that Donne's verse is rough, and that it is usually (not always) technically metrical. In other words, his verse carries derivable meters, but the tension between meter and language produces very rough rhythms indeed. Considerable attention has been given to the nature and implications of that fabled roughness. Some critics, such as Michael Moloney and Catherine Ing, have insisted that it is at least partially deceptive, and others, such as Arnold Stein and John Shawcross, have concluded that Donne's roughness is a function of his density of thought or is mimetic of voice, statement, or genre.[14]

Most modern critics of Donne have at least tacitly

accepted George Saintsbury's 1908 observation that Donne's verse is not all of a piece and that his famous roughness is much less problematic in the lyrics and sonnets than in the satires, epigrams, and elegies.[15] A few examples will illustrate gradations and suggest something of the difficulty of dealing with Donne's versification.

Among the lyrics, "A Valediction: of the Booke" provides an example of clear and easy iambic pentameter, beginning with the first line where there is only a slight tension in the third foot:

x /   x /   x /   x /   x /
I'll tell thee now (deare Love) what thou shalt doe
3 2   4 1   3 2   3 2   4 1

More complex is the first line of the "Nocturnall upon S. Lucies Day," where one must decide whether the second and/or third feet are trochaic substitutions in an iambic line:

/   x   /   x   x   /   x /   x /
'Tis the | yeares mid | night, and | it is | the dayes

or

/   x   x   /   x   /   x /   x /
'Tis the | yeares mid | night, and | it is | the dayes

or even

/ x   /   x   /   x   x /   x   /
'Tis the | yeares mid | night, and | it is | the dayes
2   3   1   4

Natural Emphasis

While these lines may remain technically metrical, some of Donne's lines, particularly in the satires, resist metricality altogether. Thus in the mostly iambic pentameter "Satire I" line 46 cannot be scanned even with great allowance for elision:

```
x  /   x  /  x  x  /    / x  /    x
Hee lost that, yet hee was cloath'd but in beasts skin
```

An elision of "hee was" would rectify the syllabification; nothing will render the line iambic.

Even among the lyrics there are examples of difficult meters. The best known is surely the first line of "Twicknam Garden," which is as unmetrical as lines from the satires. Assuming an undistorted accentuation for "surrounded," the line seems most easily to fall into a trochee, an iamb, and two anapests:

```
/ x    x  /   x  x  /   x  x  /
Blasted I with sighs I and surround I ed with teares
```

A line composed of a variety of feet was by no means unusual in this period, as a large number of songs and such poems as Jonson's "Her Triumph" will testify. But in the other two stanzas the initial lines are clearly iambic pentameter, framing, with the fourth line, the tetrameter second and third. Indeed in this first stanza the fourth line is iambic pentameter, and it is at that point that the first line begins to seem awkward in retrospect:

> Blasted with sighs, and surrounded with teares
> Hither I come to seek the spring,
> And at mine eyes, and at mine eares,
> Receive such balmes, as else cure everything.

The problem line is decasyllabic, and will render something of an iambic reading, with awkward substitutions:

/ x   x /   /   x /   x   x /
Blasted | with sighs, | and sur | rounded | with teares

This line is unmetrical even according to the revised and more liberal model for iambic pentameter offered by Morris Halle and S. Jay Keyser. They would allow what we call trochaic substitution a reasonably free rein in such a line. But the sure signal of metrical distortion, according to Halle and Keyser, is a strong (or accented) syllable in a weak position surrounded by weak syllables in strong positions, without a syntactic break. This is precisely the case with "surrounded."[16] The effect may be mimetic of the speaker's distress, but it is also emblematic of Donne's relative unconcern for metrical precision.

How to read such lines creates difficulties even when Donne's poems are generally praised, as in his own time and in ours. Yvor Winters assumes the justice of Ben Jonson's famous comment ("that Done for not keeping of accent deserved hanging") and offers some persuasive examples of bad or simply mechanical versification in Donne's works, while admirers such as Stein and Shawcross are forced to argue very carefully for Donne's rhythmic effectiveness.[17] Commonly there are two questions asked, one way or another, about Donne's versifying: is Donne's verse generally metrical, and are his poetic rhythms effective? While the answer is usually conceded to be yes in both cases, the sense of unease remains. One more question therefore should be asked: does Donne's metricality bear any relation to his poetic effectiveness? The answer is a surprising, not much.

While this truth has been tacitly recognized in a number of ways, it has not been fully stated nor its implications pursued.[18] Donne is not an effective manipulator of the rhythmic possibilities suggested by metrical forms, as Winters observed, but he is a master of prose rhythms, particularly of the rhetorical or dramatic voice. His achievement was to produce the effect of the heightened speaking voice often in spite of his meters. At best, they provide a crude frame against which (as Stein has observed) rhetorical emphases must be set. Donne's verse provides an excellent vehicle, therefore, for exploring the relation of prose to verse rhythms, an exploration very much at the heart of twentieth-century verse experiments.

The prose rhythms with which Donne adorned his verse as well as his sermons and meditations were reasonably specific. Not only did Cicero, among other Humanist sources, define metrically the heightened prose rhythms of the orator, traditions of rhythmic cursus and clausula (or rhythmic runs and closures) were recognized features of Latin prayers, the Vulgate Bible, and Cranmer and Tyndale's Englishing of those rhythms in the *Book of Common Prayer* and the English Bible.[19]

Briefly, prose rhythms are tied to phrase rather than line, and while phrasal rhythms are an unquestionable feature of all verse rhythm, they more usually work in conjunction with and in part at the direction of the emphasis suggested by the metrical model, not only in verse by such masters of aesthetic phrasing as Jonson and Herrick but in the more mimetic verse of Sidney or Shakespeare as well. In Donne the metrical emphases are frequently rejected in favor of phrasal rhythms, to the extent that Donne, more than other poets of his period and, until this century, since, requires his readers to make performance choices totally divorced from the meter.

This is apparent even in what we would expect to be his most lyrical and therefore most metrically-directed verse, the poems in *Songs and Sonnets*. Only one of these, the song beginning "Sweetest love, I do not go / For weariness of thee," seems to depend entirely on the metrical direction for its rhythmic movement and effectiveness. It moves so gracefully in line with the balladic meter that it could almost have been written by Herrick. But it is an exception. Typically even the most lyrical of Donne's poems depend on phrasal and sentence rhythms more than on the rhythms of foot or line. Or, if rime and meter clearly support lyrical features in a poem, Donne avoids the concommitant verbal euphonies that Campion or Jonson would incorporate into the lyric structure. Thus for example the lover in "The Sun Rising" addresses the sun as he pays hyperbolic compliment to his shared love:

> She'is all States, and all Princes, I,
>   Nothing else is.
> Princes doe but play us; compar'd to this,
> All honor's mimique; All wealth alchimie.

Although the second line may be scanned metrically (as a trochee and an iamb) the emphatic phrasal rhythm replaces the derivable iamb with what amounts to a rhythmic spondee. Technically English has no spondees in the Greek and Latin sense; given any two syllables one will be relatively stressed more than the other. In order to achieve the effect of a spondee one must pause between the two syllables, allowing the pause itself to replace a relatively unstressed syllable. This is not foot meter in the usual sense at all; it is rhetorical emphasis. It is, in short, a device of prose rather poetic rhythm:

> / x / /
> Nothing else | is.

Similarly, the last line may be wrenched into a tolerably metrical scansion though with considerable strain over the last half of the line:

> x / x / x / x / x /
> All ho | nor's mi | mique; all | wealth al | chimie.
>   4   3   2   1   4 3

Natural Emphasis

The real rhythms of the line are in the two five-syllable phrases (strongly reminiscent of Wyatt) with the necessary pause separating "wealth" and "al-" in order to allow for a spondaic rhythm:

$$\overset{/}{} \quad \overset{/}{}$$

All honor's mimique; ‖ all wealth | alchimie.

Donne's reaction against euphonious lyricism is evident in his imitation of Marlowe's famous pastoral invitation. "The Bait" begins with the liquid consonants we associate with Marlowe's original:

> Come live with mee, and bee my love,
> And wee will some new pleasures prove
> Of golden sands, and christall brookes,
> With silken lines, and silver hooks.
>
> There will the river whispering runne
> Warm'd by thy eyes, more then the Sunne.
> And there th'inamore'd fish will stay,
> Begging themselves they may betray.

What follows is a steady decline in the smooth sounds of Elizabethan lyricism to the heavy accentuation and cacophonies of the poem's conclusion:

> Let coarse bold hands, from slimy nest
> The bedded fish in banks out-wrest,
> Or curious traitors, sleavesilke flies
> Bewitch poore fishes wandring eyes.
>
> For thee, thou needst no such deceit,
> For thou thy selfe are thine owne bait;
> That fish, that is not catch'd thereby,
> Alas, is wiser far than I.

Even in this metrically regular lyric there are instances, typical of Donne, where rhetorical emphasis overthrows the expected

256

and unobjectionable metrical reading. In the first line of the last stanza we expect an iambic reading and there is no apparent problem with it:

```
x   /   x   /    x  /   x /
For thee, thou needst no such deceit
```

The contrastive stress demanded by the rhetorical emphasis, however, would reverse the middle feet:

```
x   /   /   x   / x   x /
For thee, thou needst no such deceit
```

Although this version is technically unmetrical (in Halle and Keyser's terms, the "no" is a strong syllable in a weak position surrounded by two weak syllables in strong positions) it seems to be the reading directed by the emphatic contrast and witty conclusion of the poem. The sense overrides the meter, and if the line is unmetrical, it is nonetheless rhetorically effective.

Many of Donne's apparent eccentricities can be accommodated without insisting that they are prose rhythms. Clearly, Donne is not somehow "really" writing prose, and it is not uncommon for a poet to foreground a tension between the underlying meter on the one hand and normal speech emphases on the other. Nonetheless, as the rhythmic power of his sermons attest, Donne's ear for the rhythmic phrase as a pattern over four or more syllables was a fine one. Consider the famous section from Meditation XVI, *Devotions upon Emergent Occasions*, which people only marginally familiar with Donne might easily take to be from a poem:

> Who casts not up his *Eye* to the *Sunne* when it rises?
> But who takes off his *Eye* from a *Comet* when that breaks out?
> Who bends not his *eare* to any *bell*,
> which upon any occasion rings?

257

> but who can remove it from that *bell,*
> which is passing a *peece of himselfe* out of this *world?*
> No man is an *Iland,* intire of it selfe;
> every man is a peece of the *Continent,*
> a part of the *maine;*
> if a *Clod* bee washed away by the *Sea,*
> *Europe* is the lesse,
> as well as if a *Promontorie* were,
> as well as if a *Mannor* of thy *friends* or of *thine owne* were;
> any mans *death* diminishes *me,*
> because I am involved in *Mankinde;*
> And therefore never send to know for whom the *bell* tolls;
> It tolls for *thee.*

(lineation mine; italics Donne's)

The section begins with a pentameter sentence: three iambs and two anapests. Its conclusion is in fact an accentual version of the classical *cursus,* or rhythmic run, known as the *planus,* the five-two pattern of /xx/x. Similar rhythmic patterns may be found throughout, though without the regular repetitions necessary for meter. It is masterful prose movement, and perfectly fits Cicero's description of the orator's rhythmic art:

> The orator links words and meaning together in such
> a manner as to unfold his thought in a rhythm that is
> at once bound and free. For after enclosing it in the
> bonds of form and balance, he loosens and releases it
> by altering the order, so that the words are neither
> tied together by a definite metrical law nor left so
> free as to wander uncontrolled.[20]

This is where Donne's skills reside, and insofar as he is able to overlay his meters with his own genius for prose rhythms, his poetry is rhythmically successful.

A theme of this book has been the interrelation between phrasal and metrical rhythms. Chaucer's somewhat variable accentuation, a feature of his tradition, received greater order through a combination of syllabic regularity on the continental model and his own good ear for accentual balance. Between Chaucer and Surrey phrasal rhythms were or were not handled euphoniously, depending on the poet's skill and his search for rhythmic artifice across a vaguely syllabic meter. With the new regularity of Surrey's iambic meters came the danger of a new rigidity as well. Gascoigne's variable accentuation and then Spenser and Sidney's reassertion of phrasal rhythms over a secure metrical base increased the flexibility and utility of iambic meters, particularly the pentameter. Gascoigne and then the rhyme controversy made explicit the theory behind the practice, and such poets as Ralegh, Jonson, and Herrick could increasingly vary traditional "rhyme" with phrasal rhythms that explored accentual analogues of classical syllabic quantity. Shakespeare is of course a master of phrasing over a regular pentameter base, in the later plays virtually ignoring lineation *per se* in favor of heavily enjambed phrases cast over an underlying iambic movement. The question, then, is whether Donne's versification is different in kind or simply in degree from that of his contemporaries. I would argue that it is so different in degree it amounts to a difference in kind, and that it has a particular characteristic that adumbrates the difference: Donne's rhythms depend far more on the choice of the individual reader, on performance choices, than do the rhythms of his contemporaries.

Consider for example the opening line of Jonson's "To Penshurst":

$$x \ / \quad x \ / \quad x \quad / \quad x \ / \quad x \quad /$$
Thou art not, Penshurst, built to envious show

For the most part the important words fall into the "strong" or accented positions of the iambic pentameter model. One reader might emphasize "art" more than "not," while another might stress "not," producing the relatively rare 4-3-2-1 ascending iambic pattern, but the distinction is subtle and will not affect the

259

meter at all. This is a fairly common example of metrical tension in the earlier seventeenth century. Somewhat less common are examples of rhythmic ambiguity, which Jonson developed into a fine art (see chapter 7). In those cases the meter is determined by the performance choice; until the reader has decided where the rhetorical emphasis should go, a given foot (or, at the most, two) cannot be confidently scanned. Jonson, as we have seen, uses this device for subtle tensions over otherwise quite regular meters. In the case of Donne, not only are such rhythmic ambiguities quite common, they will tend to wrench the poem from any sense of an otherwise derivable underlying meter. Not only is the meter uncertain until the reader has made a performance choice, the best choice may take the poem away from meter altogether, and toward commonly recognized prose rhythms.

Consider again the first line from "A Nocturnall upon S. Lucies Day." The most regular scansion is an iambic one with initial trochee:

```
 /  x    x    /  x  /  x /   x  /
'Tis the yeares midnight and it is the dayes
```

But since the speaker is referring to two midnights, the year's and the day's, rhetorical emphasis would most likely stress both. In addition, the extent to which one chooses to emphasize this double midnight will affect the amount of emphasis one will give "and," and that in turn will affect whether the third foot is an iamb or a trochee. Ultimately the meter is of very little use in directing the performance of the poem. The rhythms are phrasal, and lineation becomes important only insofar as it takes on features of oratorical phrase ending:

```
 /  x /    /  x   /  x x  x  /
'Tis the yeares midnight || and it is the dayes
```

260

In this strictly "prose" reading the end of the line has an accentual version of the classical concluding "paean," xxx′, which Cicero described as an important prose clausula (*De Oratore* III.xlvii.183). In this instance mood and even meaning can change substantially depending on how a reader chooses to perform the line, and the meter not only gives no aid, it does not even resolve into a question of one of two possible metrical readings, as in Jonson's rhythmic ambiguities. The meter, while technically derivable, becomes irrelevant. Insofar as a performer chooses to emphasize the meter, just so far will the performance tend to remove itself from the line's rhetorical effectiveness. The "drama" that characterizes Donne's lyrics is more than implied character, audience, and setting, more even than the focus on conflict and tension. It is in the very concept of the poem's rhythmic structure, which remains dependent not on the devices of the poet but on the choices of the performer.

Herbert was a master of strophic forms and mimetic constructions whose full range of artistry has only been appreciated in this century. Robert McHarg Hayes pioneered an approach to Herbert's characteristic riming of lines of unequal length, which he called counterpoint, and Joseph Summers drew attention to the various kinds of mimetic constructions Herbert achieves, which Summers described as "hieroglyphs."[21] Other critics, notably Arnold Stein, have discussed the range of Herbert's artistry at least partly in relation to his skills as a versifier. A few examples will illustrate three aspects of Herbert's remarkable verse mimesis, though a great deal more remains to be done to explore it thoroughly. In general, Herbert is a master of mimetic strophic constructions, of mimetic rhythms within and across a series of lines, and, in a summary and extension of these skills, he makes his verse mimetic of an entire Biblical poetic. The variety he achieves with the basic building blocks of English verse (mostly iambic pentameter, tetrameter, and trimeter lines in quatrain or couplet-based constructions) is a formal embodiment of what I have elsewhere called Herbert's doctrine of unhewn stones, of poetry as sacrifice.[22]

Herbert's strophic mimesis ranges all the way from the

emblematic "Altar" and "Easter-wings" to the turmoil and disarray, resolved by a concluding quatrain, of "The Collar," to such simple devices as the mending of rime in "Deniall." These represent the abundant strophic variety of Summers' "hieroglyphs," and were to influence Crashaw, Vaughan, Traherne, and ultimately the nineteenth-century English religious lyricists, notably (for the twentieth century) Gerard Manly Hopkins. Herbert's various lyric practice offers an alternative to the increasingly restrained couplet verse of the late seventeenth century.

Less immediately apparent are Herbert's mimetic skills within and across lines. Like Shakespeare, Herbert is basically a conservative versifier with a superb sense of the mimetic possibilities of subtle changes in metrical and rhythmic expectations. "The Sacrifice" offers excellent testimony to Herbert's facility with lineation, enjambment, phrasing, and metrical substitution. The poem is composed of iambic pentameter tercets, riming aaa bbb ccc and so forth, each accompanied by a refrain, "Was ever grief like mine," altered twice to "Never was grief like mine." The stanzas are decorous and mimetic in themselves. Iambic pentameter is appropriate both for discursive meditation (as in Donne's *Anniversaries*) and for tragedy. Since the poem speaks in the voice of Christ as the second person of the Trinity, the stanzas are logically rimed tercets. But since the tragedy of the poem is Christ's human sacrifice, the God-like tercets are supplemented by the refrain expressing human pain and passion. There are sixty-three numbered stanzas in the poem, possibly suggesting one member of the Trinity (the three) apparently separated from the other two (the six).

The essential regularity of the verse is supported by a preponderance of end-stopped lines. There is some phrasal variation within the lines, but whole lines are so often the rhythmic units that the pentameter line would appear to represent the basic unit of Christ's human thought when it is uninterrupted by human events around him or the chaos forced on him by the betrayers, judges, and executioners. The first ten stanzas, for example, contain only three enjambments, none of them particularly startling (ll. 5-6, 21-22, and 29-30). When Judas arrives in the Garden of Gethsemane, however, the attendant betrayal and confusion is reflected in the abundant run-on lines found in the next five stanzas. The first of these is a sharp announcement of change, missing the natural concord of the lines just as Judas misses at life:[23]

> *Judas*, dost thou betray me with a kisse?
> Canst thou finde hell about my lips? and misse
> Of life, just at the gates of life and blisse?
>
> (ll. 41-43)

The following four stanzas have two enjambments each, under-scoring the imbalance and disarray of the arrest and binding of Christ.

Though these five stanzas provide the only consistent unit of enjambed verse in the poem, other more isolated instances serve similar mimetic purposes. The "enmitie" between Herod and Pilate is emphasized by the enjambment of lines 73-74, even as the rime marks their new accord:

> They binde, and leade me unto *Herod:* he
> Sends me to *Pilate*. This makes them agree.

Enjambment imitates statement as we "passe" from line 118 to 119:

> But I the Prince of peace; peace that doth passe
> All understanding, more than heav'n doth glasse.

Since enjambment in a sense "doubles" a single line by turning it into the next, the motion from line 125 to 126 is another formal imitation of statement:

263

> Ah! how they scourge me! yet my tendernesse
> Doubles each lash . . .

The more common end-stopped lines are varied through intralinear phrasing. One of many possible examples occurs in lines 141-43, where the first two lines have balanced internal syntactic breaks while the third runs to its metrical and syntactic conclusion without a pause:

> Servants and abjects flout me; they are wittie:
> *Now prophesie who strikes thee*, is their dittie.
> So they in me denie themselves all pitie.

Another, more various, example occurs in lines 149-51. The first line has pauses after the second and fourth syllables. The second has one pause after the sixth. The third has no internal pauses. The effect is a rhythmic building to the sorrowful injunction of the third line:

> Weep not, deare friends, since I for both have wept
> When all my teares were bloud, the while you slept:
> Your tears for your own fortunes should be kept.

Metrical substitution in this period, as we have seen, usually consists of substituting a trochee for an iamb, often at the beginning but occasionally within an iambic line. Initial trochees are so common by the seventeenth century as to be scarcely noticeable, though Herbert is sparing even of those. He is even more sparing of other trochaic substitutions, and when he uses them they are almost always mimetic. He is even more seldom unmetrical, but when Christ's "owne deare people" reject him it is

With noises confused frighting the day.

(l. 103)

To keep the meter one would have to mispronounce "confused" (a nice confusion of normal speech patterns). Otherwise there is a metrical confusion, most easily read as tetrameter with anapests at the second and fourth feet.

An even more dramatic instance of metrical mimesis is the truncation of line 215, where a metrical gap of three iambs reflects the anguish and emptiness of Christ on the Cross:

> But, *O my God, my God!* why leav'st thou me,
> The sonne, in whom thou dost delight to be?
> *My God, My God –*

Italicized phrases (whether provided by Herbert or his careful printers) indicate spoken rather than interior statement throughout "The Sacrifice," and here the reader is expected to recognize Christ's words from Matthew 27:46 and Mark 15:34. By completing the text and the rime with "why hast thou forsaken me," the reader participates in the language and the experience of the cross, affirming the intimacy between Christ's human nature and the sinner for whom he dies. The refrain of this tercet is the first "Never was grief like mine." The second instance occurs at the end of the poem.

Formal and thematic coherence characterize all of Herbert's *The Temple*. "The Sacrifice," the only poem in the voice of Christ, immediately meets the speaker's response in "The Thanksgiving," a poem in appropriate elegaic couplets (rimed pentameter/tetrameter lines). The speaker's desire is to respond appropriately to the great sacrifice, but he concludes:

> Then for thy passion – I will do for that –
> Alas, my God, I know not what.

265

This is immediately followed by "The Reprisall," which formally turns the elegaic stanzas inside out (4a5b5a4b instead of 5a4a5b4b):

> I have consider'd it, and finde
> There is no dealing with thy mighty passion:
> For though I die for thee, I am behinde;
> My sinnes deserve the condemnation.

And so it goes throughout, with verse forms reflecting content and reflecting each other in a cumulative coherence of amazing versatility.

The apparent complexity of Herbert's verse forms may at first seem to contradict his stated desire to "plainly say, *My God, My King*" ("Jordan[I]") and to avoid weaving himself into the sense of his verse ("Jordan [II]"). Herbert's verse often reflects a continuing struggle for personal simplicity. In part his strophic complexity is a feature of that struggle. It is also a feature of his Biblical poetic. His poems reflect the asymmetries of the Psalms, and especially of the Sidney-Pembroke versions of the Psalms, which offer abundant examples and good authority for Herbert's formal inventiveness. In addition, Herbert's poems probably reflect his Biblically authorized doctrine of sacrifice. Like the altars the Israelites built of unhewn stones after crossing the Jordan, Herbert's poems are often composed of a harmony of uneven edges.[24] The association is suggested not only by the two "Jordan" poems, but also by "The Altar," the emblematic first poem of *The Temple's* large central section, "The Church":

By hewing the stony heart of man, God also hews and writes the speech that comes from the heart. As God's poet, Herbert throughout *The Temple* attempts to be not merely simple, but the unhampering agent of God's voice, first in "The Sacrifice" of Christ, but then and consistently in the sacrificial poetry of the struggling poet/priest. The poems are the sanctified base from which that sacrifice is made, the altars built for the reciprocal covenant of devotion and grace. As in the

A broken A L T A R, Lord, thy fervant reares,
Made of a heart, and cemented with teares:
Whofe parts are as thy hand did frame;
No workmans tool hath touch'd the fame.
A H E A R T alone
Is fuch a. ftone,
As nothing but
Thy pow'r doth cut.
Wherefore each part
Of my hard heart
Meets in this frame,
To praife thy name.
That if I chance to hold my peace,
Thefe ftones to praife thee may not ceafe.
O let thy blefTed S A C R I F I C E be mine,
And fanctifie this A L T A R to be thine.

poem, the poetic altar in general is "made of a heart," both in the sense that the redeemed stony heart is central to it and in the sense that the poet constructs his altar out of the simple phrases of God-given speech, which are then built into lines, stanzas, and whole poems that reflect the abundant variety of God's creation. Herbert's verse is therefore both simple and complex at the same time, both natural and artful. Its elements, like unhewn stones, are natural and various. Its construction, like the Old Testament altars, turns artistry into dutiful and obedient worship. Herbert's poetic is a deliberate sanctification of the mimetic artistry available through English Renaissance versification.

NOTES

1. For example, Dorothy L. Sipe, *Shakespeare's Metrics* (New Haven: Yale Univ. Press, 1968), catalogues and analyzes evidence of Shakespeare's iambic regularity; Arnold Stein, "Meter and Meaning in Donne's Verse," *Sewanee Review*, 52(1944):288-301, rpt. in *Essential Articles for the Study of John Donne's Poetry*, ed. John R. Roberts (Hamden, Ct.: Archon Books, 1975), 161-70, argues for reading Donne's rhythms according to patterns of emphatic stress directed by the poem's rhetorical organization; and Joseph H. Summers, *George Herbert: His Religion and Art* (Cambridge, Mass.: Harvard Univ. Press, 1954), relates Herbert's formal complexity to his Protestant poetics.

2. Howard Baker, "Some Blank Verse Written by Thomas Norton before *Gorboduc*," *Modern Language Notes*, 48(1933):529-30. See also Lois Potter, in vol. 2 of *The Revels History of Drama in English* (London: Methuen, 1980), 238.

3. J. E. Bernard, Jr., *The Prosody of the Tudor Interlude* (New Haven: Yale Univ. Press, 1939), 2-3: "The dramatists had comparatively little regard for the individual line beyond its integrity. . . . Their interest was in the grouping of lines."

4. *King Johan*, ed. Barry B. Adams (San Marino: Huntington Library Press, 1969). In his introduction Adams summarizes the controversy over the play's versification and offers excellent evidence to conclude that "the metrical scheme which Bale had in mind was basically a five-stress line divided in two by a break after the second stress."

5. Harry Levin, *The Overreacher: A Study of Christopher Marlowe* (Cambridge, Mass.: Harvard Univ. Press, 1952), 12. See also Alvin Kernan, in *Revels History*, 3:251:

> From the moment the Prologue in *Tamburlaine*
> speaks, the doggerel rhythms and clinking rhymes of
> the old uneducated authors – the 'mother wits' – the
> crude comedy and farce of 'clownage', are the
> dramaturgy of the past.

6. *Revels History*, vol. 3, *passim. 1 Henry VI* was probably written around 1589. See *The Riverside Shakespeare*, ed. G. Blakemore Evans (Boston: Houghton Mifflin, 1974), 48.

7. All citations are from the G. Blakemore Evans text in *The Riverside Shakespeare*.

8. Frederic W. Ness, *The Use of Rhyme in Shakespeare's Plays* (New Haven: Yale Univ. Press, 1941), catalogues the various uses of rime in the plays and provides numerous examples of such things as "speech-end rhyme," "speech-pause rhyme," and "couplet rhetoric." He makes the important point that for Shakespeare, though he was a master of couplet variety, couplets remained "embellishments rather than principal stylistic patterns" (104).

9. E. K. Chambers, *William Shakespeare: A Study of Facts and Problems*, 2 vols. (Oxford: Clarendon Press, 1930), 2:397-408. The "Summary" table, 2:398, is the most useful.

10. G. L. Brook, *The Language of Shakespeare* (London: Andre Deutsch, 1976), 165. His comment, 164: "The author of a verse play tries to make his verse approach conversational prose rhythm. He achieves this aim by varying the position of the syntactic pauses in relation to the lines of blank verse. End-stopped lines are most common in the early plays. In the later plays we find relative pronouns and auxiliary verbs separated from their verbs by the end of a line." One might add that in the later plays we find an increasing number of speeches that end in the middle of a line, the line being then (usually) completed by another speaker.

11. Richard Flatter, *Shakespeare's Producing Hand: A Study of his Marks of Expression to be found in the First Folio* (London: William Heinemann, 1948). Chapters 4 and 5, on "Pauses" and "Metrical Gaps," are of particular interest.

12. *The Poems of John Donne*, ed. H. J. C. Grierson, 2 vols. (Oxford: Clarendon Press, 1912), 2:xiv-xv, lv; T. S. Eliot, "The Metaphysical Poets," in *Selected Essays 1917-1932* (London: Faber and Faber, 1932). Most tellingly, Eliot has nothing direct to say about metaphysical versification, but in his conclusion he comments on Samuel Johnson's dislike of it: in Johnson's criticism of metaphysical versification, "we must remember in what a narrow discipline he was trained, but also how well trained."

13. John Dryden, *A Discourse Concerning the Origin and Progress of Satire* (1693).

14. Michael Moloney, "Donne's Metrical Practice," *Publications of the Modern Language Association of America*, 65(1950):232-39; Catherine Ing, *Elizabethan Lyrics* (London: Chatto and Windus, 1951), 231-36; Stein, "Meter and Meaning"; Arnold Stein, *John Donne's Lyrics* (Minneapolis: Univ. of Minnesota Press, 1962), 20-34 and 213-16; John T. Shawcross, "All Attest His Writs Canonical: The Texts, Meaning and Evaluation of Donne's Satires," in *Just So Much Honor*, ed. Peter A. Fiore (Univ. Park, Pa.: Pennsylvania State Univ. Press, 1972).

15. George Saintsbury, *A History of English Prosody*, 3 vols. (London: Macmillan, 1906-10), 2:152-66. John Hollander reaffirms that separation in his argument for Donne's complex lyricism, "Donne and the Limits of Lyric," *Vision and Resonance* (New York: Oxford Univ. Press, 1975), 44-58.

16. Morris Halle and S. Jay Keyser, *English Stress: Its Form, Its Growth, and Its Role in Verse* (New York: Harper and Row, 1971), 165.

17. Yvor Winters, *Forms of Discovery* (Denver: Alan Swallow, 1967), 71-80.

18. Grierson refers to Donne's epistolary and satiric poetry as someting other than "poetry in the full sense of the word," as "talk not song," (2:xiv). All citations of Donne poems are from this edition. See also W. F. Melton, *The Rhetoric of John Donne's Verse* (Baltimore: J. H. Furst, 1906), and Stein, "Meter and Meaning," and also *John Donne's Lyrics*. Even Hollander, who argues for Donne's complex lyricism, insists on the importance of contrastive stress in Donne ("Donne and the Limits of Lyric").

19. Morris Croll's essays on prose rhythm in this period are directly pertinent to Donne's practice. See especially "The Cadence of English Oratorical Prose," in *Style, Rhetoric, and Rhythm*, ed. J. Max Patrick et al. (Princeton: Princeton Univ. Press, 1966), 303-59. For a general discussion of the development of English prose rhythms, see Ian Gordon, *The Movement of English Prose* (London: Longmans, 1966).

20. Cicero, *De Oratore*, III.xlix.175-76. Loeb Library ed., tr. E. W. Sutton and H. Rackham (Cambridge, Mass.: Harvard Univ. Press, 1942).

21. Robert McHarg Hayes, "Counterpoint in Herbert," *Studies in Philology*, 35(1938):43-60; Summers; see also Alicia Ostriker, "Song and Speech in the Metrics of George Herbert," *Publications of the Modern Language Association of America*, 80(1965):62-68; Arnold Stein, *George Herbert's Lyrics* (Baltimore: Johns Hopkins Univ. Press, 1968); and Louise Schleiner, "Jacobean Song and Herbert's Metrics," *Studies in English Literature*, 19(1979):109-26.

22. Susanne Woods, "The 'Unhewn Stones' of Herbert's Verse," *George Herbert Journal*, 4(1981):30-46.

23. All quotations are from *The Works of George Herbert*, ed. F. E. Hutchinson (Oxford: Clarendon Press, 1941; rev. 1945).

24. Rosemond Tuve was the first to point to the Biblical poetic underlying Herbert's Jordan poems, in *A Reading of George Herbert* (London: Faber and Faber, 1952). Not only does "Jordan" suggest Christian baptism, renewal, and dedication, it also points to the doctrine of sacrifice. Cf. Deuteronomy 27:2-8:

> And it shall be on the day when ye shall pass over
> the Jordan unto the land which the LORD thy God
> giveth thee, that thou shalt set thee up great stones,

and plaister them with plaister: And thou shalt write
upon them all the words of this law. . . .Therefore it
shall be when ye be gone over the Jordan *that* ye
shall set up these stones, which I command you this
day. . . .And there thou shalt build an altar to the
LÓRD thy God, an altar of stones, and thou shalt
not lift up *any* iron *tool* upon them. Thou shalt build
the altar of the LORD thy God with whole stones:
and thou shalt offer burnt offerings thereon unto the
LORD thy God: And thou shalt offer peace
offerings, and shalt eat there, and rejoice before the
LORD thy God. And thou shalt write upon the
stones all the words of this law very plainly.

See also Barbara K. Lewalski, *Protestant Poetics and the Seventeenth-Century Religious Lyric* (Princeton: Princeton Univ. Press, 1979), 283-316. Stanley Fish has underscored the particularly didactic elements of Herbert's poetic, in *The Living Temple: George Herbert and Catechizing* (Berkeley and Los Angeles: Univ. of Calif. Press, 1978).

PARADISE
LOST.

BOOK I.

F Mans Firſt Diſobedience, and
the Fruit
Of that Forbidden Tree, whoſe
mortal taſt
Brought Death into the World,
and all our woe,
With loſs of *Eden*, till one greater Man
Reſtore us, and regain the bliſsful Seat,
Sing Heav'nly Muſe, that on the ſecret top
Of *Oreb*, or of *Sinai*, didſt inſpire
That Shepherd, who firſt taught the choſen Seed,
In the Beginning how the Heav'ns and Earth
Roſe out of *Chaos* : Or if *Sion* Hill   10
Delight thee more, and *Siloa's* Brook that flow'd
Faſt by the Oracle of God ; I thence
Invoke thy aid to my adventrous Song,
That with no middle flight intends to ſoar
A   Above

Chapter Nine

The Legacies of Milton and Dryden

*He who would not be frustrate of his
hope to write hereafter in laudable
things ought himself to be a true poem,
that is, a composition and pattern of
the best and honorablest things.*

Milton, "An Apology for Smectymnuus"

When T. S. Eliot in this century wrote of a "dissociation
of sensibility" toward the end of the seventeenth, he was in large
part simplifying and exaggerating apparent differences between
two great poets, John Milton (1606-1674) and John Dryden
(1631-1700).[1] Differences in their versification nonetheless support the stylistic and modal dissimilarities most readers instantly
perceive. Milton in his verse offers ample support for Douglas
Bush's judgment of him as the last of the Christian Humanists.[2]
Milton freely borrows syntax from Augustan Latin; balance,
imagery, and stance from the Biblical tradition; and intonational
patterns from Italian syllabic verse, as in his *canzone*-like lineation
in *Lycidas* and *Samson Agonistes*, and his highly flexible English
verso sciolto (or "English Heroic Verse without Rime")* in *Paradise Lost*
and *Paradise Regained.* His versification has proved a rich if sometimes elusive field for some excellent scholars, with his work a
virtual handbook, as well as culmination, of English Renaissance
verse skills.[3] From the headless tetrameters of "L'Allegro" and

273

Natural Emphasis

"Il Penseroso," the lyric stanzas of the "Nativity Ode," the brilliant asymmetries of *Lycidas*, the flexible multi-purpose forms of his Italian sonnets, to the lucid and sonorous blank verse of *Paradise Lost*, *Paradise Regained*, and *Samson Agonistes*, Milton both reflects and extends the achievements of Surrey, Spenser, Jonson, and the entire English verse tradition. Insofar as he preferred blank verse to couplets, enjambment to end-stopped lines, he is the last in the direct line of poets who sought to liberate the newly established accentual-syllabic regularity. Although the influence of Abraham Cowley would keep some asymmetrical verse in the poetic mainstream through the eighteenth century, the dominant direction of English verse for more than a hundred years after the Restoration was toward subtle and increasingly refined versification within the constraints of balanced, mostly end-stopped couplets.

Milton's verse is in part a heritage of Jonsonian experimentation with phrasing and rhythmic tensions. Dryden's is the heritage of Jonsonian restraint and preference for the couplet, and is the more immediately influential. While Milton incorporates the blank verse genius of Shakespeare and the rhetorical and Biblical experimentation of Donne and Herbert, Dryden follows a clearer line from Surrey to Gascoigne to Jonson to one of Jonson's many "sons," Edmund Waller (1606-87).

Waller is probably best known in this century for his song in the *carpe diem* tradition, "Go lovely Rose," a poem that matches Herrick's "Gather ye rosebuds while ye may" for lyric perfection. He was generally acknowledged, however, in his own and immediately succeeding time, for his clear, discursive couplets. Francis Atterbury, in his preface to *The Second Part of Mr. Waller's Poems* (1690), reflected the attitude of the time, including that of Dryden, when he described Waller as "the Parent of English verse, and the first that showed us our tongue had beauty and numbers in it."

The model of Waller along with the practice of Dryden and the theory represented by Thomas Sprat, Historian of the Royal Society, combined to set a course for an English poetic that was on the one hand carefully devoted to the arts of a bal-

274

anced and restrained versification and on the other hand suspicious of poetry as a mode. The development of this Baconian (and Jonsonian) approach is swift. In 1651 Thomas Hobbes, in his "Answer" to William Davenant's "Preface" to his *Gondibert*, eschewed fiction and fantasy in terms developed from Bacon. Davenant was praised for grounding his epic in history rather than fantasy, and for avoiding the imaginative creatures that had populated classical epic (with implicit reference, also, to more recent romantic epics, such as Ariosto's *Orlando Furioso* or Spenser's *Faerie Queene*. *Gondibert* itself is in what Dryden referred to as "Heroique stanzas," iambic pentameter riming abab cdcd etc., historically the predecessor of the couplet explosion in narrative and discursive poetry.

An even more important indicator of new developments appeared in 1659, in a quarto titled *Three Poems Upon the Death of his late Highnesse Oliver Lord Protector of England, Scotland, and Ireland. Written By Mr Edm. Waller. Mr Jo. Dryden. Mr Sprat, of Oxford.* Sprat, friend and editor of Cowley, presents a complex and uneven poem claiming to be a "Pindarick Ode." This is not, as it might seem, a continuing effort to loosen and elaborate English verse. In his 1668 edition of *The Works of Mr. Abraham Cowley* Sprat admires the rather free imitation of Pindar not for its lyricism, but for its similarity to prose discourse.[4] Similarly, in his *History of the Royal Society* (1667) he cites Bacon's authority for eschewing *"Fancy"* in favor of *"Reason,"* and avoiding the "easie vanity of *fine* speaking" (Part 2, section xx).

Waller's poem, titled "Upon the Late Storme and Death of his Highnesse Ensuing the same," is in couplets and begins:

> We must resigne; Heav'n His great Soul do's claim,
> In storms as loud, as His *Immortall Fame.*

The language is clear and mostly direct, as Sprat and the tradition he represents were to approve. Not only are the couplets end-stopped, the lines rely on the traditional pause after the fourth syllable to help effect the balance so much admired by the later seventeenth century.

275

Dryden's poem is in "Heroique stanzas," a form he continued to use through the *Annus Mirabilis* (1667). As early as 1660, however, Dryden had felt the metrical influence of Waller and the aesthetic impact of Bacon and Hobbes. In a dedicatory poem to Sir Robert Howard's *Poems* Dryden writes in couplets, praising "Musick uninform'd by Art." Dryden's artistic values were to be those of his time: lucid naturalness. His principal verse form was of course to be the balanced couplet, with occasional tercets often used mimetically.[5]

The great age of balanced syllabicism, the age codified by Edward Bysshe's 1702 *Art of English Poetry*, was the new age of practical men who had to make even the rhythms of poetry appear to relate to what Sprat in his preface to Cowley's poems called "useful . . . Writing." The result is to emphasize the language of talk rather than song, and to seek to combine vocal with mimetic rhythms in primarily non-fiction verse. These impulses may produce a logically syllabic poetic at first, but in the long run they project the loosening of the accentual-syllabic line, first by the new lyricism of the Romantic poets, and finally by the rhetorical, musical, and speech analogues of Blake, Whitman, Pound, and Williams.

Despite its less immediate and obvious impact, Milton's work, like Dryden's, continued to exert a presence, and, from the Romantic poets forward, a renewed influence. The differences between Milton and Dryden continue to suggest fundamental differences in English poetics. They illustrate, for example, differences between an essentially dynamic and essentially static view of human experience. These views represent not a dissociation of sensibility, but a divergence in temperament and ontological bias that goes back at least as far as the pre-Socratic philosophers. Revolutionary Milton is the poet of process and change. Like Heraklitus (born c. 540 B.C.) and the tradition he was to inaugurate in Western thought, Milton believed in a dynamic of being, sustained and made intelligible by principles of balance and measure – what Heraklitus, interestingly, called *Logos*. Conservative Dryden, on the other hand, is the poet of stability and permanence, seeking, like Parminedes (born c. 510

B.C.), the *esti*, or what is, the omnipresent one beneath the appearances. These differences between Milton and Dryden have been described in various ways: Milton's asymmetry and drama are Baroque, Dryden's balance and discursiveness are Neoclassical; Milton's individualism and stylistic idiosyncracy are Protestant, Dryden's trust in hierarchy and rigorous formalism are Catholic. All these tendencies are easy to exaggerate; certainly Dryden's "Alexander's Feast" is a complex praise of feeling and art, while Milton's "L'Allegro" and "Il Penseroso," are early exercises in balance and reason, among other things. Still, in Milton's *Paradise Lost*, Edenic joy resides in the continually unfolding variety of the tended garden; disruption, sin, and death are the products of the hierarchical, authoritarian temperament of Satan; and restored joy is divine grace infusing the painful struggle of human history. In Dryden's *Absalom and Achitophel*, stability rests in unchanging rules of succession; chaos is the product of individual wills easily swaying a changeable mob; and order is restored by Royal fiat.

Milton and Dryden are nonetheless both masters of the full range of English verse techniques. When Milton introduces "L'Allegro" and "Il Penseroso" each voice speaks for ten lines in alternating trimeter and pentameter, denouncing its opposite as an unbalanced excess. The rest of each poem is in tetrameter couplets, praising what the voice no doubt perceives as the natural moderation and balance of its point of view. Here and overall the versification is subtle and emblematic of the complex issues of perspective Milton raises in the two poems. In his "Song for St. Cecelia's Day," Dryden varies his stanza forms and enlivens his sounds to evoke (imitate would be too strong a word) the musical instruments he is praising. Milton's early pair depends for its structure on balance and contrast, while Dryden's much later poem proceeds, quite literally, to the rolling organ tones usually associated with Milton.

Despite this mutuality of skill and range, major stylistic differences (as well as ontological predispositions) remain clear. Two well-known passages from major works, each based on the premise that the word of divine authority can rout disruption, are among many that readily illustrate those differences. *Paradise Lost* begins *in medias res* with God's disposition of Satan's rebellion:[6]

> . . . Him the Almighty Power
> Hurl'd headlong flaming from th'Ethereal Skie
> With hideous ruine and combustion down
> To bottomless perdition, there to dwell
> In Adamantine Chains and penal Fire,
> Who durst defie th'Omnipotent to Arms.

(I.44-49)

Absalom and Achitophel concludes with divinely approved David's announcement that rebellion must cease, and establishes the effect of his pronouncement.

> He said. Th'Almighty, nodding, gave Consent;
> And Peals of Thunder shook the Firmament,
> Henceforth a Series of new time began,
> The mighty Years in long Procession ran:
> Once more the Godlike *David* was Restor'd,
> And willing Nations knew their Lawfull Lord.

(ll. 1026-1031)

Milton's lineation is characteristically enjambed and expansive. Dryden's is characteristically end-stopped and contained. Milton's phrasing, rhythms, and use of sounds (such as the "h" sounds of the first three lines) serve to carry forward action and achieve dramatic effect. Dryden's phrasing and rhythms define and clarify, resembling oratory more than drama. Although Milton is describing the disruption and Dryden the re-establishment of order, so that the tendencies cited are more pronounced here than in more thematically comparable passages, these lines provide clear illustration of general principles that obtain across themes and voices.

278

By the end of the seventeenth century, a period of high and divergent achievement, simple binary categories such as mimetic and aesthetic have become unprofitable. More useful is the principle of coordinates, borrowed from mathematics and used by M. H. Abrams and Northrop Frye, among others, to describe elements of literary discourse.[7] In the later seventeenth century, trends in verse style may be perceived in terms of four coordinates, along which Milton and Dryden, and Waller and Cowley, may be representatively placed:

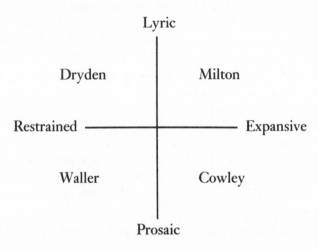

Lyric style assumes a deliberate patterning of sounds either to imitate song or to produce euphonies well away from ordinary speech. Prosaic style seeks to imitate, or to give the impression of, the speaking voice. Restrained style conveys a posture of clarification and balance, while expansive style conveys vitality and process. The approximate positions of Milton and Dryden on this graph show them to be heirs of the lyric versification of the Renaissance, while Waller and Cowley, in their influential modes at least, point toward the eighteenth-century development of sophisticated prose. The immediate result of that development was to submerge or override the lyric achievement, and particularly the rhythmic variety achieved by the Renaissance poets, and pre-eminently expressed, in their different ways, by both

279

Milton and Dryden. The turn toward the prosaic is ultimately a rejection of rhythmic versification. The directions of the lesser poets, Waller and Cowley, may in the long run have had the more important effects on English verse as it moved slowly and sporadically to the wide rhetorical expanse of "free" and experimental verse.

The disintegration of a clear rhythmic versification, the verse achieved by the Renaissance, is no doubt partly a function of changes in the language and partly a function of a less formal approach to art generally. We remain post-Romantic in our evaluation of the natural and the original; we often lack the Renaissance appreciation for *sprezzatura*, which allowed a poet such as Herrick to write with high artistry about the simplicities of nature and the value of a casual *deshabillé*. Perhaps new patterns of versification are only possible if we abandon the Jonsonian and Johnsonian traditions of matter over manner and allow the intellectual legitimacy of, for example, what Marjorie Perloff has called "poetry as word system."[8] In the twentieth century, an age which has tended toward literal minded practicality, readers often resist as not "useful . . . Writing" poetry that explores sound relationships for their own sakes. Since we seldom read out loud, we may even have lost the ability to hear those relationships. Certainly modern media of verbal communication, especially television, carry with them very little for the phonological aesthetician. Whatever choices we make in the approval of modern poetry, whatever directions our poets choose to take, it is impossible not to be aware of the current failure of poetic form. Despite yet one more borrowing from the French (free verse from *vers libre*), we have not broken the back of the iambic pentameter line, while poems in the old measures seldom carry the force of the old poems. The development of versification in the Renaissance was another example of a great national genius in a time of high adventure and intellectual daring. Like the work of Shakespeare, Spenser, and Sidney, the insights of Surrey, Gascoigne, Daniel, and Jonson provide evidence of a brilliant and increasingly conscious aesthetic achievement. No verse movement in English has matched it since. Neither has any age, except our own, approached the Renaissance sense of experimentation and possibility. If we are currently confronted with a failure of form, we are also deluged with a variety of new voices, especially those of women poets and black poets, who may well recreate English poetic.

NOTES

1. T. S. Eliot, "On Metaphysical Poetry," in *Selected Essays, 1917-1932* (London: Faber and Faber, 1932).

2. Still implied though no longer stated in the second edition (Douglas Bush, *English Literature in the Earlier Seventeenth Century* [Oxford: Oxford Univ. Press, 1962], 380-83).

3. Including such poets as Robert Bridges, *Milton's Prosody* (Oxford: Oxford Univ. Press, 1921), and Edward Weismiller, who has reviewed and reexamined virtually the entire discussion of Milton's prosody and versification, in "Review of Studies of Verse Forms" for *A Variorum Commentary on the Poems of John Milton, The Minor English Poems*, ed. A. S. P. Woodhouse and Douglas Bush (London: Routledge and Kegan Paul, 1970), 2:3, 1007, and *Paradise Regained*, ed. Walter MacKellar, 4:253-363. Weismiller's similar work on *Paradise Lost* is shortly forthcoming. For further background on the development and ascendency of the heroic couplet in England, see William B. Piper, *The Heroic Couplet* (Cleveland: Case Western Univ. Press, 1969); Felix Schelling, "Ben Jonson and the Classical School," *Publications of the Modern Language Association of America*, 13(1898):221-49; Ruth Wallerstein, "The Development of the Rhetoric and Metre of the Heroic Couplet, Especially in 1625-1645," *Publications of the Modern Language Association of America*, 50(1935):166-209.

4. In Sprat's "An Account of the Life and Writings of Mr Abraham Cowley," in *The Works of Cowley*, ff. b2v-c:

> The frequent alteration of the Rhythm and Feet,
> affects the mind with a more various delight, while it
> is soon apt to be ty'rd by the setled pace of any one
> constant measure. But that for which I think
> inequality of number is chiefly to be preferr'd, is its
> near affinity with Prose: From which all other kinds
> of *English* Verse are so far distant, that it is very
> seldom found that the same Man excels in both ways.
> But now this loose, and unconfin'd measure has all

the Grace, and Harmony of the most confin'd. And
withal, it is so large and free, that the practice of it
will only exalt, not corrupt our Prose: which is
certainly the most useful kind of Writing of all
others: for it is the style of all business and
conversation.

5. As in *Absalom and Achitophil*, where Achitophil's dangerous excesses
are underscored by the tercet:

To compass this the triple bond he broke,
The pillars of the public safety shook,
And fitted Israel for foreign yoke.

(ll. 175-78)

In vol. 2 of *The Works of John Dryden*, ed. H. T. Swedenborg and Vin-
ton Dearing (Berkeley and Los Angeles: Univ. of Calif. Press, 1972).

6. In vol. 2, part 1, of *Milton's Works*, ed. F. A. Patterson et al., (New
York: Columbia Univ. Press, 1931).

7. M. H. Abrams, *The Mirror and the Lamp*, (New York: Oxford, 1953);
and Northrop Frye, *The Anatomy of Criticism*, (Princeton: Princeton
Univ. Press, 1957).

8. In her discussion of Gertrude Stein (Marjorie Perloff, *The Poetics of
Indeterminacy* [Princeton: Princeton Univ. Press, 1981], 67-108).

Appendix A

Wyatt's Mid-Line Pause

In Wyatt's verse the mid-line pause is important for directing rhythm, though it is not consistent enough to be called "metrical." This is clear not only from careful reading of the sonnets but also from Wyatt's holograph poems in the Egerton Manuscript. Although he is not consistent in this, he often indicates a mid-line pause with a slash mark or virgule. The first few lines of his translation of Psalm 143, for example, suggest a preferred rhythmic phrasing:

> Here my prayer o lord / here my request
> complyshe my bone / answere to my desire
> not by desert / but for thyn own byhest
> In whose ferme trowgh thou promest myn empyre
> to stond stable / And after thy Justyse
> pforme o lord the thinge that I require.

Two holograph epigrams (Harrier nos. 82 and 83) on the same page of the Egerton manuscript illustrate the rhythmic rather than metrical aspect of Wyatt's use of the mid-line pause and also its importance for hearing the poetry. In the first instance, the rhythms must be perceived phrase by phrase; if we attempt to read them in relation to iambic or other foot-meter, the poem immediately becomes awkward. Further, if we try to read a whole line as a rhythmic unit we find similar awkwardness. But Wyatt's phrasal punctuation, which most experienced readers would be able to infer even if we did not have his holograph, does offer a useful guide to the poem's reading rhythms:

283

Natural Emphasis

In dowtfull brest/whilst moderly pitie, /
with furyous famyn / stondyth at debate: /
saythe thebrew moder /o child unhappye
retorne thi blowd /where thow hadst milk of late .
yeld me those lyms / that I made unto the .
and entre there where thou wert generate .
for of on body agaynst all nature /
to a nothr must I make sepulture .

Harrier comments that the next poem's punctuation is more integral than that of the one preceding, and posits that the virgules were added to the former after Wyatt saw how effectively they could work:

Off cartage he that worthie warier
could over come / but cowld not use his chaunce
and I like wise off all my long indever
the sherpe conquest tho fortune did avaunce
cowld not it use / the hold that is gyvin over
I unpossest / so hangith in balaunce
off warr my pees / reward of all my payne
At Mountzon thus I restles rest in spayne .

Other epigrams have fewer virgules than these, and Wyatt's decasyllabic poetry throughout the Egerton manuscript is sparing of punctuation generally. When virgules do appear, however, they seem to be clear indicators of phrasal rhythm, though not of a more certain metrical system. An exception is the poem in poulter's measure, "Iopas Song," whose regular rhythms are not among Wyatt's most effective. The poem is a fair anticipation of the more rigid and often uninteresting versions of this meter found in the middle of the century. The regular placement of virgules suggests a ballad stanza with a medial pause in the third line. Thus,

When Dido festid first/the wandryng troian knyght
whom Junos wrath/with stormes did force/in lybyke sandes to lyght

284

may as easily be read:

When Dido festid first
the wandryng troian knyght
whom Junos wrath / with stormes did force
in lybyke sandes to lyght

Poulters measure (a couplet of twelve and fourteen syllables, usually iambic) is essentially a long-lined version of the ballad stanza. What is interesting here is the precision with which Wyatt announces the balladic divisions of his lines and the consistency of this punctuation throughout the poem. Clearly in this song-related poem the pauses are perceived as metrical – as integral to the underlying direction of the poem's movement – while in the decasyllabic poems, including the psalms, the punctuation is less regular and part of a more general rhythmic direction.

THE
Psalmes of David
metaphrased into verse by
the noble, learned & famous
gent. Sr Philip Sidney
Knight

Appendix B

Verse Forms in the Sidney/Pembroke Psalms

The number indicates the stress accents per line with accentual feet assumed to be disyllabic unless otherwise noted. Lower case letters indicate masculine rimes, and upper case feminine rimes. Occasional notes often compare the primary text, *The Psalms of Sir Philip Sidney and the Countess of Pembroke*, ed. J. C. A. Rathmell (New York: New York Univ. Press, 1963), with Huntington Library Manuscripts HM 100, HM 117, and EL 11637.

Sir Philip Sidney

1. 5aabbcc, (3 stanzas).

2. 6a3a, (thirty-two lines).

3. 3a3a3B3c3c3B, (six stanzas).

4. 4ababb, (seven stanzas).

5. 5abbacdcd, (five stanzas).

6. 5a5B5a2B, (eight stanzas).

7. *Terza rima*, sixteen stanzas, (5ababcb, etc., concluding dee).

8. 4aaBB, (seven stanzas), and aaBBcc (eighth stanza).

9. 5abab2b, (thirteen stanzas).

10. 3aabb4ccdd, (ten stanzas).

Natural Emphasis

11. 3aaa3B / 3ccc3B, (six stanzas, three pairs).

12. 5abc / 5abc, (eight stanzas, four pairs).

13. 5a1B5a1B, (twenty lines, five quatrains).

14. 5aa3B / 5cc3B, (eight stanzas, four pairs).

15. Thirteen lines of hexameter, *one* rime: "—aine" (all different words).

16. 4aabccb, (seven stanzas), headless *passim*.

17. 5aa4bb, (twelve stanzas).

18. 6ababbcc, (hexameter rime royal, thirteen stanzas).

19. 4a3B4c3B, (ballad stanzas with internal rime in lines 1 and 3).

20. 3a5a3b3c5b / 3c5c3d3e5d, (seven stanzas, concluding 3a5a3bb5b).

21. Same as 19, but without the internal rime of lines 1 and 3; (thirteen stanzas).

22. 5AAbb, (nineteen stanzas).

23. 4a3b2b4a3c2c, (four stanzas).

24. 6A4b6A4b, (six stanzas).

25. 3abab4cc, (thirteen stanzas).

26. 3aa5b3cc5b, (six stanzas).

27. 4abab2cc, (eleven stanzas).

28. 4abbaa, (seven stanzas).

29. 4aaa, (nine stanzas).

30. 4ababcb, (thirteen stanzas, to . . . dee), tetrameter *terza rima*.

31. 5aabccb, (eleven stanzas), lines 6 and 7 have "forteresse" as three syllables. HM 100 and EL 11637 have it two syllables;

HM 117 has it three syllables. Line 27 is problematic. Rathmell prints:

> My ey, my gutts, yea my soul; grief dost waste

HM 117:

> Mine eye, my heart, yea griefe my Soule doth waste

HM 100:

> My eie, my gutts, yea my Soules greife doth wast

(in left margin: "Bowels, del. yea" in a later hand).

EL 11637:

> My eye, my gutts, yea my soule greife doth wast.

(this ms also adds an "&" in line 7 to justify syllabification for disyllabic "fortresse"; it is careted in after "work").

32. 4aa3B4cc3B, (seven stanzas).

33. 3a2a3b3c2c3b, (fourteen stanzas).

34. 3a4bb3a3c4dd3c, (ten stanzas. HM 117 divides them in half; the others do not).

35. 5aababb, (twelve stanzas).

36. 4ababab, (six stanzas).

37. 4abBA, (twenty-six stanzas).

38. 4a2a4b4c2c4b, (eleven stanzas, all lines headless).

Natural Emphasis

39. 5a4a5b4b5c4c, (seven stanzas).

40. 5a4bb5a3ccdeed, (seven stanzas).

41. 5a3a5b3b5c3c5d3d, (six stanzas. HM 100 runs all the stanzas together; HM 117 and EL 11637 arrange as stanzas).

42. 4A4b4A4bcc4Dd, (seven stanzas).

43. 3aa3B3cc3B, (six stanzas, all headless, making lines 3 and 6 trochaic).

The Countess of Pembroke

Her forms are tremendously complex, which leads to some awkward syntax, usually to produce a rime. Her meters are often not very subtle, but overall her work is very daring and inventive.

44. 4A4b4A4bb4C4b4C, (twelve stanzas). The versification is immaculately syllabic and rhythmic here as throughout Pembroke's psalms, with somewhat more reliance on "-ed" constructions to effect feminine endings than Sidney had allowed.

45. 5ababbcbc, (eight stanzas).

46. 4abab3bc4b3c, (five stanzas). Comparing this poem with the psalm versions in the Geneva Bible (1560), Bishop's Bible (1568), and Book of Common Prayer (1570) shows Pembroke's work to be sophisticated impression, not simple translation.

47. 4ababa, (four stanzas). This is another impressive comprehension of a lovely psalm. Compare 47.7 b:

1560 *Geneva:*

sing praises
everie one that hathe understanding

290

1568 *Bishop's:*

syng psalmes [all you that hath] skyll

1570 *Common Prayer:*

sing ye praises with understandyng.

Pembroke:

praise, praise our king, / Kings of the world your judgments
sound, / With Skillful song his praises sing.

(See also her interpretive conclusion: "Hee, greatest prince,
greate princes gaines; / Princes, the shields that earth defend."
vs. *Geneva:* "The shields of the world belong to God"; *Bishop's:*
"*The shields of the* earth be Gods"; *Common Prayer:* "God . . . doth
defend the earth as it were* with a shield.")

48. 4A4bb3c4A4dd3c4E4E, (four stanzas). *Headless* 4, *iambic* 3
(lines 4 and 8 in each stanza). Exception: line 5 should be
headless (if comparable to lines in other stanzas), but is iambic;
"Hill Sion, hill of fairest seeing." HM 117 has "Sweet Sion,";
HM 100 and EL 11637 have Rathmell's version.

49. 5abcdef / abcdef, with the same six rimes through seven
stanzas. The effect is rhetorical like much blank verse, but with
lyrical overtones.

50. 5ababacc, (eight stanzas).

51. 5ababb5C5C, (eight stanzas).

52. 3a2B3a2B, (eleven stanzas). A remarkably fine poem, carrying considerable conviction. Note that she uses the word
"Tyrant" (as in *Bishop's* and *Common Prayer)* rather than "man of

power" in *Geneva*, though reference is made to "the Tyrant Saul" in the *Geneva* marginal notes.

53. 4ababbcac, (three stanzas).

54. 5abab . . . , (same rimes through sixteen lines).

55. 5abccbaacbbca, (six stanzas). The same rimes are used throughout, albeit in different figurations. *E.g.*, stanza two: baccabbcaacb; stanza three: cbaabccabbac. No two stanzas are exactly alike.

56. 5aa4bb5a, (nine stanzas).

57. 5a2bb4cc3a, (nine stanzas).

58. 5ababcbcb, (four stanzas).

59. 4a2b4a2b4cc, (fifteen stanzas).

60. 3ababbcbc, (six stanzas).

61. 2ab4ab3C3C4a, (five stanzas).

62. 4ababacac, (five stanzas).

63. 5ababbcc, (rime royal – four stanzas). In line 27, Rathmell has, "High joy in God, and that God adore". HM 100, HM 117, and EL 11637 all have: "High joy in God, and all that God adore."

64. 4abab3bcbc, (five stanzas).

65. 4ABAB5cc, (eight stanzas).

66. 4aabb4C4d4C4d, (eight stanzas).

67. 4aa2b3c2b2dd3c, (four stanzas, lines 1 and 2 *headless)*.

68. 5abab5C5b5C5b, (twelve stanzas).

69. 4abab4Cc4aa, (thirteen stanzas, *headless*, rendering lines 5-6 *trochaic)*.

70. 3ababcddc, (three stanzas).

71. 4Aa4b4Cc4b, (thirteen stanzas, *headless*, lines 1-2, 4-5).

72. 5abab2cc3d2ee3d, (nine stanzas; refers to itself as a "round," line 88).

73. 5abbaccaddaee, (seven stanzas).

74. 3aa4b3cc4b, (twenty-one stanzas).

75. 5aa5B5cc5B, (five stanzas).

76. 6abab5Cc, (five stanzas).

77. 3abcdacbd, (twelve stanzas).

78. 5abababcc, (twenty-seven stanzas; *ottava rima* for this narrative psalm).

79. 4aabbc2dd4c, (seven stanzas).

80. 5ababbCbC, (five stanzas; one, two, and five have the same feminine rime, "banish'd/vanish'd").

81. 4ababccDD, (six stanzas); *c* and *d* rimes "headless.

82. 4aa5b2b4b, (six stanzas).

83. 4ab3cc4ab, (nine stanzas).

84. An interesting and complex lyric: 3A5B5A4B3CC3dd, (six stanzas; all feminine rimes except *d*).

85. 4ababcddcee, (four stanzas, all headless). Here, and with 84, and throughout, the printed stanzas in Rathmell are less complexly indented than in the mss; HM 100 is the most elaborate, but all three take great care with the appearance of the stanza on the page.

All three set 85:   while Rathmell has:

86. 4ababcc4Dd, (six stanzas).

87. 5a4B5a4B4cc, (four stanzas).

88. 4a2bb3cc4a, (thirteen stanzas).

89. 5A5b5A5bb5C5b5C, (sixteen stanzas, lyrical narrative).

90. 4aBBaBcdcd, (seven stanzas); lines 1 and 3, and 6 and 8, are headless. The result is a curious, not entirely successful, interweaving of trochaic and iambic movements.

91. 3ab4a3bcd4c3d, (seven stanzas). For line 27, which *must* be tetrameter, EL 11637 has "recompen*ces* shared," the most likely reading, while HM 117 has "-pence *shall* shared," and HM 100 makes it trimeter, "-pence shar'd."

92. 2a3b4b2a3c4c2a3d4d, (five stanzas). The first stanza seems to anticipate Part 1 of Herbert's "Easter."

93. 4ababbaba, all headless, (two stanzas).

94. 5ababbccb, (six stanzas).

95. 4a2bb5a4cc4d5d, (five stanzas).

96. 4a4B4ac4B4c, (all headless).

97. 3aabbccddc, (five stanzas).

98. 5ababbcac, (three stanzas).

99. 4aa4Bb, (eight stanzas, all headless).

100. Sonnet: 5ababcbccdcdee.

101. 5aba⁄cdc⁄beb⁄dfd⁄ege⁄fhf⁄gig⁄hih.

102. 3a4a3bc5b4a, (fifteen stanzas).

103. 2a3a5b2c3c2d3d5b, (twelve stanzas).

104. 5ababbaba, (fourteen stanzas). Some interesting images, changes, and additions. Cf. 1574 *Common Prayer*, 104.15: "wine that maketh glad the hart of man: and oyle to make him a cheareful countenance"; 1560 *Geneva*, "wine *that* maketh glad the

heart of man and oyle to make *the face to shine*"; *Pembroke*, lines 49-50:

> Thence Wyne, the counter-poison unto care;
> Thence Oile, whose juyce unplaites the folded brow:
>
> | HM 100: | unfolds |
> | HM 117: | unplaites |
> | EL 11637: | unpleates. |

See also 104.19a (Geneva): "He appointed the moone for certeine seasons" – marginal commentary: "As to separat the night from the daie, and to note daies, moneths, & yeres." *Pembroke*, lines 65-66:

> Thou makest the Moone, the Empresse of the night,
> Hold constant course with most unconstant face.

105. 5ababab5CC, (twelve stanzas).

106. 5ababcbc, (seventeen stanzas).

107. 4ababbcbc, (fifteen stanzas).

108. 4ababbccb, (five stanzas). Pembroke's use of schematic repetition to enforce syllable count can be overused, but is sometimes effective, as lines 1-4:

> To sing and play my heart is bent,
> Is bent God's name to solemnize
> Thy service O my tongue, present:
> Arise my lute, my harp arise.

109. 5a4b3c3a5c4b, (fourteen stanzas).

110. 4abba3cd4c3d, (poulters measure underlies the counterpoint here).

111. 5aa – twenty lines of pentameter couplets, whose first letters run from A-U alphabetically. Not apparent in Rathmell, but set off in bold face in HM 100 and HM 117, although not in EL 11367. In HM 117, the one homonymic rime "Well" (noun) and "well" (adverb) is distinguished by upper case/lower case.

112. 4A3B4A3B, (nine stanzas).

113. 3aa3BB3cc, (three stanzas).

114. 6a4a, twenty lines of pseudo-elegiac couplets. *Cf.* Herbert's "Thanksgiving."

115. 3a5b3a5b4cc, (eight stanzas). One of her best poems.

116. 3ababcdcd.

117. ababcdcdefef. First letters spell "Praise the Lord" – set out by Rathmell; ignored and even lost (by second line indents *passim*) in HM 117; not set out, but no indents in EL 11637; HM 100 gives it as six tetrameter lines.

118. 4aa4BB, (twenty stanzas).

119A. 4Aa2bb4CC, (four stanzas).

119B. 3a5b4a3c5b4c, (four stanzas).

119C. 2a3b4a2c3b4c, (four stanzas).

119D. 3a3b4b1a3c3d3e4e1d4c, (four stanzas). One of the better poems as well as an incredible *tour de force;* strophic construction (rather than meter/rhythm tensions) goes beyond simple iambic metricality.

119E. 4abcabc, (four stanzas).

119F. 4aaaa, (eight stanzas).

119G. 4a3b4a3b4c3a4c3a, (two stanzas).

119H. 4ababcbcdcdedefefgfghghihi.

119I. 4aabcbc, (four stanzas).

119K. 4a4b4aa4bcbc, (three stanzas).

119L. 5aba2c3c5b, (four stanzas).

119M. 4a4B4a4BC4a4C4a, (two stanzas).

119N. 3ab5c3b3c5a, (four stanzas).

119O. 5a3b5a3c5b3c, (four stanzas).

119P. 4aa4BB4cc5d4ee4FF4gg5d.

119Q. 4a4b4a4b2c4c4dd, (four stanzas).

119R. 5a5b4c2c2a5b, (four stanzas). The second line in each stanza is nine syllables, with accent-wrenching after third foot in one and two, after second foot in three and four.

119S. 3ababbcbc, (two stanzas).

119T. 4a2bb4a4cc4dd, (four stanzas).

119V. 3AA4BB, (eight stanzas).

119W. 4ababaa, (three stanzas).

119Y. 3a4bb3a, (eight stanzas).

120. Begins a sequence (through 128) of quantitative experiments; here, six unrimed four-line stanzas whose syllable count runs eleven, eleven, nine, ten. If accentual, it is a quite startling variety *passim:*

    x / ˣ / x /x x / x x
    As to th'Eternall, often in anguishes

    / x x /   / x x / x x
    Erst have I called, never unanswered

    x / ˣ / x / x / x
    Againe I call, againe I calling

Natural Emphasis

```
x   / x  /  x x  /  x  / x
Doubt not againe to receave an answer.
```

This pattern runs throughout, except for the fourth line, which seems to vary slightly:

stanza 2:

```
/ x  x  /  / x  x x /  x
Poison'd abuse, ruine of beleevers,
```

stanza 3:

```
x  / x /  x  x  /  x / x
What benefitt from a tongue deceitfull?
```

stanza 4:

```
/   x x  /  x x  / x   /  x
Flame very hott, very hardly quenching
```

stanza 5:

```
/  x x  /  x x  /  x  /  x
How? in a tent, in a howslesse harbour (like 4)
```

stanza 6:

```
/ x  x  /  x x  /  x  /  x
Faster, I found to the warre they arme them (like 3 and 4).
```

298

These quantitative experiments provide a real metrical break-through, if, as seems likely, they are heard in accentual-syllabic terms. The rule seems to be: trisyllabic feet may occur in any position, but there must be *n* and only *n* syllables.

121. See 120 rule. Five stanzas of four lines, each eleven syllables. Much trisyllabic parallelism, no absolute pattern: *viz.* stanzas one and two:

```
 /   x  / x x / x  / x  /  x
```
What? and doe I behold the lovely mountaines

```
  /    x   /   x x /   x /  x /  x
```
Whence comes all my reliefe, my aid, my comfort?

```
x  /  x  / x /  x   /  x / x
```
O there, O there abides the worlds Creator,

```
  /   x  / x x /  x /  x /  x
```
Whence comes all my reliefe, my aid, my comfort.

```
 /    x  / x x / x /  x / x
```
March, march lustily on, redoubt no falling:

```
 /  x  / x / x  x /  x  / x
```
God shall guide the goings: the Lord thy keeper,

```
 x   /  x  / x  / x /  x / x
```
Sleepes not, sleepes not a whit, no sleape no slumber

```
 /  x / x x / x x  /  / x
```
Once shall enter in Israells true keeper.

122. Syllable count, fifteen lines: 13, 16, 15, 15, 14, 14, 14, 13, 13, 15, 15, 14, 14, 14, 14.

13: Ō fāme | mōst jōyfūll! Ō | jōy mōst | lōvelý dellīghtfūll

Natural Emphasis

16: L̄oe, Ĭ dŏ | hēare Gŏdds | tēmpl̆e, ăs | ērst, sŏe
algāine bĕ frē|qŭēnted

Pembroke actually manages something akin to an *accentual* dactyllic hexameter.

123. Syllable count, ten lines: 13, 13, 15, 13, 15, 12, 13, 13, 14, 13.

124. Sixteen lines of syllabically regular elegiac verse, of twelve, eight, in pairs throughout.

125. Sapphics. Five stanzas of three eleven-syllable lines and one five-syllable. As with most sapphics in this period, the accentual rhythms respond to the iambic pentameter traditions:

```
x / x / x / x / x / x
```
As, Sion standeth very firmly steadfast,

```
/ x  x  / x  /  x /  x / x
```
Never once shaking: soe, on high, Jehova

```
x /  x  / x  / x /  x / x
```
Who his hope buildeth, very firmly stedfast,

```
/ x x / x
```
Ever abideth.

126. Six four-line stanzas of variable syllabification, mostly nine to eleven syllables.

127. Six four-line stanzas, seven syllables per line.

HM 117 substitutes for these seven poems rimed ones, beginning: 120: "In deepe distresse, trouble when I lay"; 121: "Unto the hills I now will bend"; 122: "Right gladd was I in heart and minde"; 123: "To the greate God of Skies"; 124: "If thou (O Lord) hadst not our right"; 125: "Who trusts in God, I him doth Love,"; 126: "When thou (O Lord) to Sion free"; 127:

"Except the Lord himself, the house doth build". Rathmell, 357, cites Trinity College, Cambridge, R.3.16 [his "G"] as also having "earlier or variant versions of '120-127' inclusive."

128. 4a3b4a3bcbcb, (three stanzas).

129. 4ababcc, (five stanzas).

130. 2abab4Cc, (six stanzas). Cf. Donne on first stanza:

<blockquote>
From depth of grief
Where droun'd I ly,
Lord for relief
To thee I cry:
My earnest, vehement, crying, prayeng,
Graunt guick, attentive, hearing, waighing.
</blockquote>

131. 4ababbabacc.

132. 4abab2c3c, (thirteen stanzas).

133. 4a2bb4a, (four stanzas).

134. 4aa3bbcc2dd | efef3c4g2hh4gii4c.

135. 5ababb2c5c, (eight stanzas).

136. 4a4B4a4B, (thirteen stanzas), trochaic lines 2 and 4.

137. 4abababcc, (five stanzas).

138. 5AA5bb5CC, (four stanzas).

139. 4ab2cc4bab, (thirteen stanzas).

140. 5abcdee, (five stanzas). In HM 117 a comma or other punctuation marks *internal* abcd rimes at the end of the second foot of lines following the abcd line endings.

141. 6aa6B6cc6B, (five stanzas).

142. 5ABAB3CDC5DEF3E5F, (two stanzas).

143. 5a2a3B3c3B3c3DD3ee, (six stanzas).

Natural Emphasis

144. 3ababcdcd, (nine stanzas).

145. 4ababbcc, (nine stanzas).

146. 5abab3bc5c3d5d, (three stanzas).

147. 5ababbcacdd, (six stanzas).

148. 4ababb3c4b3c, (seven stanzas).

149. 4aBaBccDD, (three stanzas).

150. 5abba (two stanzas) and 5abbacc for last stanza:

> Lett ringing Timbrells soe his honor sound,
>   Lett sounding Cymballs soe his glory ring,
> That in their tunes such mellody be found,
>   As fitts the pompe of most Triumphant king.
> Conclud: by all that aire, or life enfold,
> Lett high Jehova highly be extold.

Index

When authors or editors are cited only or primarily in the notes, only the first citation is given unless a subsequent note contains a quotation or other substantive information. Words that necessarily occur throughout the text, such as accent, meter, rhythm, syllable, and verse are cited in the index only if the reference is to a definition or important discussion of the term.

Index

Index

Herrick Robert—*Cont.*
"upon Julia's Voice," 231-32; "Zeal required in Love," 231
Hieatt, A. Kent, 154
Hobbes, Thomas, 275, 276
Hoccleve, William, 48, 49, 50, 54
Hollander, John, 12, 207*n*8, 269*n*15, 270*n*18
Holmes, Urban T., 61*n*20
Hopkins, Gerard Manly, 262
Horace, 70
Howell, Thomas, 132*n*17
Humanism, 14, 55; and Donne, 254; and Jonson, 214, 216; and Milton, 273; and the rhyme controversy, 124; and Spenser, 161; and Surrey, 101-02*n*20; and Wyatt, 70
Hutchinson, F. E., 270*n*23
Hymnody, 114, 116

Iambic pentameter, 37-38, 40, 47, *69-72*, 259; blank verse and, 89-91; Campion and, 197; the decasyllabic line and, 32, 40-42, 73-74, 77, 79, 95; Gascoigne and, 117; Harvey and, 129; *Mirror for Magistrates* and, 105-110; Surrey as inventor of, 72, 85-88, 95; Wyatt and, 73-79
Ictus, 2, 5
Ing, Catherine, 95-96*n*3, 250
Isochronic verse, 112
Italian verse, influence of, 15-16, 31-32; in Spenser, 148, 153

James I, 208*n*14
Jayne, Sears, 177*n*9
Jesperson, Otto, 6, 9
John, L. C., 180*n*32
John of Garland, 23
Johnson, Samuel, 230
Jones, Emrys, 99*n*14, 101*n*20, 101*n*21, 102*n*29
Jones, Inigo, 212
Jonson, Ben, 13, 94, 101*n*23, 170, 172, 206, 206*n*1, *209-30*, 234*n*4, 254, 255, 259-60, 261, 274, 280; and Bacon, 213-15; "Celebration of Charis," 224-26, 228-29; "Conversations with Drummond," 210-13; and Daniel, 203, 204-05, 211-12; and Donne, 212, 250, 253; and Herrick, 233; "My Picture left in Scotland," 226-27; and the ode, 154, 209, 218; "On Chev-'rill," 221-22; "On Death," 222; "On Lucy, Countess of Bedford," 227-28;

"On My First Daughter," 220-21; "On My First Son," 222-24; and Ralegh, 184-85, 186-87, 192, 210, 234*n*3; and Surrey, 218-20; *Timber*, 212-13, 214, 217; "To My Booke," 222

Kalender and Compost of Shepheardes, 161
Kalendrier des Bergiers, 180*n*31
Kalstone, David, 176*n*4
Kastner, L. E., 61*n*20
Keats, John, 152, 233
Ker, Walter C. A., 235*n*12
Kernan, Alvin, 268*n*5
Keyser, S. Jay, *see* Halle, Morris
Kinsley, James, 66*n*64
Kinsman, Robert, 96*n*4
Kiparsky, Paul, 17*n*8
Kyd, Thomas, 239
Kyng Alisaunder, 26-28

Laistner, M. L. W., 59*n*2
Langer, Susanne K., 20*n*22
Langland, William, 56-57
Latham, Agnes M. C., 206*n*2, 207*n*3
Latin verse, classical, 112; dactylic hexameter, 125-26, 197
Latin verse, rhythmic or medieval, 16, 21-23, 42, 70, 111, 113; and the rhyme controversy, 125-27
Lawler, Traugott, 60*n*8
Layamon's *Brut*, 28-29
Leech, Geoffrey, 19*n*16
Lefranc, Pierre, 206*n*1
Legge, Sr. M. Dominica, 60*n*14
Leicester, Robert Dudley, earl of, 193, 206*n*1
Lever, J. W., 180*n*32
Levin, Harry, 268*n*5
Lewalski, Barbara K., 181*n*41, 271*n*24
Lewis, C. S., 49, 57, 62*n*34, 95*n*2, 95*n*3, 97*n*8
Liburnio, Niccolo, 89
Lodge, Thomas, 193-94
Lovelace, Richard, 210, 230
Lucan, 184
Lucas, St. John, and C. Dionisotti, 63*n*35; and P. Manstell Jones, 63*n*35
Lucretius, 217
Lydgate, John, 46-55; influence of, 69, 70, 72, 97*n*8; and *Mirror for Magistrates*, 105; and rhyme, 126
Lynn, Karen, 50-51
Lyric verse, 25

306

Index

Index

Pope, Alexander, 1, 2, 210, 229
Pope, Evelyn F., 178n18
Potter, Lois, 268n2
Poulet, Georges, 19n19
Poulters measure, 70, 78; decline of, 139, 168, 194-95; as English heroic line, 91; Gascoigne and, 114-16
Pound, Ezra, 276
Preminger, Alex, 177n12
Prescott, Anne Lake, 180n31
Prouty, C. T., 131n4
Provençal verse, influence of, 23, 24-25, 70
Puttenham, George, 98-99n11, 176n1
Psalm translations, compared with Biblical versions, 174-75; Sidneian, 138, 148, 169-75, 287-302; Sternhold and Hopkins, 114-15; Wyatt, 70
Pyles, Thomas, 60n14

Quantitative verse, 11-12, 125; Campion and, 197-201; English efforts at, 128-30; Gascoigne and, 112-13; Sidney and, 144-47. See also Latin verse, quantitative
Quinones, Ricardo, 19-20n21
Quintillian, 213

Ralegh, Sir Walter, 183-93, 206n1, 210, 216, 259; "A Vision upon . . . the Faery Queen," 184, 185-86; "Calling to minde," 188; "Commendation of the Steele Glas," 184, 185; commending Gorges' Pharsalia, 184, 185-86; and Gascoigne, 110-11, 131n4; History of the World, 184; "Nature that washt," 188, 189-91; "The Nimphs Reply," 188-89; Ocean to Scinthia, 192; "Passionate Man's Pilgrimage," 192
Rathmell, J. C. A., 182n42
Raw, Barbara C., 59n6
Raynaud, Gaston, 60n13
Renoir, Alain, 49
Renwick, W. L., 178n14
reverdie, 25, 86
Rhyme, verse system of, 111, 126; controversy over, 105, 124-30, 183, 197-206. See also Rime
Rhythm, 7-10, 13-15; phrasal, 258-59; prose (and Donne), 254, 257-58, 270n19
Rhythmic verse, Latin, see Latin verse, rhythmic or medieval
Richardson, David A., 176n7
Richmond, Henry, earl of, 101n20

Ridley, Florence, 102n25, 102n26
Rime (or end rime), 29, 59n3; and accentuation, 38-39; distinguished from rhyme, 133; feature of rhyme, 126; feminine endings, 170
Rime Royal, 38, 106, 114, 148
Ringler, William, 144, 181n36
Roberts, John R., 267n1
Robinson, F. N., 61n26
Robinson, Ian, 41, 42, 47, 63n41
Rolle, Richard, school of, 66n70
Rollin, Roger B., 235n14; and J. Max Patrick, 235n14
Rollins, Hyder E., 102n30, 207n9
Ronsard, Pierre de, 125, 154, 180n30, 181n37
Roydon, Matthew, 195
Rudenstine, Neil, 181n35
Rudnick, Michael, 207n5
Ryding Ryme, 112, 142
Rymer, Thomas, 178n18

Sackville, Thomas, earl of Dorset (1536-1608), 108-09; Gorboduc, 109, 238, 239
Saintsbury, George, 4, 49, 65n53, 95n1; and Donne, 251; and extra syllables, 134n25; and Epithalamion, 154; and the Faerie Queene stanza, 148, 178n18; and Wyatt, 95n5, 97n8, 100n17; and Wyatt and Surrey, 101-02n24
Samuels, M. L., 63n41
Sapphics, 173
Schane, Sanford, 17-18n9
Schelling, Felix, 281n3
Schick, Joseph, 48
Schirmer, Walter, 52
Schleiner, Louise, 270n21
Schwartz, Elias, 97n8
Scottish Chaucerians, the, 53, 66n60
Sebillet, Jaques, 131n12
Sells, A. Lytton, 59n1
Seymour, Edward, duke of Somerset, and his party, 106
Shakespeare, William, 13, 70, 89, 193, 216, 237, 239-49, 254, 262, 274, 280; All's Well, 241-42; AYLI, 243-44; Ham, 244-46; 1 Hen VI, 238, 240; 3 Hen VI, 240-41; and Herrick, 233; KJohn, 243; Lear, 11, 246-47; MND, 241; Much Ado, 243; MWW, 243; Oth, 246; R&J, 241; sonnet 30, 5, 6, 7-8, 10; Tempest, 243, 247-49
Shawcross, John, 250, 253
Shepherd, Geoffrey, 57-58

308

Index